ANTHOLOGY ONE

THE ALSOP REVIEW PRESS

For more information visit www.alsopreview.com

ISBN 0-976-19540-2

Orders, enquiries, and correspondence should be addressed to:

Alsop Review
122 Broad Creek Road,
Laurel, DE 19956

ANTHOLOGY ONE

Poetry, Fiction, Essays

• Jaimes Alsop, Editor •

 THE ALSOP REVIEW PRESS

Credits

Kim Addonizio
Courtesy of BOA Editions, reprinted by permission.

Kelli Russell Agodon
You Can Never Have Too Many Rosaries, Post-Valentine's Day with Waitress, Fifty-Six Knots, *Small Knots* (Cherry Grove Collections, 2004).

Karen Alkalay-Gut
A variation of Love Soup first appeared in *Prairie Schooner*.

Jan Lee Ande
Contemplation (View), *The Chester H. Jones/National Poetry Competition 1999 Anthology*. The Well, *Bellevue Literary Review*. Journeyman, *Reliquary* (Texas Review Press, 2003) First published in *Cairn*

David Anthony
On the Suicide of a Friend, *Artemis Journal*. For My Daughter, *Mindfire Renewed*. Warming, *Edge City Review*.

Jeffery Bahr
Appearances, *Alaska Quarterly Review*. They Don't Know Their History, *Beacon Street Review (2002 Prize winner)* Genealogy, *Rattle*.

Kate Benedict
Here From Away, We Are Refugees, *Here from Away* (CustomWords 2003), Contemplative Observances, *Voice of Many Waters*, ed. Kay Snodgrass, About Words (Reston, VA), 1997 and Geneva Press (Philadelphia), 2000

David Cazden
The New Geomoetry, *Porcupine Literary Arts*. Sunstroke, *Conspire*. Melanoma, *The Chiron Review*.

Rachel Dacus
Riddle, *North American Review*. Fertilizing, *Rattaplax*. Thunder-Edged, *Prairie Schooner*.

Julie Damerell
In the Heat of an October Night, *Moveo Angelus Literary Arts* (online). Mary, you can, *Dust on Our Palms* (online, 1999) and *Needing Blue* (H&H Press, 2001). Baptism, *Conspire* (online) and *Stagger* (online). Fourth Grade Recess at Our Lady Queen of Hope, *La Petite Zine* (online) and *miller's pond* (print). Summer's End, Maryland, *Desert Moon Review* (online).

Kelly Madigan Erlandson
Rising, *Manzanita Quarterly*

Rhina P. Espaillat
Discovery, *The Formalist*. Guidelines, *Garden Lane*. Parable, *Margie Review*. Translating, *Oberon*.

Larry Fontenot
The Other Side of Ice, *The Poet's Canvas, Issue 17, 2001*. Swimming Lesson, *Pebble Lake Review Vol 1, Issue No. 3, Summer 2004*. Seduction, *Sulphur River Literary Review Vol. XVII, No. 1 Spring, 2001*.

Michael Graber
A Fantasia for My Four Year Old Daughter, Mistakenly Given an Overdose of Demerol, *Spoon River Poetry Review*. Paris, Tennessee, *River City*.

R. S. Gwynn
Ballade Beginning with a Line by Robert Bly, *Edge City Review*.
Ubi Sunt for the 70s *is forthcoming in Tar River Poetry*.

Neile Graham
Wearing Nothing but the Midnight Sun, *Arc* The Walk She Takes, *TickleAce*.

Rafael Guillén
Estoy Hablando, El Miedo, No, *I'm Speaking*, selected poems by Rafael Guillen, pub. 2001 by Northwestern University Press. Apenas Si Recuerdo, *Poetry Society of America* for Poetry Month in 2002.

Steve Harris
Nightingales, In the Circle, *Avatar Review*. To Her Son, *Samsara Quarterly*. OxyContin, *Taint Magazine*.

Lola Haskins
all selections from The Rim Benders (Anhinga Press, 2001).

Jim Hayes
The Man Who Used to Fish, The Auction, *Iambs & Trochees*.

Andrew Hudgins
Had It Coming, *The Great River Review*. The Circus the Trees and The Tooth Fairy, *Shenandoah*. Our Neighbor's Dog, *American Poetry Review*. Imaginary Friend, *Antioch Review*.

Richard Jordan
Through The Ice, *Cranky*. One Way to Go, *Harpur Palate, the literary journal of Binghamton University*. Whenever Light Arcs, Bait, *Pacific Review*.

Rose Kelleher
Rosa Rugosa, *Worm*. The Rectangle, *Anon*.

Peter Krok
How Do You Explain It, *Asphodel*. Desire, *One Trick Pony*. Hands of a Ball Bearing Worker, *New Zoo Review*.

Dorianne Laux
All Credits to BOA Editions, used by permission.

Fred Longworth
After the Animal Show Filed Bankruptcy, *Melic Review*, Workshopped to Death, *Poetic Voices*.

Frank Matagrano
Driving Down Route 80 without a Radio, *Northwest Review*. Waiting with Alexandria for Her Mom, *3AM Magazine*. Throwing a Shoe at the Branch, *Another Chicago Magazine (ACM)*.

Chelle Miko
Appraisal, 1973, *32 Poems Magazine*. In the Habu Hour, *The North American Review*.
How To Make An Agnostic A Martyr, *Eclectica*.

Steve Mueske
After Reading of an Amazing New Device That Brings Back the Dead in Lifelike
Holographic Images, *Redactions*.

Ginger Murchison
Small Craft Advisory, *Atlanta Review*. Vocabulary, *Shout Them from the Mountain Tops: Georgia Poems*,
edited by the Georgia Council of Teachers of English, 2004.

Joyce Nower
Private Parts: Erotic Poetry by Women, in a somewhat different form
in *The Longest Revolution*, CWSS, 1982.

Shann Palmer
Bread 'n butter pickles, *Conspire*. The Nature of Belief, *Stirring*, November 2000.
Picture Perfect, *Nuvein*, Spring 2004.

Jennifer Reeser
Why It Wasn't You, The Fall, *An Alabaster Flask*, Word Press, 2003.

Sue Scalf
Alchemy, *South by Candlelight*. The Baptist Ladies Travel to the Factory Outlets, *The Southern Review*.
Genesis, *Ceremony of Names. (Also won Hacknet Award)*

Deborah J. Shore
The Round Glade, *Avatar Review*. Fall Line, *Artemis Journal*

Robert Lavett Smith
Walking Across the Sea of Galilee, *The Distillery*, The Skull of Billy The Kid, *Plainsongs*

Ernest Slyman
The Things We Wish For, *Dream Forge*. I'm Baggy In Because, Therefore and Why and Little Piggy
Everything, *The Mandrake Review*. Kew Forest Park, *Sparks*.

Robert Sward
Selections from "Dog Door to Heaven," from *"Collected Poems, 1957-2004,"* Black Moss Press, Winter, 2004.

Robt. Ward
My Secret Kept Alive, *Fulcrum Annual, 2004*

Dedication

For Carla Kandinsky and the Berkeley writers group. For Ray, Bob, Mark, Jenna, Chuck, Paul, Michael, Janet. For B.C., Mike Billard, Jack Hunter, Lewis Gresham and Linda Thomas Harms. For AnnaLynn, Chris, Fiona-Maria, Jennifer, Andrew, Karen, Rachel, Rob. Sandy, Martin, Jack , Joyce and all the former staffers, columnists and editors of the Review.

~

For Jamie Wasserman

~

For Dorianne Laux

~

For Robert Ward for his enormous help putting this together. For all the writers and poets who have appeared on the Review, in Octavo and posted on The Gazebo over the years. For the members of St. Agatha's. For Jim Dostal, Dylan Rhodes, Kim Addonizio, Karen-Alkalay-Gut, Jon Teets and Robert Sward.

~

For Wendy

Contents

Foreword

Since its inception in 1995, *The Alsop Review* (www.alsopreview.com) has steadfastly pursued its goal of bringing some of the best in contemporary poetry and art to the World Wide Web in an elegant, understated format that presents but does not overpower the work. Over the years, many people have had a hand and/or a voice in shaping *The Alsop Review*, and we have sought to acknowledge them on a separate page. A history of the *Review* may be viewed on the website, as may be the archived poetry we have published, various columns on a variety of subjects, the online magazines (*Aside* and *Octavo*), and the Gallery.

Also associated with the *Review* is the workshop, *The Gazebo*, a thriving online community of writers (of both prose and poetry) where the members critique each others' work and engage in discussion on a huge variety of topics, some of them only peripherally relevant to the literary field. *The Gazebo* may also be accessed from the *Review*'s website.

Without our friends, our supporters, and most importantly our contributors and their faith in us, *The Alsop Review* would not exist.

Now, nearly a decade after our founding, we are making a long-anticipated move into the world of "real", paper publishing. *The Alsop Review Press* is already hard at work collating, designing, and preparing for publication half a dozen books of poetry. But we thought it fitting that our first published work should be this: *Anthology One*, which comprises work sent to us when we announced to our friends and contributors that we were inviting their participation in this book.

In this sense, *Anthology One* is a "thank you" to an extended community we have come to think of us our family-in-spirit. The work spans a variety of *genrés*, is uniformly interesting, and sometimes (we like to think) luminous. We bring it to you (the reader) as we begin this journey, and give it to you (our contributors) with our thanks and our promise of many wonderful books to come.

— Jaimes Alsop, Editor

Kim Addonizio

Kim Addonizio is the author of three collections of poetry from BOA Editions:
The Philosopher's Club, *Jimmy & Rita*, and *Tell Me*, which was a
Finalist for the 2000 National Book Award.

Her collection of stories, *In the Box Called Pleasure*, was published by Fiction Collective 2.
With Dorianne Laux, she co-authored *The Poet's Companion: A Guide to the Pleasures
of Writing Poetry* (W.W. Norton). Her work has received two NEA Fellowships and other awards,
and has appeared in various zines, literary journals, and anthologies.

What Do Women Want?

I want a red dress.
I want it flimsy and cheap,
I want it too tight, I want to wear it
until someone tears it off me.
I want it sleeveless and backless,
this dress, so no one has to guess
what's underneath. I want to walk down
the street past Thrifty's and the hardware store
with all those keys glittering in the window,
past Mr. and Mrs. Wong selling day-old
donuts in their cafe, past the Guerra brothers
slinging pigs from the truck and onto the dolly,
hoisting the slick snouts over their shoulders.
I want to walk like I'm the only
woman on earth and I can have my pick.
I want that red dress bad.
I want it to confirm
your worst fears about me,
to show you how little I care about you
or anything except what
I want. When I find it, I'll pull that garment
from its hanger like I'm choosing a body
to carry me into this world, through
the birth-cries and the love-cries too,
and I'll wear it like bones, like skin,
it'll be the goddamned
dress they'll bury me in.

Night of the Living, Night of the Dead

When the dead rise in movies they're hideous
and slow. They stagger uphill toward the farmhouse
like drunks headed home from the bar.
Maybe they only want to lie down inside
while some rooms spins around them, maybe that's why
they bang on the windows while the living
hammer up boards and count out shotgun shells.
The living have plans: to get to the pickup parked
in the yard, to drive like hell to the next town.
The dead with their leaky brains,
their dangling limbs and ruptured hearts,
are sick of all that. They'd rather stumble
blind through the field until they collide
with a tree, or fall through a doorway
like they're the door itself, sprung from its hinges
and slammed flat on the linoleum. That's the life
for a dead person: *wham, wham, wham*
until you forget your name, your own stinking
face, the reason you jolted awake
in the first place. Why are you here,
whatever were you hoping as you lay
in your casket like a dumb clarinet?
You know better now. The soundtrack's depressing
and the living hate your guts. Come closer
and they'll show you how much. *Wham, wham, wham,*
you're killed again. Thank God this time
they're burning your body, thank God
it can't drag you around anymore
except in nightmares, late-night reruns
where you lift up the lid, and crawl out
once more, and start up the hill toward the house.

Kelli Russell Agodon

Kelli Russell Agodon is the author of *Geography*, winner of the 2003 Floating Bridge Press Chapbook Prize. Her poems have appeared in the *North American Review, Seattle Review, Crab Creek Review, Calyx, Rattapallax, River Oak Review, Parnassus, Byline, blink*, the print version of *Poets Against the War* edited by Sam Hamill (Nation Books) and other national literary journals and anthologies. Her first full collection of poems entitled *Small Knots* will be published in the summer of 2004 by Cherry Grove Collections.

Fifty-Six Knots

I can count the women in my family
between the wooden beads of my rosary.
They are the small knots, the tightness,
the holding—
the ones embracing the fragility of sons
and fathers between their soft bodies,
and the lives they watch leave them.
I can count the number of prayers
spoken by men at the dinner table,
disguised as promises
they slip out the backdoor
even before the apple cobbler
has been removed from the oven,
the smell still hot in the hands of the burned.
I can count the number of nights I have
listened to Hail Marys bleeding
from the walls, and how many times I have
wanted to break the chain
sending the fifty-five beads scattering
like the families who prayed to them;
I imagine collection plates around the world
filling with broken rosaries, imperfect
virgins escaping beneath stained-glass skies.
In the whispering corner of the church
a suffered woman unties
each knot, the sound of beads baptizing
the marble floors, the sound of women
leaving the church hand in hand in hand.

You Can Never Have Too Many Rosaries

Like lilies, they seem to multiply each season.
Having slid from a Bible, find them
mixed with lingerie, wrapped around
the straps of a black bra, a rose-patterne
thong tossed across the rug. Spread them
across the photo of your mother,
use broken ones to hold back the curtains
in the kitchen, the hair from her eyes.
Carry them in your pocketbook with the snapshot
of your son, the picture of the girl who came
with the wallet and the twig of lavender
you picked from the abandoned fairground.
Remember, faith fits in the tightest pocket
of your jeans, in the cracks of your palms,
and in the fine roots of strawberry plants.
It is the song that continues to play
after the band has gone home. Worn
like a loosened necktie, let the beads hang
down your shirt, over the wine stain
like long fingers reaching for your belt.

Post-Valentine's Day with Waitress

I looked for the crumbs of January in a poem
about snow. I chanted the words, O terrible
white beauty and the waitress raised her eyebrows,
tapped her pen against her wrist. She asked,
"Are you reading poetry?" the way someone
asks, "Are you wearing pants?"
The idea seemed so unusual, that I imagined
she had never undressed for anyone.
I told her that I could still remember
the lines from a poem someone sent me
one Valentine's—
When you appear all the rivers sound in my body.
She told me that sometimes she can hear the ocean
from her apartment window. She thinks
that all water tries to speak to us, even the coffee
brewing behind her on the counter.

Karen Alkalay-Gut

Considered Israel's premier poet, **Karen Alkalay-Gut** teaches poetry at *Tel Aviv University*.
She has also launched her career as an artist with an installation about body sculpture
that coincides with the completion of her tenth book of poetry, *"The Love of Clothes and
Nakedness."* Living in Israel and publishing in a language foreign to most of the
inhabitants, she has found various strategies of coping – founding the *Israel Association of
Writers in English*, making friends with Hebrew translators (who are responsible
for the publication of three books), working with other media such as music and art,
and enjoying the Internet as a window to the world.

Love Soup

I

On
this night I dream we accompany our child
to the ritual baths,
built
deep into the ground, below the vision
of those involved
in daily life. So none
unschooled in congress
can see the lovers
in their profound
rites, examining their bodies,
learning nakedness,
immersion.

I
awake to the stroke of a hand,
move my body flush to my old man.

II

What
wisdom can we leave our children about love.
It is our generation
which first exposed
our sores to the air, formed elegant tattoos
from
our scars, wrenching joy from pain

that danger shows. We are sitting
in the cafe,
watching our daughters walk past the men
they might
have loved and meeting
mirrors of their misery, those
who cannot
give them joy,
and making the wrong men
miserable.

III

This
woman, whose breasts
tumble from her heart, takes her measure
in
another's eye - the greater
he is, the larger the reflection,
and
the farther away
the more of herself she sees

And in the evening
she makes love
to her own body - washing her hair,
massaging her
fingers before
her manicure

IV

And of that man whose
voice
is honey hunger I know
nothing; of his flat -
the living
room
with its two arm chairs
facing the music:
receiver, tape
deck,
compact disk, speakers —

the wall-to-wall record collection
(God
he pulls them out as if he knew
where each one was blind folded).

All
those people in all those songs
all alone in their albums

V

"I
slept with Jagger"
my friend from California writes
after years
of dreaming
of sleeping with Jagger
"and all the time
I was thinking
of
my dream
of sleeping with Jagger"

VI

Why can't Mick
get satis
faction? We were assured
it, or our money
returned.

And
in bed the other
looks nothing like
the perfect people
in movies.

We
have been promised too much
to take our pleasure
as it comes.

VII

I
can't get no
satis

Nothing's
better than more

Less than
all
will not satisfy

When what we want
is possession

VIII

In
the dark ages before
the Joy of Sex every
touch was its own

IX

Will
you teach me love,
She asks.
He turns his back

Thank you.

X

What
do we owe each other in the game of love,
What do we owe ourselves
and
what choice do we
have — so many people
in bed with us,
like
Russian dolls

one mother inside the other,
or action shots on
low speed film
endless shadows seeming
to move as one.

XI

How
interchangeable are genitalia
and how specific desire

XII

Obsessions
are easy:
loving someone who doesn't
love back. So pure.
Hitting
ball after ball
into an empty court
you don't expect to return

Then
it comes back
and the game becomes
complex
almost
impossible

moving,
changing,
dangerous.

XIII

The closer you get
the
less you see
the more you become

The more you become me
the

less you are
a lover

Keep your distance
stay near

XIV

What
if you fall
into a warm bath
of love soup
and as you lie there,
sated,
the soup cools, congeals,
catches you in its clammy
vegetable
grasp

XV

The oldest woman I know,
lectures in rest
homes on Truth.

At the movies,
the scene turns sexy
she clasps
her breast, whispers
over and again, "O, my heart, my
heart"

And
Yeats ends hungering
for a girl in his arms

XVI

You
awakened this poem

I sought you for that
thought of that shudder

strength
you would open
that wonder
you didn't know

Then

XVII

A
young man in my dream
serves me lentil soup
with a deep smile
I
am thrilled to share.
I was hungry and you fed me
pottage, I say,
and see
he looks like the boy I loved
many years away,
like the
orderly
who cared for my father
with warm gentle hands
those
days he was dying.

George Amabile

George Amabile has published in The USA, Canada, Europe, South America, Australia and New Zealand in over a hundred anthologies, magazines, journals and periodicals including The Young American Poets, The Penguin Book of Canadian Verse, The New Yorker Book of Poems, Saturday Night, The New Yorker, Harper's, Poetry, American Poetry Review, Poetry Australia, Sur (Buenos Aires), Poetry Canada Review, Canadian Literature, and Margin (England). He has edited The Far Point, Northern Light and has published seven books. The Presence of Fire (McClelland & Stewart, 1982), won the CAA National Prize for literature, his long poem, "Durée", placed third in the CBC Literary Competition for 1991. His most recent publication is Rumours of Paradise / Rumours of War (McClelland and Stewart).

The Patriot Act

Altogether now, Baaa, Baaa, Baaa.
Another telling blow for Democracy, struck
like a coin: skull, and blackboard pointer, the kind
used at Military briefings. Ahh...
yes, there's something dangerous in the wind.
You'd better believe it. This is no time to fuck
around, asking questions, remembering history.
Our freedom's at stake, so bite the bullet and be
what you know you're supposed to imagine you are—
unique individuals with exactly the same
ideas, beliefs and obsessions, but of course not
the same incomes, that would be rude, a blot
on the sacred mammaries of the D. A. R.
whom we will honour today by changing our names.

Number

They've always been
useful; nothing
personal about them
though, lately,
with the crackling
of cervical vertebrae
and Peter Pain's
electric-spear-thrust
sciatica they seem
to glow with the radiance
of a clock dial or an LCD.

Time isn't always
money, but these days
it disappears with equal
speed and I find
myself counting,
checking my watch:
how long before the
decanted Cabernet is fit
to drink, four ounces of red
meat twice a week, at least
thirty brisk minutes a day
on the treadmill or out
in the air, afternoons
at sixes and sevens, a gill
of eighty proof scotch with one
ice cube before dinner,
and remember, ninety
seconds in the microwave
will draw the brilliant greens
of paradise from broccoli florets.

But then the sky darkens
and fills with sapphire ice,
a reminder of the all
that cannot be reckoned,
or measured, or known.

Hard Times

Crumpled cellophane, gone
amber and crisp
with age, rags, rusted springs,
soup cans lined with teflon, papers
and letters no one will read
again.
The broken leg
of a table pokes through the rubble.
A rat crawls to the tip
and sits there, sniffing.

It's as though he can feel
the bright bead
of the varmint rifle nestle under his chin.
He looks at me,
his black eyes empty
of fear, inquisitive, almost
intelligent, as if
he might be able to say
something useful about life
as a veteran opportunist
in the fields of rot and waste.

My head fills
with an irresistible urge
to sneeze, but his nose twitches
and all that's left
of him as my breath
explodes
is the lash of his tail.

Jan Lee Ande

Jan Lee Ande comes from a long line of Anglican clergy, was initiated into Tibetan Buddhism by
Kalu Rinpoche, and later joined a Roman Catholic community. Besides an M.A. in Asian Studies
and a Ph.D. in history of consciousness, she has an M.F.A. in poetry from San Diego State
University. Ande's first book, *Instructions for Walking on Water*, won the 2000 Snyder Prize from
Ashland Poetry Press. Her second book, *Reliquary*, won the 2002 X.J. Kennedy Poetry Prize from
Texas Review Press. *Pigs & Fishes*, sixty-four poems inspired by the ancient Chinese *I Ching*, is in
submission. Her poems appear in *New Letters, Image, Nimrod, Notre Dame Review, Mississippi
Review, Bellevue Literary Review, Poetry International* and the anthologies *Place of Passage*
(Story Line Press) and *Jubilation* (Beat Books). She teaches poetry, poetics, and history of
religions at Union Institute & University.

The Well

It is written that in the days of Abraham the Father,
the Philistines filled up his wells with rock and mud.

So Isaac's servants dug in the valley and found there
founts of flowing water, and before one, built an altar.

If a man lifts a thirty kilogram bucket from a well
one hundred meters deep, how much work does he do?

Let f^1 equal the gravitational force. Note the work
is positive, that the man expends energy lifting the bucket.

What happens when a child falls twenty two feet
down an abandoned wellshaft in the heartland?

Why does the rescuer who labored two and a half days
to bring her back into the light, take his own life?

Note the work is negative, that the gravitational field
surrounding the bucket gains energy as it is lifted.

How far down in the mingled wellspring of creativity
do syllables abide? Is it so dark near the quickening

water that blue stars shine and then set, taking
their blackened light back into the fountainhead

Contemplation (View)

A few angels come here for the view,
and the illusion of time ticking on its way.

On the outstretched arms of Christ the Redeemer
in Rio—they reach a familiar perch.

Poised on his languid fingers, they gaze down
at the world and its scurryings.

Here the hallowed laws of heaven are far above
and the curious ways of people below.

They keep messages tucked up their tidy sleeves
or folded neatly beneath wings.

These things named for them they find pleasing:
angel food cake light as clouds,

the angel network with its proclamation of deeds,
angelica in the belly of male musk deer,

angel fishes swimming inside a glass globe,
their compressed bodies and sad mouths.

Before leaving this world, they descend Angel Falls
(Venezuela quick as a thought in the mind's eye)

sailing over earth's longest waterfall—the rush
of white froth, a multitude of tongues

Journeyman

Once you looked like Clark Gable, big ears
and high cheekbones, your hair black and sleek.
Women swooned. I loved you more than rainfall
or cedar trees. Carpenter of my childhood,
maker of teepees and boats, what happened
while you were gone to a far house, a new family?
A lifetime later you returned, pallid and doddering,
leaning on a mahogany cane. Now you slump
in a wheelchair too wide to pass through the door.
At times you ascend to totter down the hallway.
A blue joke falls from your lips on the days
the mouth muscles tighten into speech. How papery
your skin, the veins purple, standing like winding lines
on a map. The twisted fingers of your left hand
suddenly curl into a fist, never to loosen.
I want to turn from you, and then you whisper
that when you held my half sister in her coma, kissed
the frail limbs, you felt her soul fly from her body.
I will make a wooden boat the size of a child's toy
to hold a pinch of your ashes, the faded photograph
of you and me on Juan de Fuca Strait¾
me steering, you facing the camera, tanned,
shirt sleeves rolled up, a cigarette dangling
from your mouth that still manages its lopsided smile
as we navigate the waters marked on old maps:
mare nostrum, mare incognita

David Anthony

David Anthony is a British businessman who lives with his family in Stoke Poges, close to the churchyard where Gray wrote his *Elegy*, a source of much inspiration.

Warming

The seasons' course seems strange to me,
more strange than I remember;
wild flowers bloom unseasonably:
primroses in November.

The young pretend to blame us all.
Well, youth's a great dissembler:
May was forever I recall
and there was no November.

These days I'll take what nature sends
to hoard for dour December:
a glow of warmth as autumn ends;
primroses in November.

On the Suicide of a Friend

God help the kids! I heard the neighbours say—
so quick to judge though mostly they were kind.
They saw the sorry mess you left behind
and thought you took the coward's selfish way.

The coward's way? No, not that I can see.
Despair's a snare. They say a fox will gnaw
its fettered foot and sacrifice the paw.
What desperation drove you to break free?

Nor were you selfish. Just beneath the calm
the darkness gathered; I have known it too.
It touched those near. It's my conviction you
believed you were protecting them from harm.

God—if there's a God—will grant you rest:
you failed, we all do, but you did your best.

For My Daughter

It's funny how I never saw you grow.
I seem to miss what's nearest as a rule,
far too preoccupied—a busy fool
blind to the way the seasons come and go.

What shall I give since now you're going too
and will be gone a while? Although you're brave
and self-assured I know I rarely gave
a sign to show how proud I was of you.

I give it now, with love; but love's no gift:
it's yours by right. Because you're going far
I'll give a gentle light to be your star
and all my hopes to hold when life's adrift.

I'll give them all though all I have would be
no gift beside the gift you were to me.

Talking to Lord Newborough

I'd perch beside your gravestone years ago,
a boy who thought you old at forty-three.
I knew you loved this quiet place, like me.
We'd gaze towards Maentwrog far below,
kindred spirits, and I'd talk to you.
Sometimes I asked what it was like to die—
were you afraid? You never did reply,
and silence rested lightly on us two.

These days the past is calling, so I came
to our remembered refuge on the hill,
expecting change yet finding little there:
my village and the Moelwyns look the same,
Saint Michael's Church commands the valley still—
but you, old friend, are younger than you were.

*(Lt. William Charles Wynn, 1873-1916, 4th Baron Newborough,
whose grave overlooks the Vale of Ffestiniog in North Wales)*

Jeffery Bahr

Jeffery Bahr lives in Colorado and runs a software development company.

Genealogy

Outside, it's cold like the day
my father's grandpa drowned
while Sigrid salted cod on walls
of stacked antlers. Their sons
and daughter fled to Eden
Prairie. One, my father's uncle, lost
a claim in Manitoba, another crashed
a Huppmobile. One died ice-fishing.

My father's mother, pink and vicious, made
him cover the bidet with plywood
when we lived in Teheran. Made me drive
all over Fairfax County in search
of Carnival glass. Told me "Never
marry a woman for her looks." My mother's
dad lost his lungs to mustard gas. Her mom

never gambled. Betty lived in Hollywood
working at the studios, roller-skating
with a man who would later play
Tonto. She rented a room
in a house with a victory garden until
the Tamuras were shipped
to Utah, then married Dad, who left
to kill Koreans. On the ship

to Japan to join him in Kobe, my sister
scared me with stories of dwarves. My children's
mom is small and pale, like the pages
of an appointment book, except when speaking
Spanish. Then, her hands become larakeets, her eyes
marcasite. Her grandfather knew the Franks
before they moved to Holland, and he
to Pasadena, where he never met

my mother who skis like she's waltzing,
or my father, who came home and built
a barbeque of brick, or my sister the shrink,
or my brother who sells drugs, or my other sister
for that matter. They all live
in California and no one
ever dies. There's a boy

at the bus stop who dances
in place: knit cap, heavy coat, an extra
chromosome, perhaps. Sometimes he raises
his arms and spins. The world starts with him.

Appearances

Harry's in town but hasn't called to dine and cover
six years of silence: Rachel's dead and what did he do
with all her kimonos? They always conjure up my blue gown
the day Kyle's head crowned, steel shears showing up
to cut the gray cord tethered to sudden blood - Rachel
never wanted kids. She and Harry lay on teak to harbor sway

and searched for new stars. Now, men catch neutrinos
just before the miracles of novae, like the ghost ring before
your sister calls to say your parents are fine and phoned
from Ouray. A small surprising thing can *not* be there,
and then it is: Rachel's malignant visitor. The cat
on your chest licking your chin at midnight. Harry's only stint

as godfather. The river raft threw Kyle into the Lower Klamath,
water and white skulls of rock, Harry probing the rough
with a paddle, me gripping the yellow rope, the bloodless
face of the river guide, Kyle's blanched hands
on Harry's wrist, his head breaching.

They Don't Know Their History

Junie tilts the miniblinds: "You're achieving love
through successive approximation." Barker elevates
a sun-striped creamer into a go-cup of MJB. He's thinking
St. Exupery, the wooded glen, the fox. Xeno's paradox,
Junie like a spelling bee. It's an old Lexus

but the aerial still sniffs for overtures. Driving to Idaho,
snow-fences stripe the road heat. "Now's your namesake,"
Barker triple-skips off the silence. Junie's tall and capable
of stripping a wall to the lath: "When did you lose your faith?"
Little America looms, men with dogs in their cabs.

Barker has a thing for motel sewing kits, and symmetry.
He once weighed two madrigals. In bed she says
"I'm you, at rest." He elbows her doubt. With a logo'd pen,
she writes MISSING on his lowest rib. Junie places an ice bucket
on his chest. They are a day from dinosaurs.

Junie pooh-poohs half-life, the notion of quarrying
bones: "They have beggared stone." He thumbs
a stolen bible. The ranger recommends fishing
at Jones Hole and every language echoes off the walls.
Barker's surprised at the weight of the rocks in his pockets.

A road home, Barker smug as an empty
ashtray. The car's an age spot in the high desert,
Junie reads *The Art of Drowning*. He remembers
capturing the Horsehead Nebula with slow film
and dry ice.

Deborah Batterman

Deborah Batterman's work has appeared in Many Mountains Moving, Sistersong, Palo Alto Review, The MacGuffin, Stray Dog, and Dunes Review. She has an essay in Surviving Ophelia (Perseus Publishing). Online, her fiction is in Three Candles and Standards: The International Journal of Multicultural Studies, and will appear in an upcoming issue of prosetoad. A story of hers is among the "Notable Online Short Stories of 2003," selected as part of storySouth's Million Writers Award for Fiction. Over the years she has worked as a writer and editor for a wide range of publications and organizations, and now serves as writer-in-residence to a variety of schools in New York and Connecticut.

Defensive Driving

Blame it on the coffee. Leaking out from a paper cup with a badly designed lid. She reaches for the cup, just for a sip, a good swallow to bring down the level of coffee enough to keep it from leaking every time she hits a bump in the road. She doesn't see the next bump as she's sipping and the coffee spills over, this time on her white pants. She lets out an unrestrained "Fuck!"

"Two dollars," says her daughter. "You owe me two dollars." This is an agreement she, the mother, has come up with to bring down the level of fucks in her household. It was her idea, really, a sense of two-way behavior modification. She writes out an agreement: *Your father or I say fuck, we give you two dollars. You say fuck, you give us one dollar.* It is unilateral, nonnegotiable. And it has the desired effect. Everyone in the household – father, mother, daughter – has learned a little restraint.

Her daughter is smiling. She is smart enough to understand that respect begets respect. And she likes this easy way of earning a buck, though she has to admit the dollars are not exactly flowing. If her mother had thought of this idea sooner, she'd have a lot more money. As it is, she takes what she can get.

The mother should be smiling. Her daughter is not reprimanding her. She's playing a game they both like. But somewhere between the sip and the spill, the reminder and the smile, a deer has run into the road. The mother has only one hand free. Later, when she thinks about what happened, trying to settle on the precise sequence of events, she cannot recall putting the coffee cup back in the holder protruding from the dashboard. She can recall two hands on the steering wheel, a car swerving out of control toward a tree. And that unequivocal sense of acting on instinct. Propelled like a disembodied spirit, she knows she will not hit that tree head-on. She knows she will not let her daughter be hurt. She turns the steering wheel, the car sideswipes the tree on her side. No one is hurt, really, just a little rattled. No one is crying, just a little shaken. Like the coffee cup, she thinks, which is really to blame for the mess. In her post-accident daze, when she hugs her daughter (and hands her two dollars), so glad that no one was hurt, she contemplates suing Toyota. What were they thinking when they put the cup holder above the control panel and radio? Anyone with half a brain knows a cup holder should be designed in a way that lets the cup rest on something. Anyone with a quarter of a brain would see that cantilevering the cup holder for easy reach means obstructing the driver's access to heat and air control. Not to mention the sound system – CDs and cassettes, preset radio stations – she counts on to keep her awake, alert, at the touch of a finger. The more she thinks about it all – the spilled coffee, the deer appearing out of nowhere – the more she considers suing Toyota.

"Love you," says the man in orange as he walks into the classroom, talking into a phone. There are fifteen other people in the room, not a peep from any of them as the man wearing an orange jumpsuit enters the room. He clicks his phone shut, slips it into his pocket. He is also carrying a boom box. She slips a note to her husband, sitting next to her. *Do you think Orange Man is the instructor?* He leans over and whispers, "More likely a drug courier who has racked up too many parking tickets and now figures it's payback time." He raises his eyebrows, starts writing on her small yellow notepad. Her eyes follow, word for word: *You don't really think that's just a boom box – do you?* She is now convinced he has seen *Lethal Weapon* one too many times and has gone to sleep too many nights with *Law and Order* reruns thumping through his brain.

Orange Man wends his way to the back of the room, takes a seat. Lenore does not have to turn around to know he has pulled his phone from his pocket. A conversation begins. She imagines he is talking to his mother. He asks, *How are you feeling? Did you take your pills?* He does not say, *Love you.* He does not say, *I'm sitting in the back of a classroom waiting for an instructor who is already half an hour late.* There is a dummy, frighteningly real at first glance, on a hospital bed near the window, and a screen that gives authenticity to the hospital room setting, and a skeleton, none of which he says anything about. There is a poster, too, with a picture of a healthy infant and a message about her (his?) nine-month journey to a healthy delivery. All of which have nothing to do with the reason he is sitting with fifteen other people on a Saturday morning, waiting for the instructor.

His words ring out in an otherwise silent room. There is fidgeting and pencil tapping and stolen glances, but no one, with the exception of Orange Man, says a word.

Don't forget to take your pills.

See you tomorrow.

A short, balding man with wisps of hair stuck to his scalp like a sticky paintbrush, finally gets up, goes to the office of this alternative high school which is transformed into an adult education center on weekends. "He'll be here in twenty minutes," he announces when he returns. "If he's not here," he tries to be funny, "I want my money back." Mutiny is in the air.

The twenty-minute countdown is Orange Man's cue to light up a pipe, turn on his boom box. Eddie Murphy, sounding like a cross between Stevie Wonder and Sting, belts out the opening lines to "Roxanne." Lenore's husband Alan immediately identifies the soundtrack to *Forty-Eight Hours.*

"This instructor better come soon," he whispers, "or Orange Man is going to blow us away." Lenore is beginning to worry.

Should I tell them the reason I'm late? thinks the instructor as he hands out workbooks. *Or just let it rest with my apologies? It 's not as if I did anything* wrong – *the car wouldn't start, needed a battery. It could happen to anyone.* He looks around the room, apologizes for being so late, without explaining why. There is something inherently wrong, he reasons, with a firefighter moonlighting as a National Traffic Safety Institute instructor telling his students that he inadvertently left the low beams on. All night.

How it happened would be easy enough to explain. He normally kept the car in the garage, but the driveway had recently been paved, so he had to park on the side of the road. It was early evening when he returned home, the rain had slowed to a drizzle, making the windshield wipers useless. Making him forget the low beams were still on. His next car, for sure, would have lights that go off automatically.

A hand goes up. "This course is supposed to be six hours," says Balding Man. "Since you were – " he clears his throat, "– late, what time can we expect to end?"

"Tell me your name," the instructor says to Balding Man.

"Arthur. Arthur Mandel."

"Okay, Arthur – " his eyes scan the room, fix on the hospital bed, which jars him. He hopes this is not a sign, teaching a course on safety in a room normally used for . . . what? First aid? He looks around, sees pictures of infants, quickly seizes on the neo-natal nursing paraphernalia. *Everyone – everything – doubles as something else,* he thinks. *Even rooms.* "If everyone agrees to a shorter break," he says, focusing again on Arthur, "we will leave here as scheduled." Heads nod. It is the only bit of enthusiasm Lenore has observed since walking in here. The instructor – Bruce – sits at the desk, asks for an around-the-room roll call. It is his opportunity to size everyone one, give them names of his own. Sean (the Deer Hunter) is here to reduce the points he's gotten for running cars off the road in his Chevy pick-up. Marion (the Librarian), who should probably have given up her license by now, thinks a refresher course in rules of the road is a good idea. Matt (the Teenager) figures six hours of one Saturday of his life is a small price to pay for the privilege of driving his father's (or mother's) Beemer. Balding Arthur is obviously here for the insurance rate reduction. Juan (Disco Man) in his noncamouflage orange thinks DWI is a skill to be acquired The archetyping stops at Lenore. In her late forties, attractive in a Lauren Bacallish way, she exudes intelligence.

"Lenore," says Bruce, "what are you here for?"

She turns to her husband Alan, who is the reason she is here. *We get a reduced insurance rate of ten percent,* he had told her when he signed them up for the course. *Think of it as a refresher.* She cannot say the words *insurance* or *refresher,* they sound so stupid. The only words that come out of her mouth are, "A deer. I'm here because of a deer."

Her daughter has been terrified to get into the car with her since the accident, though she never admitted it until this morning. Eyes still closed when Lenore slips into her room to say they are leaving, Emily rolls over, reaches for her mother's hand. She is fifteen and already counting the days, still many months away, when she will obtain her driving permit. "Do they teach you how to relax more behind the wheel?" Her voice is sticky. "That's what you need." She pats her mother's hand, mumbles something about the tree she sees coming at her when she closes her eyes at night. The tree she can almost hear breathing when she gets into the car with her mother.

For the entire twenty-minute drive to the school, Lenore sips her coffee – Alan is driving – two hands on the cup. Each sip, each passing tree takes her deeper into a riddle that has become unsolvable. *Did I step on the gas, meaning to step on the brake? The ground was wet, the side of the road slick with mud. Did I slam down on the brake, out-of-control into a skid?* Up ahead she spots two baby deer nibbling in a field. Alan sees them, too, and slows down. Just in case they dart across the road. There is no sign of a mother nearby and they are too young, really, to be off on their own. Which means only one thing.

*

Women like her should not be driving, thinks Sean. *Not in this neck of the woods overrun with deer.* He pulls at the rim of his cap, runs his fingers through the long scraggly hair coiling down his neck. Thinks what a thrill it used to be hunting deer. *These days you do people a favor, getting rid of some of those fucking deer. If you do it right, get some fresh kill, you can even make a buck.*

"I once hit a deer," calls out Marion. "It was not a pretty sight."

Another one who should never get behind a steering wheel, thinks Sean. He turns to look at Marion, who is brushing wisps of silky grey hair from her face. "My front windshield was shattered." She takes a sip of water. "I'm lucky to be alive."

Sean sits back in his chair, crosses his arm. *What a fucking waste of time.* He flips to the opening page of the workbook, following Bruce's instructions to read the first three pages.

. . We believe that by the end of the workshop, you will have learned many eye opening things about yourself and other drivers. . . .

He wants to blurt out, *Gimme a break.* He wants to say what is so painfully obvious – that driving a vehicle skillfully requires a certain instinct and assertiveness (not to be confused with aggressiveness) lacking in most females and many males. It is not simply about getting from one place to another.

. . . Each student is ultimately responsible for his/her learning . . .

He glances over at Lenore, who seems very attentive in her reading. She reminds him a little of the woman who is, ultimately, responsible for his being here. The woman going 30 mph in a 45 mph zone. Okay, maybe she was going 40, like the trooper said, but it felt like 30. And there was no "improper passing," as far as Sean could tell. It was a broken line just turning solid. There were no oncoming vehicles, there was no danger. The three points he got for that violation, coupled with two incidents of "following too closely" brought him smack into the DMV danger zone. The only way he can avoid license suspension is to torture himself with this NSTI Traffic Survival Workshop. It is, he thinks, a fucking act of survival to sit through six (five, thankfully, since the instructor was late) hours of this bullshit. Everyone (with the exception maybe of the kid sitting behind him) is reading intently. No one (with the exception maybe of the kid yawning behind him) really comprehends what a great distance there is between the page and the steering wheel.

*

Those school bus days are over
It's the open road for me
There's nothin' that can stop me
The day I get those keys
    to the car
The day I get those sweet keys
    to the car

The Teenager (Matt) is scribbling. In his head he hears the rhythm of the blues. In the margins of his workbook, he is composing a song. About driving.

The instructor is talking about distractions. Animals. Cell phones. Children. Pets. Coffee.

"When you're behind the wheel," he says, "your mind should be on one thing, and one thing only. Otherwise, you're an accident waiting to happen." He looks over at the Teenager, who is doodling.

"Loud music," he says. Matt perks up. "Another distraction."

"I don't know about that," responds Matt. He slouches back in his seat, taps his pencil against the desktop. "Personally speaking, it helps me stay alert."

There is some laughter. Matt thinks that this mostly 'older' group (old enough, with the exception of Sean, to be his parents, maybe even grandparents) has forgotten what it is like to get those keys – *those oh so sweet keys* – to your first car. It is almost impossible *not* to gun the engine, push the envelope of speed limits. His girlfriend says it's hormonal – this need on the part of males (mostly) to drive fast. And it is a need. She knows a lot about hormones, so he believes her. All he knows a lot about is driving. Fast.

Which is why his mother signed him up for this day of atonement. It has nothing to do with driving, really, it's all about atonement. I mean, what's he gonna learn here that he didn't already learn in drivers' ed?

Forgive me, mother, for the sin of smashing up your car. She would not speak to him for days, and when she did, finally, start speaking, all she did was nag him about his reckless driving. For all the days the car was in the body shop, Matt was without wheels. He listened to (loud) music a lot. He ate a lot. He understood, maybe for the first time in his short life, the full meaning of being grounded. When the car was released, shiny as new, he was ready to fly. Only she wasn't so ready to unclip his wings. She liked hearing him play music, even if it was loud. She liked seeing him eat. Since he'd gotten his license two years ago, he'd become like a ghost, flitting in and out of the house. The car – the one he smashed up – is supposed to be his when she gets a new one. Suddenly she is not in such a hurry for a new car. Sharing, the control over her son's life that it brings, suits her just fine. The state trooper had clocked him going 65 mph on a winding two-lane road. The fact that he walked away with just a scratch over his left eye after skidding into a rail guard is a blessing. The mere fact that he is alive is a miracle. His mother, who believes strongly in miracles and blessings, sees this as a wake-up call, coming as it did a few days before Yom Kippur. His father, from whom his mother is divorced, sees this in less mystical terms: he was in a top-of-the-line car (BMW) with air bags, he was wearing a seatbelt. On one thing they do agree: a little humility is in order, and the Teenager will have to take one of those defensive driving workshops before he ever gets to turn on the ignition of a car again.

*

"The sun," says Orange Man. "Now there's a major distraction."

From the corner of her eye, Lenore senses movement. It is the Teenager, Matt, slouching further into his chair, his legs sticking out from his cargo shorts like monstrous caterpillars. This is just too embarrassing for him – being here – and his body is squirming for a way out. If he stands up, his shorts will drop to below his belly button, something Lenore will be spared having to look at since his shirt, like his shorts, is meant for someone twice his girth. This is a style she does not understand. The boys, friends of Emily who come into her home, remind her of the stick figures she dressed, as a girl, with cutout paper clothes. Nothing ever fit quite right. Nothing was expected to fit quite right.

Orange Man is going full throttle now, about his trip to work every day across the Tappan Zee Bridge. "I drive good," he says, "but man, I tell you – that trip home on a sunny day. The glare . . . it like blinds you. There must be one, two accidents a day." He clasps his hands behind his neck, leans back. "I think, maybe, there should be a law making people wear sunglasses." No one, not even Bruce the instructor, responds. Juan turns his statement into a question. "Don't you think it would a good idea – making people wear sunglasses? Sure would cut down on accidents."

Arthur looks at his watch, shakes his head. He would like to turn around, tell Juan what a moron he thinks he is. He would like to tell the instructor that he needs a course in classroom management. If there is anything Arthur has learned from thirty years of teaching high school mathematics, it is that students have lost their sense of place. They have forced his hand, beaten him down, given new meaning to the law of diminished returns. The art of teaching is a very far cry from what it was when he started out thirty years ago. Safety, in these times, is an illusion.

"You can't make people wear sunglasses." Arthur is curt. He turns to Bruce. "Can we move along now?"

"Why not?" argues Juan. "You make 'em wear seatbelts – why can't you make 'em wear sunglasses?"

Sunglasses? thinks Marion. *What did I do with my sunglasses?* She fishes around in her purse, cannot locate the sunglasses. She hopes they are in the car, envisions them on the passenger seat where she probably placed them when she took them off.

Or did she ever put them on today?

The passenger seat, that's where they must be. She must be careful not to sit on them . . . She catches herself, just in time. She has never really liked driving. All those cars tailgating, hurrying past her – to what? To where? She laughs to herself. *To the next stop sign.* Of all the things that Howard's death deprived her of, it is those late afternoon drives, falling asleep in the sun, her head against the window, that she misses most.

Alan thinks (no, he knows) Juan's train of thought is *cannabis*-driven. Requiring motorists to wear sunglasses is something that would only occur to someone who has smoked a lot of dope. Juan thinks (no, he knows) that his suggestion is brilliant – as brilliant as the sun glaring into his windshield on his way home from Victor's Home Entertainment Center in Rockland County, where he works as a home entertainment specialist (otherwise known as a salesman). He wonders why no one else has thought of it before. Alan smiles at the corollary to the blinding that results from sun glare. It is a condition he calls night vision. This is something he has personally experienced on more than one occasion, an ability to see more clearly, at night, under the influence of marijuana. He thinks (no, he knows) it is best not to bring this up.

"There are certain things – behind the wheel of a car – over which we have no control," says Bruce. His strategy is one of deflection, avoiding confrontation at all costs. He directs the students to the workbook.

Traffic collisions are caused by four main categories of factors . . .

"Environmental factors – weather, road layout, sun glare –" he looks over at Juan, "are the least within our control, followed by distractions inside and outside the vehicle." He gets up from his chair, sits on the desk. "The other two factors – vehicle maintenance and your mental/physical state – are much more within your control."

Juan's hand goes up. Bruce acknowledges him.

"My wife – she's a fanatic about brakes. Ever since the time the brakes gave out on the parkway. We didn't have an accident – thank God – but she was scared out of her mind, I know it. That's just the way she is. And me – all I'm trying to do is slow the car down. That is what you're supposed to do – right?"

All eyes, with the exception of Matt the Teenager (who is doodling) and Marion (who is nodding off), are on Bruce. They want an answer. They are demanding an end to Juan's inane digressions. This is a group growing more hostile by the minute.

"We'll talk about brakes later," says the instructor. "Right now I want to talk about a condition responsible for 13 percent of all traffic fatalities nationally." He looks at Marion. "DWD," he says, walking over to the chalk board and writing the three letters. "Driving while drowsy – that's something everyone has control over. I can't stress this enough." He reads directly from the workbook: *Eighty-seven percent of crashes from falling asleep at the wheel are fatal.*

Marion's eyes, rolling, follow along.

We build up a 'sleep debt' for every hour of sleep that we need, but don't get. Caffeine and other stimulants only mask the problem.

Coffee, she thinks. *Did I turn off the coffee maker? I was in a hurry, did I even drink the coffee?*

"Sleep debt," Bruce says the words again. "There is only one way to make up that debt." He looks at his watch, thinks this is a good time for a break. Marion gets up first, leaves the room, for a cup of coffee. *They've got this debt thing all wrong,* she thinks, putting her quarters into the coffee machine. *Sleep is something you* don't *do when you're in debt – you're up half the night worrying about how to make ends meet.* Howard – dear Howard – had a larger insurance policy than she was aware of. It helped her pay off an outstanding loan and some credit card bills. It helped her sleep off all her worries about debt.

*

Lenore gets a busy signal, tries calling again. Emily answers. Lenore can tell, by her distracted, one-word replies, that she is on-line. Multi-tasking the way only a teenager can. On the phone, on-line, doing homework, listening to music. All at the same time. Any suggestion on Lenore's part that she try doing *one thing at a time* is met with a frown.

"What time did you wake up?"

"Eleven."

"What are you doing?"

"Nothing."

"We should be home around four."

"Okay."

"I would like you to get outside – take a walk – do something besides staring at a computer screen having silent conversations." This is the new dynamic in the art of conversation, thinks Lenore. You see the words – shorthand, incorrectly typed – instead of hearing them.

"Actually, I may go to the mall later. I'll leave a message on your voice mail, if I do." She tries hard to sound uncertain about her plans. It is the only way she can get away with the scheme she has in mind. Her plan is simple: make the call just before dashing out the door. Her mother, who hates to be one of those people answering phones, having loud private conversations in public places, usually leaves her cell phone turned off, just checks periodically for messages. She is counting on her mother to be predictable.

*

Only this time, the phone is on when she calls. It was Alan's idea. "Turn on your phone," he whispers when Arthur forces everyone out of the room, except Lenore, to whose head he is holding a gun.

It all happened so fast.

Right after the break Bruce launches into his talk on 'driving with skills and sense.' What do you do if your brakes get wet or fail? If your car goes into a skid? If your steering fails? If your tire blows out? The thought of any one of these mishaps terrifies Lenore. Conceptually she knows what to do – move in the direction of a skid, don't step on the brake. But it all happens so fast – the urgency, the moment off-guard that precedes an accident. It is the thing on which accidents thrive. The off-guard moment. And the assumption that not everything in the universe happens for a purpose.

What was it that set him off? she thinks, her heart pounding as she watches everyone head out of the classroom. Was it the inane cartoon about the top-of-the-morning, hat-tipping Mr. Walker transformed into the scowling hell-on-blacktop Mr. Wheeler? Or was it Juan, digressing again, this time about the wife who never touches alcohol? They were in the middle of a discussion on the long-term and short-term effects of alcohol.

Brain cells are altered and many die . . .

The lens is responsible for bringing far and near objects into sharp focus. Alcohol distorts this, sending a fuzzy picture to the brain . . .

They were had just finished the segment on road rage, were onto DWI (now on the chalkboard under DWD). Driving while intoxicated, the sin of all sins behind a wheel. Juan starts in again, about how even if he has just one beer, his wife drives.

Who the fuck cares? thinks Sean.

I could use another coffee, thinks Marion.

It all happens so fast, even Arthur is not sure of the precise trigger. He knows only that he has a gun in his pocket, and Lenore is directly in front of him, and Bruce is a very poor excuse for a teacher, and looking at him from the perspective of a student does not give him the empathy it should. On the contrary, it convinces him that he, Arthur, should be doing what he does well, not sitting here listening to the drivel of dim-witted Juan who, he has to admit, looks and sounds a lot like the bitch who brought him down. The stupid bitch whose lies forced him into early retirement. Why else would he be sitting in this stupid class, for which he paid forty-five dollars in order to save about ninety on his insurance policy? Where's the logic here? Where's the justice?

Lenore's phone rings. She pulls it from her bag, hoping it is Alan. She wants to know what to do.

"Hi, Mom." Emily is surprised to hear her mother's voice. She expected – wanted – her voice mail.

"This is not a good time to talk, Emily."

"That's cool," she says. "I just wanted to let you know I'm going to the mall."

"Fine," says Lenore. Her eyes never leave Arthur and the gun pointed at her heart. She does not ask who she's going with, who's driving them, which she normally does. She does not say a word when Emily, guilty before the fact, tells her that Michael is taking Kara and her to the mall.

"Fine," says Lenore. This is not the response Emily expects. Michael is seventeen and Emily has a crush on him. She thinks she should be allowed to drive with him. She argues (on average twice a week) that Lenore has to learn to let go. Her tenacity does nothing to alter Lenore's usual response: she wants him to earn a few more miles on his own. Soon enough, she figures, her chauffeuring days will come to an abrupt end. No more drop-offs and pick-ups. The relief that might bring is no measure against the loss.

"Are you okay, Mom?" Emily's words stumble out before she has a chance to stop the clock, take them back. Every moment on the phone brings her that much closer to the dialogue she has so far managed to sidestep.

Lenore is curt, distracted. "I'm fine." Emily thinks this defensive driving course must be doing her mother a great deal of good. "Love you," she says before hanging up.

"Tell them to get the principal — and the superintendent — down here," says Arthur. He is under the mistaken impression that she is talking to someone outside the room. "Tell them I'm not letting you go until I get my job back."

Is that what this is about? thinks Lenore. *A job?*

"I want my job back," he says again. "I want my dignity."

*

Outside the room a strategy session is in the works. Bruce wants to call the police. Sean thinks they should wait.

"This guy is not going to hurt anyone," he says.

"He has a gun," Alan reminds him. "He's holding my wife hostage."

"I can take him," insists Sean.

"No-No-No," says Alan, shaking his head. He is looking through the small window of the door, where he sees his wife, a gun pointed at her, talking on her cell phone. *Who could she be talking to?* He is not about to risk her life with a Rambo-type rescue. "First of all, we don't even know what he wants."

"A distraction," says Juan. "We need to create a distraction." Everyone is paying attention. It is the only intelligent thing he has said all day.

"I still think we need to first find out what he wants," says Alan. Juan pulls his phone from his pocket, hands it to Alan. "Call her," he says. "Find out what the crazy man wants."

*

"I did not get a fair shake," he says to Lenore. The phone rings, again. It is Alan.

"How are you holding up?" he asks.

"Okay."

"Who were you just talking to?"

She does not want to say her daughter's name, not in the presence of this psychopathic balding man who is having a nervous breakdown at her expense. "Home," she answers. Her voice is about to break. He understands the code.

"What does he want?"

She hands Arthur the phone. "Tell him what you want." Arthur repeats what he has said to Lenore, then gives her back the phone.

"That's it?" her husband says.

"That's it."

"I'll get to work on it," he says. His voice sounds uncannily like Bruce Willis in *Die Hard*.

She clutches the phone. Arthur clutches gun, looks down at it.

"Funny how I got this," he says. "I'm rummaging through my wastepaper basket, looking for a phone number I'd written on a scrap of paper. My fingers touch something cold, metallic. I pick it up." He adjusts his glasses, wipes beads of sweat from above his lips. "The boy who dropped it in my basket probably expected to retrieve it. He was mistaken."

Arthur's eyes, through his glasses, remind Lenore of bullets. She cringes.

"Ever hold one of these?" He asks.

Lenore shakes her head.

"There's a weight to it – a weight that has the contrary effect of making you walk with a lighter step. I suppose I should have turned it in – along with the piece of shit who dumped it on me – but I got to like the feel of it. I carry it everywhere. It isn't so much the power it renders – though that is an undeniable reality. For me, it's more about altering the equations of prediction and probability. I am a man of mathematics, after all, a lover of algebra and geometry. And what is the universe, if not a geometric construct? I have spent more than half my life trying to instill in students a love of teasing apart fractions, coming to grips with odds, both in abstract and concrete terms. Seeing the pure beauty of a perfect right angle. And this is what I have to show for it – " He looks down at the gun, his thumb rubbing the barrel. "Odds change dramatically when you're holding one of these. A once predictable outcome is turned on its head . . . though when you come to think of it, how many things ever turn out the way you expect them to?"

An inexplicable calm overtakes Lenore. The off-guard moment has passed. She is moving in the direction of the skid, not slamming on the brakes. She asks Arthur why he lost his job.

"Stupid lying bit –" he looks at Lenore, cannot say the word he is thinking.

"This girl – Hispanic, not too bright – not that that necessarily goes hand-in-hand, but in this case it did. She was not doing very well in my class. She said I gave her a low grade because I was a racist. I said I gave her a low grade because she cut class half the time, and when she came to class, she never paid attention. Someone puts it in her head to blackmail me. I don't believe should she would really go through with it – concocting a story about how I tried to seduce her. Do you see where this is going? Can you see how ridiculous this is?"

The phone rings. Arthur is startled. Lenore answers the phone.

"Tell him the principal is on his way," says Alan. He does not tell her he is lying. He does not tell her they've decided to call the police.

*

"I still say I can take him," insists Sean. "Someone creates a distraction by the window, I run in, grab the gun." He bends over to tie an unlaced sneaker. A pair of sunglasses falls from his shirt pocket.

Sunglasses, thinks Marion. *I need to find my sunglasses.* She leaves the building, goes to her car, where she finds the sunglasses on the passenger seat. Relieved, she gets into the car. She is tired of looking at letters strung together, making no sense – DWD, DWI. She wants to go home. She starts the car, inadvertently putting it in reverse instead of drive. She steps on the gas pedal, expecting to move forward. When the car moves in reverse, she is startled. Instead of stepping on the brake, she keeps her foot on the gas pedal. Until the car lurches backward, comes to a screeching halt in the hedges alongside the building.

It is a moment of pure instinct for Sean. He hears the collision, sees Lenore (and Arthur) running toward the window. In less than the time it would take to shoot straight into the heart of a deer, he has wrestled the gun from Arthur. He hands it to the police when they arrive. Arthur is mumbling when they take him away. Something about a girl he never touched. And students with no sense of place, no interest in learning – real learning.

Something about coming to grips with odds.

Everyone else goes back into the classroom, to collect their things. There is silence, no one saying a word. Except the Teenager, who raises his hand. He wants to know, um, even though we didn't, like, do the whole course, um – we're not gonna have to come back, are we?

*

Lenore is sitting in the backseat of a car being driven by a teenager. His name is Michael. Her daughter Emily is in the front passenger seat. Emily is more amused than mortified. She figures this is a small price to pay for her transgression. Michael doesn't mind, he thinks it's pretty cool actually, to a point. It's a phase he knows will pass, this proving himself to Emily's mother. He's a good driver, he knows, and a careful one. He would never (knowingly) do anything to endanger Emily. Lenore knows better. She knows how little of it really has anything to do with knowing.

Kate Bernadette Benedict

Kate Bernadette Benedict's collection *Here from Away* was published by CustomWords in 2003.

Here From Away

Do not expect a welcome. People here
are harsh, our inclement disposition matches the weather.
Our complexions are cracked leather,
callus gnarls our unextended hands.
Our jaws are set; we neither smile nor sneer.
You are not welcome, you are not unwelcome in these lands.

"From away" is how we'll speak of you,
if speak of you we do. You will agree: the designation
suits. An old affiliation
marks your speech and lineates your mind.
Though you plant a field or occupy a pew,
we'll recognize what's plain: you are not our kind.

What of that field? It will yield, or not yield.
You own the deed but such a claim is temporary.
What of that pew, the momentary
respite from estrangement you hope to find
there? Certain ruptures simply can't be healed.
Certain quests are futile, insubstantial, ill-defined.

You quit the bright Cosmopolis to settle
in this other place, this land of sharp cliff and rough shore.
And though that parting tore
you at the root, now you quarter into new clay.
Who knows how long you'll last? You lack our mettle.
But here you are among us, uninvited, from away.

We Are Refugees

In groups of two or three, we steal through breaches in the mountains.
In throngs, we shamble over trance-inducing sands.

We left our city to the interlopers, with their new weaponry.
We left our village to feral cats and the few dying elders.

We carry dry foodstuffs in woven cloths, and motionless infants.
The Holy Book we left behind, with our intricate carpets.

By this walking we know we live. Do our bowed heads still venerate?
We cannot say; nor do we speak of bleeding or any particular
lack.

A little water may flow out of rock; we chance upon a small oasis.
To extinguish a morning's thirst, to move on: it is enough.

There is nothing to want anymore, nothing to expect.
Nevertheless, a child is delivered, ululating in the reeds.

At night, when you fly over, count the holy prayer beads of our fires.
By day, with your instruments, note the many colors of our robes.

We hear from all directions sounds of strafing and detonation.
Is there no place left where we came from, then? None where we are going?

Contemplative Observances

Let this small apartment be a cloister.
I'll be a pacing monk at morning prayer.

Let the windows of my ears shut against tumult,
let the clattering of garbage trucks be quieted.

The pure light of dawn suffuses the corridor.
Let my soul be thus illumined.

Let it darken also, for the maelstrom is infinite,
and the absolute an all-in-all of colors, a perfect black.

It's what I quail before, in my hooded bathrobe.
It's what body knows and unknows. Knows.

My arms are open for a Pentecost.
I wait for tongues, a tribulation, the flame, the lamb.

I wait for the annihilation.
Let every sense and synapse acquiesce.

Reason has brought me here, the mind my beacon.
Reason will allow the exaltation.

Faith will accomplish it, one day.
As the carrion is taken by the vulture, I will be taken.

It will be all I hope for.
It will be nothing I hope for.

It is nothing I return to now.
A bare plank floor, a pall of dust.

And in each ball of dust, a galaxy of mites.
And in the essence of each mite: *alpha, omega*.

Bruce Bentzman

Bruce Bentzman's stories and poems have appeared in *The Free Cuisenart, Gruene Street, In Vivo Magazine, The Morpo Review, Snakeskin, Southern Ocean Review*, and *Zuzu's Petals Quarterly*. He describes himself as "a practising Peripatetic Minister of Secular Humanism."

The Gospel According to Judas

I'm not really all that bad, you know. If He was alive He'd tell you. I did Him as much service as anyone. Why is everyone blaming me for His death? What I did He predicted I would do, He expected it of me, it was no different than had He instructed me to do it. And truthfully, He forced my hand. He manipulated me as readily as He did that witless Simon.

Let me tell you about, Simon. We call him Peter. None of these fellows from Bethsaida were very smart, but Peter in particular was dumb as an ox, and big as one. Mind you, he was broad as a soldier, and although he was a fisherman from a family of fishermen, he kept a short sword at his side. You have to be careful, the guy is quick tempered, but slow in everything else. Slow wit and slow feet, any of us could out run him. Besides, Jesus kept him in check. He believed everything Jesus said, not that he really understood. He was always asking Jesus to explain the parables. What an oaf. Let me tell you how Peter got his name.

There was among us two Simons. The other one was a Zealot. Anyway, Jesus decided to start calling Simon of Bethsaida, Rock. Jesus told Simon, "I shall call you Rock, because like a rock you will be the foundation on which my Church shall be built." That big jerk was so proud and grateful, and while he was gloating to his brother Andrew, Jesus leaned over to a few of us and whispered out of the corner of His mouth, "and like a rock, people will be stumbling over him trying to reach my true teachings."

Really, Rock didn't have a clue. Meanwhile, Philip, who speaks Greek, changed Rock's name to Peter, which in Greek means rock. He didn't want his fellow countryman bouncing around proudly announcing himself as Rock. Others would have seen right through that. Smart as a rock, that's Peter. One day Peter tried walking on water in imitation of Jesus, right? I've never seen Jesus walk on water, I haven't a clue how Peter ever got it into his head that Jesus could. You guessed it, he sunk like a rock.

Okay, so I've got some bad things to say about some of the others - and believe me, a lot of them would as easily tell you disparaging things about me behind my back. We didn't always get along. Peter was the least liked, which is not to say he wasn't my friend.

Peter is a big man with a sword, but let me tell you, the guy lacks determination, can't make up his own mind, and such a whiner. No one respected him, least of all his younger brother Andrew.

Andrew was always playing practical jokes on his brother. Heating a danarius in the fire, then placing it where Peter would find it, pissing in a cup of wine and offering it to Peter, putting camel dung in his brother's food. And Peter would go running off to Jesus whining, "how many times am I suppose to forgive my brother? Seven?" And Jesus, who enjoyed these jokes as much as the rest of us, tells him, "Seventy-seven." Now of course Jesus was using the incident to teach us something, that we should be endlessly forgiving of others. But that's not how Peter understood it. He starts keeping count, thinking he will one day reach seventy-seven and then beat the dung out of his bratty little brother.

As for the others, there is my old friend Thomas. Dear Thomas, I knew him before I met the others. I can't explain his infatuation with Jesus. He and I always debated religion. He liked me because I was not a good Jew, always suspecting the value in the rituals and practices of my countrymen. Thomas was not unlike me in this. He was even uncertain if he should remain a Jew. He abstained from wine and wouldn't touch any meat. It was Thomas who introduced me to Jesus and His band of disciples.

Our paths crossed in the street. I was on my way to the Temple to start a new life lending money when he saw me and called to me. He was smiling and his arms were outstretched. "What makes you so happy," I called back. And he came closer and whispered to me, "the Messiah has come and I am His disciple." This I had to see and I allowed him to lead me.

Jesus was a handsome man, tall, with large, dark eyes that held your attention, and a deep voice that held your ear. The others called Him Teacher, or Master, but none called Him Messiah to His face. When we were introduced, He greeted me with sincerity and our friendship felt old from the start. When I asked if He was the Messiah, He said, "other have called me by this name." It was not an answer and I told Him so. So He added, "the Messiah is different things for different people. What the people would expect of their Messiah might not be what the Lord intended for a Messiah. What do you expect from the Messiah?" I told Him I didn't know. And He said, "then you are welcomed to follow me, Judas, and see what I do, and ask yourself if my acts are those you would expect from the Messiah."

His round eyes studied me. "I can see that you are one who is not satisfied in your life." Was it in my stance or dress that gave me away? Who can be happy obeying their father's instruction, so of course I decided to follow Jesus, and call Him Messiah, but never to His face, if only to get me out of my father's house.

The second thing that Jesus noticed about me was the small chest of money I carried. He admired the craftsmanship, a woodworker Himself, and the finely tooled goat's skin in which the box was covered. I proudly pointed out that I had made the box, that such boxes had been my father's trade and that I had learned it from him, although I didn't much care for the work. Because of that box and the money inside it, it being my money up until that moment, Jesus appointed me treasurer of His small band.

But I was telling you about all the ardent disciples and there are others. Let me continue with crazy Simon the fanatic. He was always taking me aside and trying to convince me to join the Zealots. And when we were gathered together, Simon would mumble remarks as if in defiance of whatever opinion was being expressed. He would even sneer as he whispered under his breath, so I always suspected it was some insulting remark. How it was that he was willing to submit to following peaceful Jesus I cannot fathom? These fanatics, under cover of night, will sneak around looking for the rare Roman soldier foolish enough to be alone, and then they will murder the unfortunate fellow, slicing his throat before he can scream. Disgusting.

Then there is Thaddaeus, Matthew, Bartholomew, and the other James, the son of Alphaeus. These last four fellows are too quiet for my tastes. These four are all of a kind, and Thomas fits right in with them, young men with thin beards and gaunt bodies - well, except for the bulbous Bartholomew - and they are quiet, always preferring to show there sincerity in good acts and never a thoughtful word to explain themselves, they are completely devoted to Jesus - they are like sheep. Or so I thought.

Just because I associated myself with this small group, don't think that I was willing to accept everything Jesus said. Still, He reinterpreted the old ways into practices that made sense. But He insisted on expressing Himself in parables. I challenged Him on this once.

"So what you are saying is that the Pharisees are only following the letter of the law," I said, "but that it is a hollow practice because they've lost sight of the reason for the tradition. And so it is better to live and act in accordance with the purpose of the law and not merely to practice a tradition exactly, yet without sincerity."

And Jesus smiled at me and said to me, "you among my disciples are the wisest." Yeah, He really said this to me. But I didn't let it rest there, I didn't let Him turn my attention back with a compliment. I tell Him He ought to speak plainly. And He said, "but there is far more than can be revealed by the plain truth, a full wisdom that can only be yours when you enter the Kingdom of Heaven." And that's how He spoke. The guy would never let you nail Him down. Just when you thought you had His meaning pegged with the exactness of Greek reason, He wiggles out with some vague remark.

"How can I understand," I complained, "if you won't tell me exactly what it is you mean."

And He said, "then I would only be creating more laws for you to practice without understanding their purpose. I cannot show you a thing if you cannot see, and I intend to open your eyes so that you can see more and beyond the little I show."

On another day I wondered about Job's first wife and children. Why did they have to suffer to appease God's wager?

And Jesus said to me, "I promise you sufficient amends will be made in the Kingdom of Heaven for those who suffer in serving the Lord. The family of Job were not forsaken for having served the purpose of the Lord. Great will be their reward for trusting in the Lord."

"So you say," I said to Him, "but where's the proof?" I often demanded of Jesus that He give me evidence, show me some miracles that I could not explain. It is said that He did miracles, but I didn't see them. That men who claimed to be blind could see following His touch, that sick men could be cured by His blessing didn't impress me. I've seen many a sick man get well without Jesus.

"You do not believe your eyes?" He asked following a so-called miracle. I told Him, these things I have witnessed before, performed by holy men who said they represented other gods. I don't know why these people were sick or blind, and I don't know why they've become well, but I do know a good salesman can make people buy what they never intended to buy when they woke that morning, and many a medicine has worked on another, but never do they seem to work on me.

He put His arm around me and walked me away from the others to whisper in my ear, "Judas, what are you afraid of?" This was not unlike him. I think he had something different to tell each of us in confidence, especially my friend Thomas, the two of them often in the shade of a tree privately conversing.

I turned to Him and found His eyes sincere. Never has anyone been so concerned for me and my happiness, certainly not my own father. My tongue spoke what I would've kept concealed, what I didn't know myself. I am afraid of only one thing, I told him, death.

"Then I will save you," said Jesus matter-of-factly.

You can save me from death?, said I.

"I will save you from your fear."

One day Jesus took the whole lot of us to visit His family. The family of Jesus was very poor, yet how I did envy Him. We stayed in His mother's house for a short visit. I didn't see His father, who had recently abandoned the family. I never learned why. They never spoke of him. Still, I envied Jesus. I, who also had but one parent, a cold and critical father, and no siblings, my mother dying giving birth to me, would have traded places with Jesus. His mother was tall and proud, like a marble column. She bore no weakness and raised that family even without her husband. She evidently cared for all her children, but Jesus most of all. Jesus had younger brothers working as carpenters in a shop that by rights He should have inherited. Maybe He abandoned His father's work because of His mother, who held her first born so highly, she felt He should be spared from doing any labor. And although she embraced each of us warmly, even me, a stranger to her household - O, how dearly I enjoyed that embrace - it was Jesus that she coddled. She smothered Him with hugs and kisses as if He were her young babe and not the eldest male of the household.

I could not bear it. Yes, I was truly jealous, for I had no such mother to nurture me. Andrew and Peter would talk about their mother, also named Mary. The only Mary I knew was a little whore in Bethany. I'll come back to her, later.

I tell you, I would have traded my wealth to have had a tender mother to embrace me and approve of me, instead of a father who gave me no better than my trade and money sense. All the others, Thaddaeus, Bartholomew, even Simon the Zealot, they all had mothers who loved them.

That day in His house, Jesus called me brother, and His mother, hearing it while she served us food, said, "in which it follows then that I should call you son." She really said this to me, and said I was always welcomed. What joy that moment and those words brought to me. They became my family. So it was, when Jesus asked to see the contents of my chest, I let Him freely take of my inheritance, mixed with the money emptied from the meager pouches of the other disciples, to offer His mother.

Jesus had nothing against amassing wealth, but He thought it vile to hoard wealth. He thought little of our wants and luxuries, but whenever the chest seemed too heavy, He would cast much of it away to the needy, the money's only purpose being what good it could serve.

Well, we were in Bethany one night, while on our way to Jerusalem. Jesus wanted to celebrate Passover in Jerusalem.

O Jerusalem, beautiful, beautiful Jerusalem, can there be a lovelier city in all the world? Yet they claim Rome is grander still. I would have liked seeing Rome. In Rome do they have streets like the Street of Flowing Honey?

What if none of you have ever been to that street? What if you have never heard of it? You might be Pharisees reading this, faking blindness, as if the street doesn't exist? Let me tell you what you're missing. It is the only street in the city shaded from the sun. They have draped colored sheets from rooftop to rooftop the whole width and entire length of that splendid way. It is scented with incense and perfumes. The stuff comes wafting out of the many promising doorways. Framed in each window the most beautiful women from every land sing their invitations. They use names like Venus, Aphrodite, Cleopatra, and even Bathsheba. No man lured to navigate into that perilous strait could pass through without coming to rest on its soft shores. That is no one except, perhaps, Jesus.

What hope had I of visiting the Street of Flowing Honey, especially now that I was in the company of Jesus? It is an expensive street. Jesus would foil the pleasure I would have, if He knew. He could have walked into that street pure and untouchable, and He would have instructed those many delectable beauties, and He would not have put them to the good use for which they were intended.

What can I write, but the truth? It had been a long time for me and I would not let Jesus prevent my enjoying myself. So while we were in still Bethany, I visited that lady acquaintance of mine named Mary.

Bethany is not Jerusalem. There is but one house of Lot where I could be satisfied. Nor was it hard to find me, Jesus having sent Peter to fetch me. Glad I am he found me too late.

O my, yes. When I reached the door of that house, she recognized me, even remembering my name. She called out my name. My eyes were not yet used to the darkness of the interior, and I could just make out the shadow of her form as she danced across the room on those small feet, fleet and graceful like a gazelle, leaping into the air and embracing me. If I told you that her hair was like a flock of goats descending from Mount Gilead, her breasts like twin fawns of a gazelle, I would not be lying.

While she stood, I allowed myself to slip down the length of her body, embracing and nuzzling each descending inch until I was on my knees, my arms clasped around her firm legs. Her fingers caressed my head. She invited me with the words of King Solomon, "Let my lover come into his garden and taste of its choicest fruits."

I responded in kind. I also quoted that wisest of men, "How beautiful you are and how pleasing, O love, with your delicious delights! Your stature is like that of a palm-tree, and your breasts like clusters of fruit. I declare, I will climb this palm tree and I will take hold of its fruit." And I reached up and caused Mary to squeal and laugh as we tumbled and entwined like grape vines. That was how I wanted to spend my life, staring into the deep pools of her dove-like eyes. She was the thing Jesus could not give me. And in her grasp I did not think of death.

Before Peter arrived, I had showered Mary with some of the money that had been entrusted to me. She began by washing and massaging my sore shoulders and tired legs. She coaxed me and I came to her. It was in that happy state that Peter found me.

Imagine my surprise that the two of them should know each other. They were neighbors, or some such thing, growing up in the same village. And he starts telling her about the coming of the Messiah, how Jesus came to rescue us from our labors and from our pains. He told her of the many miracles to which he bore witness - miracles I never saw. But I digress.

Anyway, it was easy to see my tempting little Mary was becoming enamored with the idea of Jesus maybe rescuing her.

Rescuing her from what? She never seemed especially unhappy to me. She gave of herself most thoroughly and never concealed her enjoyment. Perhaps she was neither skilled nor as beautiful as the daughters of Lot in Jerusalem, but she seemed far more sincere. Perhaps that sincerity was only for me - I used to like to think so. And Peter was telling her how Jesus was God Himself, in the form of a man and walking the world.

So it was that Mary put on her finest clothes and allowed Peter, who had come to fetch me, to also lead her back to Jesus. And she carried with her a beautiful jar of carved alabaster, which I thought she would probably present to Jesus as a gift.

We arrived at the house of one Simon the Leper, so called not because he was a leper, but simply because he was so ugly. Jesus saw me enter the room and smiled. He didn't ask me any questions. There was nothing stern in His expression. It was as if He wasn't angry for my wandering off, yet He didn't hesitate to have me found and brought back. Did He know I spent some of the money from the box? He didn't seem to care. They were all reclining around a table upon which were placed sweet treats, and I saw the cups of wine and immediately put Jesus' good mood to the influence of the drink.

Peter pointed to Jesus and Mary went over to Him. She stood in awe before my Master. He looked up at her and tendered one of His irresistible smiles. And what do you think she did? This woman, who not long before laid naked beside me rehearsing wedding vows, broke open her precious jar and poured the entire contents on my Master's head and hands, and on His feet. The fragrance filled the house. Then she took her long hair and with it cleaned His feet.

I was indignant. "Why this waste of perfume?" I complained. It was expensive perfume, made of pure spikenard, worth three hundred denarii at least. And you know what Jesus said to me?

"Let her be," He said, "don't bother her." Here is my Master, who normally gives away what wealth our little troop manages to acquire, who had just had me dragged back from my little pleasure of far less cost, and now He was tolerating this same woman, she who took money from me, who was now wasting a fortune cleaning His feet?

"But Master," I cried, "if she hadn't broken the seal, if she'd only used less, this perfume we could've sold and the money we could've given to the poor!"

"Ah, but what she has done is a beautiful thing," He said through an enormous grin. Of course it was. Doing beautiful things was her profession.

"But what about the poor?" I said.

"The poor you will always have among you," He retorted, "and you will have plenty of time to help them when you want, but you will not always have me."

At the time I couldn't understand what He meant by this. He was not yet very old. Did the others not call Him God, would He not always be with us. Meanwhile, how often would I have the opportunity to be with women before I am too old and decrepit?

He leaned close to me and said, "I am going to die."

"We're all going to die, Master."

"No, no," He said and He brushed the air away as if He had left the wrong words suspended there. "I am going to die very soon. She has prepared my body for my burial."

What could I say? He said it loud enough for all to hear. What did it mean? Was He sick? At the time I didn't understand that Jerusalem would be the undoing of our happy little clan. All went astray in Jerusalem.

By the time we had arrived to Jerusalem, the fame of our Master preceded Him. A great sea of people spilled out of the city's gate to greet the Son of Man. They were the poor, the sick, the hopeless, and they were unruly. We didn't see the Pharisees. We didn't see the Romans. It was difficult just to keep at our Master's side. Nor would they allow Him to merely walk into the city, but placed Him on a young ass and shaded Him with palms. In this manner, we entered the city, being pushed and pressed.

Once inside the wall, Thomas nudged me. "Come with me," he said. I glanced at his face and immediately I knew something was not right. So it was that we abandoned our leader to the people and I permitted my old friend Thomas to pull me out of the crowd and into a side street.

He rushed me through narrow streets and would not answer my questions. He found the particular place he was looking for and brought me inside. It was a foul place, a home for thieves and beggars. I was astonished that Thomas would know of such a place. Here we waited. When I asked what was it we were waiting for, he said, "there is a traitor among us." I occupied the time drinking the poor wine they served while Thomas watched.

"A traitor," I said. "Who, and why? What is there to betray?"

"I don't know," he said. "Did you see the way Bartholomew slinked off as soon as we entered the city?"

"So what," I said. "Maybe he is going to pay a visit to the Street of Flowing Honey; or, what is still more likely with him, he is going someplace to dine."

"No, it's something more than that. Haven't you noticed how often he has suspiciously went off on his own?"

"But we all have," I answered, and wondered if they hadn't been as curious of me.

"We have followed him," Thomas said. I asked him who he meant by we. "Simon - he was the first to notice Bartholomew's particular wanderings from the Teacher. Simon has been following him." So that was how Thomas learned of this place for thieves and beggars, it was also a meeting place for conspiring Zealots.

"What is this, Thomas, are you so suspicious of your fellows?" I asked. "Have you been following Thaddaeus, or Philip, or Andrew," and here I became daring, "or me?"

"Oh, Simon, everyone knows where you go." This was news to me. "Do you think we care about your passion for women? But Bartholomew, that's a different matter. He has been visiting the homes of Pharisees." And so we waited, nor was it very long before Simon arrived with the fat Bartholomew in tow.

With violence Simon shoved Bartholomew at our table. Bartholomew came crashing to his knees knocking over my drink. The barkeep cried out and Simon shouted at him to mind his own business, at which I believe the barkeep was probably an expert. Bartholomew was quaking like a full wineskin, begging us to rescue him from that bully Simon. When I asked Simon what it was all about, he told us, "I caught this traitor at the door of one of the Sanhedrin."

"Bartholomew, is this true," I asked in my most honeyed voice. He started to deny it, but Simon gave him a kick and put a hand on the hilt of his short sword. "No need for that, Simon," I said to him. Then I asked Thomas, "and why do you bring me here? Why do you involve me?"

"Are you not the Teacher's best friend?" That's right. Those were Thomas' exact words, I swear. He went on to say, "He has favored you and it is obvious He regards you His best pupil." So it wasn't just me who thought I held this special place of honor with the Master.

"Still, why involve me, why not take him to Jesus?" I asked.

"You know what Jesus is like," answered Thomas, "he'd spare this scoundrel, even if it meant putting His own life at risk."

"Yeah, and didn't He say He was going to die soon?" added Simon. "He sees into the future and knows what this fat friend of the Sanhedrin is planning."

I told Simon to remove his hand from the sword. I had Bartholomew get off the dirty floor and sit at the table, the side furthest from the door. I had Simon sit at the opposite side. Thomas and I sat between them and could keep them apart. I opened up the money box I always carried with me and ordered more wine. Simon would have preferred cutting a confession out of Bartholomew, but from experience I knew how wine could dissolve caution and clear the throat.

It wasn't long and we had it out of him, Bartholomew was indeed a spy, at every opportunity informing the chief priests of what Jesus was telling the people. But why report it to the priests? What did they want with the information? And why resort to a spy when they themselves could come and listen to Him speak? Jesus always made free with His wisdom.

Bartholomew explained that the priest were afraid that their appearance might be construed by the people as condoning the Master. Furthermore, they thought that what He told His disciples in secret might be of far more value to them than what He freely presented to the crowds. In another time the Sanhedrin might have brought Him to trial for blasphemy, but not now under the Roman occupation. The priests were hoping to gather proof of a conspiracy against the Empire.

"And so what did you intend to tell them tonight?" I asked.

"What could I tell them? There is no hope of revolt stemming from our Master, is there, Simon." With these words, and the courage of his wine, Bartholomew squinted and stared at Simon. "We all have our reasons for seeing Jesus imprisoned, don't we Simon? Tell them, Simon, what you told me."

"And why not," Simon grumbled, first turning to look at Thomas, than at me. "He is supposed to be a leader of our people, a second Moses. If He is truly the Messiah, He will bring down our enemies."

"Simon thinks if Jesus is locked away," explained Bartholomew, never taking his eyes off a humiliated Simon, "that the people would gather into a force to free Him, and with the

Lord's hand to assist, Jesus would be leading an army. It's just a question of putting Jesus to the test, isn't it Simon?

"Then there is you, Thomas," and Bartholomew directed his words at my friend. "You, too, see Jesus as a second Moses and hope he will create a new moral order. You want to see Him bring about ten plagues to bring down the Romans. You think if He is cornered, He would defend Himself and you need those grand miracles because you want to believe He is sent by our Lord.

"And you, Judas," and Bartholomew turned his gaze towards me. "You think we don't know how you have been squandering the money entrusted to you? Perhaps you would simply like the Master locked away so that you can make off with whatever is left in that chest you guard."

"And you, Bartholomew?" I asked. "You are the only one among us who acted on his whim to see Jesus imprisoned, what is your reason? Did you need further proof that He is the Messiah?"

He answered, "I went, yes, and you probably won't believe this, but all the time I was revealing what He taught us, I was hoping the priests would never find fault with His wisdom. I suppose I, too, was putting Jesus to a trial, but I never intended to be the cause of His capture. I went to them with my reports to hear their arguments against Jesus. No different than any of you, I need to know if He is really the Messiah."

"And now He says He is near to His death," remarked Simon, "so it doesn't make much difference. If He dies He cannot lead His nation against the Romans."

"Die!" responded a startled Bartholomew. "Why should He die? The priests have no longer any right under Roman law to execute anyone."

"But you heard Him at Simon the Leper's house," Thomas reminded Bartholomew.

"And don't you remember Lazarus at that dinner," I reminded Thomas. "Surely if our Teacher can raise the dead He has no need Himself to fear death. But if He was to die, what would you do after He is dead?" I asked Simon.

"If He does not raise an army to lead against the Romans, then I will seek some other Messiah," he answered.

"And you, Thomas?" I asked.

"I don't know," he answered.

"Ha! Thomas is uncertain about everything," Bartholomew said. "He couldn't find his way out of the sun without someone to guide him."

"And you, Bartholomew?" I asked.

"I will serve the Lord," he announced, "either through the Master or without Him. I have always meant to become a priest."

"You will make an excellent fat priest," I told him.

"And you, Judas," asked Bartholomew, "what will you do if the Teacher dies?"

I said, "what, me? I shall find a firm woman with smooth skin that has not been parched by the sun, and with her I shall fulfill the Lord's commandment to be fruitful." This was sufficient to make the fellows laugh.

"I bet you were hoping it could be that beauty who came to supper the other night and poured perfume all over our Teacher," said Simon.

To which Bartholomew added, "I don't think any of us missed your reaction to that. You were certainly jealous."

"I was not jealous," I said.

"Well, it doesn't matter now, you certainly have no hope of fulfilling the Lord's commandment with her," said Simon, "not now that she has been blessed by Jesus. I understand that she has returned to her father's house and will probably marry the neighbor."

I wondered how much they knew to be teasing me so. At that table, only my friend Thomas should have known that Mary was someone special to me. Thomas, who sat opposite me, was not laughing with the other two. His eyes pitied me. I forget what Thomas then said, but he diverted the conversation elsewhere. Good friend, Thomas. By this time the wine had relaxed the others and we were all once again friends.

It was night when our gathering left the bar. The other three returned to the fold of their Shepherd. I said I had somewhere else to sleep. Bartholomew, who was as drunk as Noah, laughed and challenged me, saying that I was probably on my way to spend the night in the Street of Flowing Honey. I put on an embarrassed face, as if to suggest he had found me out, but I went to the Sanhedrin.

During the next few days I made several visit to the house of a chief priest. That first night, at that late hour this son of Aaron was awake, his servant willing to let me in, once I told him I was a disciple of Jesus. I found the old keeper of the flame in a room among his scrolls studying by the light of an oil lamp. On the second visit, a deal was struck. Thirty pieces of silver. Oh, what I could have done with thirty pieces of silver. It was enough money to go to Rome and start a new life. And it could have been enough to take another with me, if Mary had wanted to come.

On my third visit there were several chief priests and a contingent of Roman soldiers. No one had mentioned soldiers. Why were they necessary? I found out too late.

I lead this contingent to my Master, and when I greeted Him with a kiss, He asked, "would you betray me with a kiss?"

Betray Him, how could I betray Him? Did the people rise to defend Him? They didn't. They betrayed Him. Did our Father in Heaven deliver Him from bondage? The Lord our God betrayed Him. Did Jesus call upon the unlimited powers He claimed to possess to protect Himself? None of these things happened. He submitted. He allowed Himself to be bound and led away. And they killed Him. O Lord in Heaven, hallowed be Your secret name, how could you let them kill Him! Why? I don't understand why? I never meant for Him to die, why did you use me this way? And to be crucified? Why so ignoble a death?

The citizens of Jerusalem now hate me. Some dark night they will grab me off the streets and surely stone me to death in an alley with no outlet. My own people hate me. Mary, His mother, she must hate me, now. And the other Mary, beautiful Mary, my Mary, that Jesus blessed in the house of Simon the Leper, will she not hate me too? What reason have I to live?

What good were thirty pieces of silver to me? I never took that money to see the Master killed. I have caused the death of an innocent man, a wise man, a good man, which was never my intent. The silver became poison to me. I threw it back at the priests in the temple and shouted at them to use it to bury my Master. He shall surely get a splendid funeral for all that silver. Maybe He had planned it that way all along, for I believe He planned His death. He had said, "it remains only a single seed, but if it dies, it produces many seeds."

He said He would take away my fear of death and He has.

Janet Bernichon

Janet Bernichon is a registered nurse from Long Island, NY is a major contributor to
Intensive Care: More Poetry And Prose By Nurses, University of Iowa Press. She also has
written for Newsday's Commentary. Janet is a Pushcart Prize nominee.

Eden Revisited

The first time
after the divorce
she pulls the sheet up
to her neck
covering her self-conscious
underwear, covering
what she got used to-
the rolls and sags
that won over years
of crunches and carrot sticks.
She never really believed
they could stop time.

She rehearsed.
Like a kid practicing kisses,
she prepared before a mirror
her best angle, contorted
into a still life study
of perfect arrangement,
flesh that had settled
into comfortable form.
Over time, marriage molded her
to a husband. Almost as one,
they took shape. It seems

unnatural now,
aroused and undressed,
back again in Eden
overgrown with embarrassment
untended for years.

The Line Is Always Busy

Standing on the corner of her life,
in a dimly lit phone booth,
Sharlie presses her blue denim butt
against the plexiglass. Her baby
forgive me forgive me forgive me
call nothing more than breathing
on the answering machine.
He stays away
since she got caller ID
and an order of protection.

She warms up
under the florescent light,
after her long walk in the battering
wind, cowering from cars
nearing the curb. She is afraid
of aluminum pots, unlocked doors,
of being alone. She cringes
at the stench in here.

Someone pissed in the booth. Some
man like a dog marking his territory
or a cat spraying his intentions
or a drunk not knowing the difference
between a pay phone and a pay toilet
or some crazy urinating liquid
Krypton on some invisible
superman he knows lurks in there.

And that man really calls
those numbers scratched
into the glass or written
on a wall in lipstick or marker,
with round gloom
longing for blond fate
to answer.

And she does—
her date with death late.
There are worse ways to go
than by crimes of strangers, muses
Sharlie. How slowly time
bleeds out its final hours.

"Hey you, I need to use the phone."

Faux is dressed to kill
in her low cut
blood count and
virus pooled in bruises
skittering across her pale
skin. In a cell dead
zone, she needs
to press her lips against
the mouthpiece, held as a prayer
in her palm, and talk dirty
for her next fix. Sharlie pulls

her collar up and pushes past
neon skull and cross bones
back into the street, wind blown in wake
of a passing car. Faux talks
like a Charlie Parker solo.
Have need, will travel.

In the rear view mirror,
Desperation, life tossed
on the back seat, watches the booth
recede into its aftermath.
It sneers and speeds up.
Destination? Stick
a pin in a map, it will be there

phoning its obsession
calling the cops, beeping
its connection, ringing
the suicide hotline,
dialing a prayer

Death Row

The hallway does not go on forever.

A spirit's long
stemmed ruination
lives in their condemned skin,
under the mesh of light,
that yields to the night.

Walking on their knees
to the necropolis
do they find deliverance?
Does it come through the mesh
and blind them to the scars
on walls splattered
with slaughter?
Does it blind them
to written epitaphs
angrily clutched in protest-
it's right
it's wrong.
Does it matter?

The floor is littered
with human parts, obstacles
not impeding their progress
of dying to dead.
There are no doors, no windows,
no fresh air to circulate
no white noise
no thunder,
only broken wings bleeding,
perishable, weeping.

as they walk, and walk again.
Walk until time runs out

Robert Brueckner

Classically trained in flute — he studied with members of the Chicago Symphony Orchestra, and played in that organization's training orchestra — **Robert Brueckner** made his living playing and teaching until age 30, when he opted for a more lucrative career in advertising. His musical skills served him well, and he wrote and produced commercial music and commercials until he became bored with ads and fascinated with multimedia and the Internet. He now designs and develops Web sites and interactive vehicles for Web delivery, including the Alsop Review site. When not working or writing poetry and fiction, he plays the piano and is an avid cyclist.

Corners of the Eye

From my porch I see dryads come
out of their forest each night,
damp as oysters in the nude
and glowing foxfire violet.

They could almost be tattoos
on the arms of a dark islander
who fashions logs into vessels
that glide on silent lagoons;

or dancers whose moves entice
the sifting shades, engulf
them for as long as it takes
to consummate a *pas de deux*.

I must pretend I'm sightless,
cannot feel the subtle pull
of tree-fog light on retina,
or in an instant they will flee.

Creatures, conjured from wood
come alive apart. They wonder
why we refuse to speak their name
or say the man in the moon is a lie.

A Woman Combing

You see her in tangerine light
making shadows on the stone,

facing away from the light,
head down as if in thought.

Her gown strap unsupported
genuflects across one shoulder

and the tortoise-shell comb moves
like a loom, jacquard weavings

that pull back and forth through
working fables yet to come.

There are men in the distance
hunting boar in sparse woods

but here is a scene of women
who have greeted each other

with a kiss. They admire a swallow
drinking from a marble fountain.

The one holds the other's hand
in a way that means nothing

or everything, and they may be
sisters, or mother and daughter,

or someone's long-dead ancestors.
Like the sudden rearing of a horse

she throws back her hair in an arc
as light from the infant sun warms

her cheek and raises her eyebrow,
as she catches your eye and sees

you've been holding your breath
as the story unfolded from her hair.

sumi-iro-na kami-no-ke

Your ink-hued hair and wheaten skin, in shade
your eye, like darkest life, obsidian —
in light reflect *sakura-bana* glints,

a perilous vitality, which seems
most precious when it quivers on the twig
in paper white, when just about to drift,

when just about to fall, *josei*, so light,
the bright of death floats all around — but still
your charcoal hair, your iris flashing jet.

Sunrise Breakfast
Pennsylvania Turnpike, 11/24/03

For hours skeins of spun-sugar fog
catch at my burrowing headlights.

My mind waters for light, images
beyond these two incandescent swabs

probing the vacant yawn of night
which lies about everything.

Then the merest arc of cantaloupe
impeaches the darkness, peeks out

coquettishly from whipped cream,
sly and luminous on pale blue china.

All at once my lips form an *O*:
I ought to stop and help myself.

There in Black & White

About the smiles: people smile for pictures.
They're always made to stretch their lips, show
some teeth to others who will see this shot

a hundred years from now — in case one
could care how people hid what they really felt
on a warm June night in nineteen thirty-six,

a night picnic beneath a stalwart oak
where the hunters had caught up to the two
and pulled them up like piñatas to be

beaten as the world blacked out — or steers,
to judge from the dark stains on the front
of their trousers. Cars drew up in a circle

like wagons, ringed the women and kids
and roasting flesh somewhere in southern Indiana
where even from a black-and-white photo

I could hear the crickets and June bugs
and smell the hayfields, the cooking flesh,
feel a breeze stir the hairs on my forearm.

Firelight showed a girl like my cousin Pam
who gave the best smile of all, a warm
caress from someone capable of love

and ready for it too — you could tell
from the way her grinning, hopeful boyfriend
had his arm around her, looking at her

smile, or past her smile, thinking about
her breasts, her warm flesh on a warm
June night when the satisfying labor

of gelding and hanging had been done
and now thoughts could turn to lighter
pastimes, such as how to get the smiling

girl to yield. But she was ready for it.
His look said this was going to be the night —
and to think it only took something as simple

and fine as the stringing up and burning
of two men. They called it a barbecue,
not a picnic, certainly not a chore

because it was all about good folk
getting together to do what they do
when feeling right: sing some songs,

have a few beers — later get laid,
if lucky as this boy with his muscular arm
around my cousin's waist, her warm smile

and lovely breasts. And maybe that smile
didn't hide anything at all, and this
was just the perfect ending to a perfect day,

all there in black and white, a fond memory
lying at the bottom of an oaken hope chest
inherited from a great aunt who'd made us

lemonade and laughed at our shenanigans
as Pam and I scrambled warm and happy
after fluttering bugs in the porch-lit night.

Julie Carter

Julie Carter lives with her husband in Ohio where she works
as a sales manager for a manufacturing firm.

Visitation

This is the grey beginning,
the cold dinners from a machine
at 2 a.m., the quarter's clink.

There is a way to sleep,
head canted just so, that the long
smooth muscles in your neck
suspend your skull. There's an angle
when your body balances so sweetly
on the armless chair. The aide
knocks again, rattles with her cart
and you swim toward the surface—
lose your place.

No tincture can make coffee
drinkable, no cream alchemy. The cup
tips in its bin, you are burnt
opening the porthole to set it right.

No aspirin, no gauze. You lap at the remnants
of grit-wallowed tea. Your jeans squeak
on the vinyl, grip, keep the pressure
from the foot you have wedged against the bed.

This is the blue echo of voice after voice
speaking up for the deaf. We're not
all here. We have assigned hours.

Snatchers

My dead uncle came out of the restroom
casually, like last year's cancer
was of no concern. He's taller now,
and the grave leached the grey
from his beard. I was tempted
to offer him popcorn, a drink,
or to sidle close enough to feel
if he still radiates.

The dead flock to crowds, darting
at an eyelid's edge (Isn't that?
Isn't that? It can't be. He's gone.)
where a jowl's droop recalls
Francisco Franco, a whisker's droop
Wild Bill. I have outlived
too many faces; they reappear
in theater lobbies or grocer's queues,
and cannot remember whose souls
once enlivened their skin.

Revelations

A stronger wind reveals the shape of things,
as leaves peel back from blackened twigs, or hair
displays our curving skulls. A kite's frayed strings
uncoil like asps, then snap. The lawn chair's wings
emerge when it takes flight. The skirt betrays
the thighs while mortar cracks in walls once square.
Deep-footed oaks tug at the ground and craze
the hunching concrete walk. A draft surveys
the floorboards like a tomcat. Snow falls up
and drifts the sky. Every straight thing bends
to greet the ground. Although our faces cup
the wind in hollows, skin can't comprehend
the jut of bones, the way the cyclone's maw
can find the sharp spear heart inside the straw.

Lens

The branches spread like Rio Jesus, gold
with carotene and sunburn, at the curve
of highway twenty-two. My husband folds
the map in threes and mutters at my nerve
in spying miracles in autumn trees
or Virgin Mary rutabagas. He
is for agnostic things, at best, so please
keep silent my whimsical piety
and drive. The windshield seems to magnify
the sun to burn our corneas away
like sidewalk ants. A driver cruises by;
perhaps he wonders why the trees today
are so disguised and strange. The sun can pass
no secrets through shatter-resistant glass.

Arrest

If I could hide within the hoops of bone
the surgeons cracked and spread like swallow wings
to free your heart, I would. You cannot doubt.
I'd ease beneath the surface of your skin,
breathe only when you breathed, stop up my ears
to any noise but hushing blood. And when
you died no one could pry me out again.

David Cazden

David Cazden, from Lexington, Kentucky, is currently poetry editor of *Miller's Pond* magazine. His poetry has recently appeared in *The Chiron Review* and *Rattapallax*, as well as online at *Tryst* and *The Pedestal*. His first chapbook, *The Joy Of Cooking School*, is forthcoming from H&H press.

Sunstroke

All I wanted today
watching you tend the garden
in the humid hunger of August
was to make you a perfect glass of water
like a perfect martini.

I went inside where the refrigerator had frozen over,
my thumbs digging into the ice.
I poured the water like a soothing voice.
I did not sense the dancers
of your spirit and body break stride.

Your feet turned inward on the parched surfaces of the yard.
You fainted in the flowers.
You felt that they held you
and swore they spoke the holy language.
You fell near the unbearably thin legs of crickets
sparkling in the grass.

And I held your head
as if it were a huge blossom,
the ambulance lights flashing
in a rapture you thought was yours,
green then red, the dancers circling
together again, behind all that I saw in your eyes.

The New Geometry

When nights were square
they would not ease into our arms,
not like the rounded nights of marriage.

Square nights fit beneath the windows,
arrived in envelopes with locks of hair,
without a note or invitation.,
addressed in our own writing.

Night's corners bumped into us
with bare-shinned suddenness.

You appeared in my apartment
against bachelor button blue
tinted walls.

Sitting on un-cushioned furniture,
I found freckles halfway down your neck
where the sun left off

and night's reluctance
took its photograph:

first the chairs
around the wooden table

then scalloped shapes, like hands, appeared.
I went pale

when the window closed its shutter
and you were over
exposed. This
I thought, is what occurs
whenever a night lingers
a moment too long.

Melanoma

Every month the doctors check
each stretch of her,
down to the paper ribbons
wound between the toes.

But I see only skin
the color of mocha,
freckles of cinnamon and clove.
As auburn hair falls upon the table

she tells me how they examine
the neck, the elbows, the delta
of the back, where a cool rain pours,
and I ask can I see the scar

so she pulls a sleeve away
from the center of her arm
revealing seared streaked skin
the color of pork left on the barbeque.

This is the opposite
of what a kiss might do,
an unraveling of flesh,
the threads tied down.

She stares at me through glasses
thick as bowls of water.
At twenty five she already talks
beyond the afternoon. And after

our awkward conversation
I return to editing her poem,
erasing a few lines,
as if my hands could change
a story not my own.

Wiley Clements

Born in 1928 and raised on a one-mule farm in rural Alabama, **Wiley Clements** now lives in
Lewisburg, Pennsylvania where he retired after a long career, first as a military journalist and
later as developer of a half-dozen HMO's from the northern plains to the mid-Atlantic coast.
Though a chronic writer of metrical verse since childhood, his first book of poems,
Yesterday, or Long Ago, was published just this year by Clock and Rose Press
of Harwich Port, Massachusetts.

The Last Age

I hear time's wingèd car so I
afoot will go
to find a plot in which to lie
so deep that no
alarm will break again the long
sleep I knew,
or did not know till in a throng
I battled through,
became myself and gladly strong
to worldward grew.
Let the stones be cut and set
at head and foot;
I have some time for pleasure yet
before I put
my fiddle and my gun away,
my Nell and Jenny,
Dolly, Deb and lusty Faye,
my last of many.

Letter to Ezra (1970)

Dear Mr. Pound, I write
To say that I regret
I missed the chance you granted me
so long ago in Wash., D.C.
I wish we'd met.
Yet I can truly say
I could not fathom why
the note I sent, although naïve
and importuning, should receive
so strange reply.
I wrote to you in fall;
you answered in the winter:
an envelope addressed to me
in your own hand, presumably,
but in it-no letter.
I saved it, souvenir
of you and your condition.
Years after, peering down inside
I saw what you had meant to hide:
this cramped inscription:
Next Saturday at 2pm-
They read my mail, you know.
By then I had a family,
and you were free in Italy
where I could not afford to go.

The Other

I feel a consciousness around me,
a formless interest waiting, waiting,
patient as immortality,
asking nothing, nothing stating;
only waiting.

Incident at Stirling Castle

(September 1842)

MacKim an I stuid furth that day,
in tairtans bleck an green;
the Bleckwatch baund begaud tae play
God Sauf oor Gracious Quean.

Victoria rade throu the yett,
a gret lord by her side.
"Which heroes do we decorate?"
she askit, an he replied
wi a hauty glence at me an MacKim,
"Your Highness, these are they."
"How odd a phrase," she says tae him,
"Whose English is it, pray?"
"Madam, it's Your Majesty's'."
"Not ours, my lord. We'd say
not 'these are they,' but they are these
we honour as best we may.
Let each be made a captain, please,
and paid a captain's pay."

Sae lown a quean, sae strang a wit,
the strangest o thaim aw;
MacKim an I wad ser her yit
gin muntains aw doun faw.

Terese Coe

Terese Coe's poems and translations from Ronsard and Rilke have appeared or will soon appear in *The Formalist*, *Verse Daily*, *Leviathan Quarterly (UK)*, *The Edge City Review*, *The New Formalist*, *The HyperTexts*, *Electric Acorn* and other journals and e-zines.

Sappho, Remembering Atthis
(Adaptation from Sappho)

You, renowned as a goddess,
she took most delight
in your singing. Now she,
unique among Lydian women,
is bright as the moon among stars
when the sun sinks low,
and clings with fair graces
to the salt sea
and the flowering lea,
alive with white dew's traces.

Soft roses, chervil,
fragrant melilot
all bloom. Often,
as she goes out,
she remembers gentle Atthis
with a smart;
then grief sets her down
and devours her tender heart.

Cretan Artemis (Rilke translation)

Consultant: Claudia Grinnell

Wind of the green foothills: wasn't her brow,
somehow, an agent of light? Even crest
of the roebuck's headwind: did you give her shape,
her deerskin tracing her unknowing breast

like some mercurial foreboding?
While she, as if from distances around,
she'd known it all already, tucked in tall
and cool, stormed along with nymph and hound,

testing her bow, and bound
by the high sling of her quiver,
now and then summoned

to strange outposts only,
and forced to subdue her fury
by cries from the birthing ground.

The Houdini of Tahini

Known as Houdini in cavern and souk,
his NSA code *Yokohama*,
he sweats in his burka, a ladylike spook,
while everyone looks for Osama.
He's not on the Khyber, he's not in Kabul,
there's nothing in Tora and Bora—
we know he departed with all camels full
and a box that belonged to Pandora.
He could be a Saudi, could be a Pak,
could be a plant for the Commies—
whatever he could be, we just want a whack—
before he blends in with the swamis.
Last seen on the edge of Mazar e-Sharif,
he was crouched by a hookah, sedated—
now satellite infrared tells us the thief
has been transubstantiated.
Known as Houdini in cavern and souk,
his NSA code *Yokohama*,
he sweats in his burka, a ladylike spook,
and searches himself for Osama.

Rachel Dacus

Rachel Dacus's poetry and prose have appeared or are forthcoming in various publications, including *The Atlanta Review*, *Flyway*, *Many Mountains Moving*, *Prairie Schooner*, and *Rattapallax*. In addition, her work has been included in the anthologies *Ravishing DisUnities: Real Ghazals in English* (Wesleyan University Press, 2000), *The Poetry of Roses* (Abrams, 1995), and *The Best of Melic* (Melic Review, 2001). Her poetry collection, *Earth Lessons*, was released by Bellowing Ark Press in 1998.

Riddle

Thirty-three hundred wing beats a minute
—in figure eights from those jointed hands—
keep the ghostly wings
hovering between worlds.
To see them folded and the bird
a minuscule sphinx on a maple twig
was something like seeing time
suspended. Eternity's long beat.
A clawed foot lifted
and pawed behind what must
have been an ear. Christmas trees whirling!
The throat feathers flashed red, green,
red—an indecisive stoplight
gone wild, freezing me,
then just
gone.

Fertilizing

It's the opposite of grieving,
scattering nitrogen pellets
around shagged bud unions,
feeding high-season hunger.
Thorny canes, more likely to sprout
pine cones than blossoms,
rock in the wind.

Feeding roses that might have been
cut when you died, I learn
to trust unlikeliness.
If I penetrate the shade
beneath each bush too deeply,
tossing nutrients, a stab draws blood.
I look up, sucking the wound
under spiny branches that caliper
the span of a cloud and measure
the richness of cabbage
and coffee feeding calloused feet.

You untangled branches.
Master gardener, you cherished
each new leaf and fed
its lavish urge. Blood's pulse
distances. You step out
and away from life in the dark soil.
And I lean in, and toss.

Thunder-Edged

Sun under chin,
she rambles after them
as they garden the hillside.
Brushed with light, she rides
low among slim stems,
thunder-edged.
Slipping through holes
in wind, she rolls
under a flower's hem.
Buttercup, they call
her, but tuck her into a null
crib to listen to thin
mosquito hours. Again
and again, no one.
The child's ear hums
with moon's footfall
on the hill, a cloud-tall
lady who kindles the lights.
By day, rolled up tight,
she is given to those who prick her
scalp with needle fire. She blurs
and shrinks into thickets,
rooting fists on stone.
In the shimmer of alone,
how she spins
light, how sparks flee
the first wound, how it brims.

Ruth Daigon

Ruth Daigon was founder and editor of POETS ON: for twenty years until it ceased publication. Her poems have been widely published in E mags, print mags, anthologies and collections. Daigon's poetry awards include "The Ann Stanford Poetry Prize, 1997 (University of Southern California Anthology, 1997) and the Greensboro Poetry Award (Greensboro Arts Council, 2000). The latest of seven books is "Payday At The Triangle" (Small Poetry Press, Select Poets Series) based on the Triangle Shirtwaist Factory Fire in New York City,1911 was published in 2001 and one of her many readings was performed in The Lower East Side Tenement Museum in Manhattan, the area where the fire occurred. "Handfuls of Time" (Small Poetry Press, Select Poets Series), her last book, was published in 2002, Her poetry was published by the State department in their literary exchange with Thailand and their translation program has just issued the first book of Modern American poets in English and Thai in which she appears. Garrison Keillor featured her poetry on his morning show Poetry Almanac

Incompleteness is All We Have
(Charles Bukowski)

If we love each leaf, each
small animal, the rind, the seed,
the flesh of fruit,
then hidden in the basketry of shadows
could it be you, could it be me,
could it be anyone.

Mother is water,
we hear with our eyes,
see with our skin
and listen to visible echoes.
Why do we long for temporal magic?

If incompleteness is all we have
and time is a crack in the lens,
let us settle for urban grit,
astral dust and spend the hours
gathering hawthorne berries
to soothe the heart.

Bittersweet

these are the falling years for them
they will go deep and remember
how they flew the ecstatic moments
and returned to a nourishing earth
and what they never knew they invented

caressed by a wind
stirring their deepest sleep
they walk the paths of earth
step by step stone by stone
until parachutes of light announced the dawn

youth was once a gift they could afford to lose
but now as the moments spin retreats
every day is strung
and restrung like broken beads

the storehouse of the past guards
the silken clefts of the body
the straight secret of the spine
the winged scapulae
with their recurrent hints of flight
and the blind hours before dawn to midnight's blaze

the heart recalls
the suddenness of trees
and flawless entrance of morning light
spring blooms and impermanent buds
flowers so fragile and generous
willing to fade
giving way to the fruits of summer

ripe and bursting to bloom
the juice flowing from within
abundant
and the rich life reaching down to the roots again

Dark Duet

lovers creates their own patterns
as they move through light
reaching for the stillness

locked in parallel dimensions
trusting their feet
the arms extensions
the wrapped hearts
a fierce joy spilling from them
in spasms of delight

their bodies forget time and place
and without effort
shake off the cadence of the hours

leaning hard into each other
they move in abstract figures
he spins her out
and brings her back
holding her body tight until he knows it by heart

in a dream of possibilities
a touch more than touch
they become artless motion
gestures purer than language
in the dark duet they now perform

where the passion lies in absence of passion
and deep movements from a crimson center
the bodies learn their sweet particulars
reaching for the beat below the beat
the tender compromise

breaking through a flow in time
the pure silk of movement
they surrender and extend
in exuberant gestures
and sensuous rhythms of the dance

Inside the Moment

On scrubbed autumn days, nothing grows
but absence. She's at the pond
sighting wild geese overhead
and the sun trapped in civilized ripples.

Along pond's perimeter a silence
waits for winter. Slow currents
prod a scum of leaves
from one shore to another.

2

Frost sets in with its brittle stalks
and heapings of salt hay. Winds
blow in the same bare place.
Winter's breath adds another layer to the year

Fixed in that perfect tense
like a bird hanging midair
frozen inside the moment,
she surrenders to the silent population of the snow.

3

The weather vane grinds on its swivel.
Her eye blots out images of green, finding comfort
in bare limbs. A snowflake resting in her palm
makes of her life a crystal moment.

She's wrapped in frost-thinned moonlight
and a twilight of voices humming
love songs, birth songs, death songs.
All the melodies she left behind
return and take her into their arms.

Chains of Radiance

I have outdistanced this body
that slipped from me
like a fish
floating free of itself

The great sea travels underground
with tongues of tides that sing the earth open.
Harnessed by water I plunge into the current
then turn and swing into the deep

mouth cupping air
body riding the wetness
arms reaching beyond themselves
thrust contain recover, thrust contain recover

The water's granular with light—
chains of radiance
tilting and twisting.

My body, a wet suit
filled with flesh and longing,
rises wingless to the surface in sunlit strokes
over ocean's veined landscape

In a damp continuity
water enters me entering the water
Backward strokes reveal wrinkled maps of hands,
where they've been, where they're going,

reshaping surfaces,
changing rhythm and direction,
rescuing stillness from its own weight
and then becoming stillness again

The smell of rain's skin
mingles with my breath
and blood moves through me
as an unseen light.

All the oceans I contain
flood through me
as I float embraced by the depth
in intoxications of calm.

Music to make your Rib Harp Sing

Morning rises from the slot of earlier mornings
heavy with green counterpoints of sound
swelling the air with grace
or harmonies freezing the soul

and below the sieve of heaven
intoxicating calm and music
inviting us to enter the wild light
and call it love

After all the unbridled cadenzas
let the air circulate
let the light enter
let the quiet fold in upon itself

Before the unending flow and spiraling echoes
let there be intervals older than time
alphabets of silence
and the quick breath of the moon

Birds on windowsills
telegraph their hunger
as a worm sings in the throat of a robin.

The ocean glistens
with a thousand voices,
the shore foaming harmonies

and the blood pumping toward the heart.

Time Warps

Walking tames the wilderness.
Inching over a segment of soil, we find
dill growing wild through sidewalk cracks.
and we can almost hear the voices of the dead
made perfect by their absence

We walk familiar fields.
Choose a tree.
Count the leaves and branches
down to invisible roots deep in earth

These are the clear days
fragile as air
where the hours grow pale
just below the ribs of night.

.

We live in collusion with the sun
and conspiracies of light
and climb secretive into the atom's heart
while the sky's perimeter draws near and nearer.

After the summer heat
the sun floats pale moving inward
withdrawing its rays
its ring of steady warmth
while the years burn down to autumnal heart beats
and the black honeycombs of generations
fall between the dried leaves covering the earth

Let them go
            Let them all go

Between a hard rim of daylight
and the trough of night
swift seizures of dark appear and disappear
and time means nothing at all.

All the Old Dreams

The day is full of eyes,
a desert of faces
the corridor crowded with weeping images
and the moon casts an icy blue light.

Our flaming origins
pushing through earth's crust
bring us to air
and we breathe

Now morning invites us in
to examine the future
where we study
the catechism of seed, fruit, core

Through cracks in the universe
we view a world green and blameless
a drum in the desert, an eye, a window
a dialogue of light

The flawless entrance of dawn reveals
a suddenness of trees
and all the old dreams
fading to whispers

and before the nuclear dawn
I look up at the pale abundance,
the legendary space where hope remains
pure with wonder
fragrant with remembrance.

Seasoned Syllables

In the cold kiss of evening
and the deep throw of heaven
our apprenticeship begins.

We taste the honey of spring
the pitch and pulse of wind.
Light crawls toward us
and sound leads us to its source.

Words surround us with the smell
and spread of their soft flesh
and seasoned syllables. We're covered
with the dust of mother tongues.

Days expand. Wild grasses
weave a new language,
our thoughts advancing
like an army of fire ants.

We lick our lips
tasting the flavor of youth.
a time of fruitful innocence
like the inward glow of the plum as its juices flow.

Julie Damerell

Julie Damerell has been writing poetry and prose since 1997. Her writing can be found here and there, in print and on-line., http://juliedamerell.com. She edits the web version of *miller's pond* and teaches at Monroe Community College in Rochester, New York. Her chapbook, *Needing Blue*, is available from her or her publisher, H&H Press, http://handhpress.com/.

In the Heat of an October Night

Black before time, the sky spools yellow
through treetops, illuminates maple skeletons.
Thunder tumbles across sullen fields, spills fear
from chasms that spit dark, then darker.
We ignite candles, gather flashlights, rummage
for a cache of candy.

Shadows thrown by fingertip flames drop
from walls, shift left to right, lengthen to reveal
secrets normally wound tight within our frames:
we're more alone than we thought, more afraid
than we admit, less defined by day than night.

In the absence of color, the absence of clamor, desire
assumes shapes recalled to the tune of water on glass,
the hollow of night, a flicker of light wrapping bare trees.

Mary, you can

refuse to cloak the dead.
Deny the stain of his life,
your sheet muddied
across prayer-laden years.
Sinners desperate for mercy
will knot hopes in the linen
you could have floated skyward,
white rising like wild swans.
Let wings and warm breezes bear
the promise of redemption.

Baptism

She set me on the water,
then let go knowing
I would not call.

She did not pull me back,
did not let me be the one
she loved most.

I see my face at sixty,
wrinkled from the wash of days
looking for a woman
with eyes the color of leaves.

I wonder if this mirror is the water,
if she looks like this,
if she sees me.

Fourth Grade Recess at Our Lady Queen of Hope

Mary Angela sails above our sea
of pixie cuts and Peter Pan collars,
the flap of her ribbons matching
our chants with Double Dutch and flying hands.
We beg her to tell.

White fear tucked tight
as blouses in plaid jumpers,
we want the facts
between slaps of rope
and Buster Browns on blacktop,
make her jump until she spills
the bloody words.

Summer's End, Maryland

The Chesapeake furls its way to shore
drawn to rock weary of wanting
another shape. Like ashes coughed into a summer
gust, osprey scatter from dead branches.
My fingers no longer hold your goodbye.

Love is no more
than river willing a shift
in stone, no less than heron's wing
glancing a reef. Drawn by currents
nudging one to another,
love is the wrinkles of land and sun,
memory in our weathered hands.

Kelly Madigan Erlandson

Kelly Madigan Erlandson's work has recently appeared or is forthcoming in *Crazyhorse*, *Barrow Street*, *The Massachusetts Review*, *Puerto del Sol*, *Hawai'i Review* and *South Dakota Review*. Her manuscript "Born in the House of Love" won the Main-Traveled Roads Chapbook Award in 2004.

Waves

At the shore while dolphins ferried up the sun
and night relinquished its grip on the underside of waves,
some soft thing in you began to fall or turn away.
The slow walk home, at your feet the clattering
of crabs across packed sand. Something gave
and fluttered out behind, like words the beach wind
steals, and we can only wave, cup our ears, and hope
they'll say again what we have missed. But even
words repeated vanish here, the length between us
past the reach of voice. I like to think you had already
gone, the motions of returning home a route the body
memorized. You were in the house and dropped
your glass — the paramedics ushered in the door —
but if you had a choice I think you stepped aside
from us this morning, at the shore.

Before She Decides

They are in a dark plum thicket
and she is too far above the ground,
can feel the lift and fall of walking
but is not walking. Beneath her
are the shoulders of a boy
who is willing to carry her for years

but he is unsteady as a shirt
unbuttoned in the wind and she
is like a feather on the surface
of a river with round stones
in its bed. She already knows
he will fall and because she is above
him she will fall further

but that doesn't matter yet, the night
held up all around her
like great bolts of cloth for her choosing.

Rising

There is something in us
that wants to be seen in relief
against something else entirely,
mammal against ledge of shale,
woman with dark hair, her back to you,
standing at the edge of the table,
bread dough billowy in front of her,
the whole kitchen filled
with the yeasty smell.

Without the context it is hard to say
what she means, hard to know
if her forearms are strong enough
for the work ahead, or if her eyes are closed,
or if she has a son, if the son has dark hair,
if she'll wait for the bread to rise, if she'll
punch it down or let it just keep rising.

Rhina P. Espaillat

Rhina P. Espaillat has four poetry collections in print: *Lapsing to Grace* (Bennett & Kitchel, 1992); *Where Horizons Go* (Truman State University Press, 1998), which won the 1998 T. S. Eliot Prize; *Rehearsing Absence* (University of Evansville Press), which won the 2001 Richard Wilbur Award; and *Mundo y Palabra/The World and the Word* (Oyster River Press), a bilingual chapbook.

Translating

This is an art difficult as marriage
whose medium is the stony grit of language
that rends—and renders—message from mirage.

Not the clear eye of love that reads, if briefly,
all there may be and wills to fasten bravely
on what is not, choosing to find it lovely;

no, this is harder, this is love in action,
not contemplation; this is live dissection
cobbling the monster into breathing fiction,

discarding this, salvaging that. One wish:
synchronous motion like those parts that thrash
in porno flicks to be not quite one flesh;

and one fruition: how the face, the phrase,
through long devotion manages to fuse—
not sum, not seamless—into compromise

that's neither old nor wholly new, but rather
echo dopplering off, off by a feather,
but circling back, miraculous, together.

Discovery

Lifting the phone to call, he heard her laugh
on an extension: something had been said,
but what? and who had said it? He was half
tempted not to replace it in its bed
but hold it there by his astounded ear
to hear her laugh again in that old way
he had not heard since—when?—some distant year.
But also half afraid what she might say
into some other ear elsewhere. He dropped
the phone into its cradle, and the room
went loudly still, as if his life had stopped
like a stopped clock, as if it were a tomb
haunted by sounds he knew he used to know
but had forgotten missing long ago.

Parable

You dream a man before you with a stick
tugs at a rope that binds a muzzled bear.
A crowd collects. And though it makes you sick,
now that you've bought a ticket to this fair
you follow too, one with the rubes around
a ring of straw. You join those passive faces
to watch the prod, the dance, without a sound,
as one wretch puts another through its paces.
You dream indignant speeches you would make
if you could speak, dream you could rise and fly
this small-town golgotha, and howl awake—
were you unmuzzled—each indifferent eye,
but for the knotted noose that makes you stand,
your pointed stick, the ticket in your hand.

Guidelines

Here's what you need to do, since time began:
find something—diamond-rare or carbon-cheap,
it's all the same—and love it all you can.

It should be something close—a field, a man,
a line of verse, a mouth, a child asleep—
that feels like the world's heart since time began.

Don't measure much or lay things out or scan;
don't save yourself for later, you won't keep;
spend yourself now on loving all you can.

It's going to hurt. That was the risk you ran
with your first breath; you knew the price was steep,
that loss is what there is, since time began

subtracting from your balance. That's the plan,
too late to quibble now, you're in too deep.
Just love what you still have, while you still can.

Don't count on schemes, it's far too short a span
from the first sowing till they come to reap.
One way alone to count, since time began:
love something, love it hard, now, while you can.

Larry Fontenot

Larry Fontenot has had poetry published in Texas publications such as Chachalaca Poetry Review, Chapultepec Press, Maverick Press, The Northwest College Review, Red River Review, RiverSedge, and Sulphur River Literary Review. National publications include Eye Dialect, Melic Review, Moveo Angelus, Mystic River Review, The Poet's Canvas, Snow Monkey, Sol Magazine, and Urban Spaghetti. His poem "Wile E. Coyote's Lament" was published in The Year's Best Fantasy and Horror, 12th Annual Collection in 1999. A chapbook, *Choices & Consequences*, was the winner of the Maverick Press 1996 Southwest Poets' Series Chapbook competition.

Seduction

It is, of course, that moment a man recants
his own death and begins a long descent
into memories bunched among mortal fiber.
With an earful of noise he begins
to count backward from infinity to zero

until one foot strokes the other, one hand
wonders what the other is doing.
Confusion, again and again, whispers
a litany of forgiveness. Words, as go-betweens,
perform in the manner of servants

anxious to please, anxious to tell a story,
even if it is a lie. Like rain draining
through empty flower pots, this is how we learn
longing. This is how we learn language.
No wonder we fall silent so soon.

Swimming Lesson

The girl leaned over the polished lip,
reached down into water made blue
by the pool's painted bottom,
tugged hard on my hair
to pull me up from certain death.
(An act she came to regret later in our life.)

So I learned early to avoid even the shallow
end of public pools, to conceal my failings.
For years I only showered,
once going three days
without bathing when the hotel
in Mexico had nothing but a tub.

I understand this about water:
it pulls you to it as gravity
pulls apples to ground,
as death drags men toward
the center of the earth,
if only by a miserly six feet.

Swimming is attitude, the man says,
look ahead and never down.

But for me any stretch of water suggests a glance
back at dangers I've survived, then forward
to some immense failure that will drown me.
Though water is transparent,
you seldom see disaster coming.

Nothing now seems as clear
as that first wave of love in the last row of a theater,
when the fifteen-year-old beside me entwined her
hands in mine and kissed my cheek.
Then, after leaving the latest Elvis movie,
she invited me to a pool party the next weekend.
I eagerly accepted, not knowing
I was already out of my depth.

The Other Side of Ice

She's so girlish
he's embarrassed to stare.
It's not just her youth or beauty
but the careless way she floats
her arms out from her body,
the reckless sweep of her legs
when she strolls to the bar.
Watching her is like hunting
fish under ice, chasing an elusive
creature through luminous fields.

Past midnight he's caught
nothing but the flow of air
spun by shifts of conversation.
What saves further humiliation
is being too old, once again,
to be rewarded this sweet moment,
this elliptical beauty curving over him
like the path the trout takes before it disappears
into a spirited river whose waters
would surely drown him.

Jack Foley

Jack Foley is an innovative, widely-published poet and critic who, with his wife, Adelle, performs his work frequently in the San Francisco Bay Area. For the past several years he has hosted a show of interviews and poetry presentations on Berkeley radio station KPFA. His current show , " Cover to Cover," which can be heard by streaming audio at www.kpfa.org, is on every Wednesday at 3:30 p.m. Pacific time. His poetry books include *Letters/Lights—Words for Adelle* (1987), *Gershwin* (1991), *Adrift* (1993, nominated for a Bay Area Book Reviewers' Award), *Exiles* (1996), and (with Ivan Arguelles) *New Poetry from California: Dead / Requiem* (1998).

Adrienne Rich,
The School Among the Ruins: Poems 2000-2004
(W.W. Norton)

How I've hated speaking "as a woman"
for mere continuation
when the broken is what I saw.
　　—Adrienne Rich, "Terza Rima," *Fox: Poems 1998-2000*

All kinds of language fly into poetry....
　　—Adrienne Rich, "A Long Conversation," *Midnight Salvage: Poems 1995-1998*

But who　at the checkout this one day
do I address　who is addressing me
　　—Adrienne Rich, "Address," *The School Among the Ruins: Poems 2000-2004*

The School Among the Ruins: Poems 2000-2004 is Adrienne Rich's most recent volume. It follows *Midnight Salvage: Poems 1995-1998* (1999) and *Fox: Poems 1998-2000* (2001). Each of these volumes is not an attempt to produce an individual "masterpiece" but a kind of way-station in a ongoing engagement with poetic language. "By 1956," Rich writes in "Blood, Bread, and Poetry" (*Arts of the Possible*, 2001), "I had begun dating each of my poems by year. I did this because I was finished with the idea of a poem as a single, encapsulated event, a work of art complete in itself":

I knew my life was changing, my work was changing, and I needed to indicate to readers my sense of being engaged in a long, continuing process. It seems to me now that this was an oblique political statement...It was a declaration that placed poetry in a historical continuity, not above or outside history.

Rich describes herself as "a writer in a country where native-born fascistic tendencies, allied to the practices of 'free' marketing, have been trying to eviscerate language of meaning" ("Arts of the Possible," *Arts of the Possible*). As a poet, she says in "Blood, Bread, and Poetry," she feels "more and more urgently the dynamic between poetry as language and poetry as a kind of action, probing, burning, stripping placing itself in dialogue with others out beyond the individual self." Poetic language connects us "with all that is not simply whitechauvinist/ malesupremacist/straight/puritanical—with what is 'dark,' 'effeminate,' 'inverted,' 'primitive,' 'volatile,' 'sinister'"; it constitutes "writing...that may not be male, or white, or heterosexual, or middle-class." In her earliest encounters with poetry, Rich writes, "my...mind did not shut down for the sake of consistency"; later she came to realize that poetry "reasserts the claim to a complex historical and cultural identity, the selves who are both of the past and of tomorrow." "We are," she insists, "trying to build a political and cultural movement in the heart of capitalism"; at the same time she confesses to "the fragmentation I suffer in myself." In reading Simone de Beauvoir and James Baldwin, Rich writes, "I began to taste the concrete reality of being unfree, how continuous and permeating and corrosive a condition it is, and how it is maintained through culture as much as through the use of force."

What kind of writing is contained in *The School Among the Ruins*? Does the title refer metaphorically to poetry, which, Rich says, is "a kind of teaching" ("Blood, Bread Poetry")? How does her complex vision of poetry connect to the actual poems she produces? In what way does her poetry assert "freedom" and not merely the ruminations of the individual self—or, worse, the ruminations of late Capitalism?

To begin with, Rich's poems are by no means conventionally "clear." The book opens with "Centaur's Requiem":

your hooves drawn together underbelly
shoulders in mud   your mane
of wisp and soil deporting all the horse of you

your longhaired neck
eyes   jaw yes   and ears
unforgivably human on such a creature
unforgivably what you are
deposited in the grit-kicked field of a champion

tender neck and nostrils   teacher   water-lily suction-spot
what you were   marvelous   we could not stand

Night drops   an awaited storm
driving in to wreck your path
Foam on your hide like flowers
where you fell   or fall   desire

The poem is a puzzle piece which remains resonant—indeed, becomes *more* resonant—as one considers it, but never fully declares its "meaning." A "centaur" is of course a creature from Classical mythology; the creature has the head, trunk and arms of a man and the body and legs of a horse. (The notion of such a creature may have arisen from an imperfect perception of men riding horses.) Since the poem is a "requiem," this centaur must be dead—yet the poet seems to feel "desire," tenderness towards it. The poem resembles Rilke's "Archaic Torso of Apollo," with its famous concluding line, "*Du mußt dein Leben ändern*" ("You must change your life"), so it is possible that Rich is looking at a statue of a centaur, perhaps one that has sunk into the mud of the "grit-kicked field" in which she encounters it.

In any case, the creature is, or has been, "marvelous"—an entity which seems to connect us to some realm of authenticity. Further—in a book whose title poem involves a "school" and teachers—Rich calls the centaur a "teacher." *Why does the centaur have long hair?* Is this poem an oblique lament for the sixties or for the seventies—for a time of power? "The movements of the 1960s and the 1970s in the United States," Rich writes in "Arts of the Possible" (1997), "were openings out of apertures previously sealed, into collective imagination and hope...They have been relentlessly trivialized, derided, and demonized by the Right and by what's now known as the political center":

I've been struck by the presumption, endlessly issuing from the media, in academic discourse, and from liberal as well as conservative platforms, that the questions raised by Marxism, socialism, and communism must inexorably be identified with their use and abuse by certain repressively authoritarian regimes of the twentieth century: therefore they are henceforth to be nonquestions.

Is the centaur—still potent even in death—an emblem of "Marxism, socialism, and communism"? "Capitalism," Rich goes on, "vulgarizes and reduces complex relations to a banal iconography." What kind of "iconography" are we dealing with here? Is this a political poem? Is it a lament for a time in which "marvelous" creatures such as centaurs were freely imagined by humankind? Is it a lament for poetic fictions? And why does the creature cause desire? Isn't Rich known to be a lesbian feminist? Why should she feel desire for a creature which is part man and part horse?

The questions I am raising here are not, in Rich's term, "nonquestions" and they are not questions which can be easily or definitively answered—not something which can be handled by the evening news. Rich's language deliberately moves us into a realm in which nothing is certain but which opens us to the process of *questioning*. In Capitalist society, Rich asserts, "everything...tends toward becoming a *thing* until people can speak only in terms of the *thing*, the inert and always obsolescent commodity" ("Arts of the Possible"). The centaur is a *thing* and it may be "obsolescent," but it is not a commodity: it is a linguistic—or "poetic"—fiction; while it can be speculated about, it cannot in any way be bought. Indeed, its "being" is pure speculation: no one any more believes that centaurs "really" exist in any form except poetic fictions, speculations, "possibilities."

It is Rich's great perception to realize that *speculation itself is political*—that "questioning" in a society in which "distinctions fade and subtleties vanish" ("Arts of the Possible") is a political act. Her poem does not assert that Capitalist society is a bad thing; instead, it thrusts us into a realm in which questions, ideas—thought—arise. Further: it speculates about something which *had* power and which might yet be involved in some sort of resurgence. Like "Marxism, socialism, and communism," the centaur is really nothing but a bundle of ideas, a myth. Can one "kill" a myth? The poem is fragmentary, incomplete—Rich refers to her own feelings of fragmentation—but it *points towards* a wholeness which it cannot manifest. It stands, as Rich says, not as a piece of merchandise but as something "unforgivably human."

The School Among the Ruins is full of poetry like that—a poetry of questioning and of struggle rather than what Rich calls "the sweetly flowing measures of my earlier books" ("Blood, Bread, and Poetry"), which is not to say that the book is necessarily difficult or "obscure." There are a number of love poems in it, poems in which the poet turns away from heavy political questions to indulge herself in the sweetness of sentiment

> There's a beat in my head
> song of my country
>
> called Happiness, U.S.A.
> Drowns out bouzouki
>
> drowns out world and fusion
> with its *Get—get—get*
>
> *into your happiness before*
> *happiness pulls away…*
>
> break out of that style
> give me your smile
> awhile

("This Evening Let's"—a very amusing title)

There is also a fine tribute to French poet Guillaume Apollinaire and French songwriter Georges Brassens, "After Apollinaire & Brassens":

> what flows under the Seine
> Mississippi Jordan Tigris
> Elbe Amazon Indus Nile
>
> and all the tributaries
> who knows where song goes
> now and from whom
> toward what longings

(Rich's volume, *Midnight Salvage* has a beautiful, partial translation of Brassens' song, "Chanson pour l'Auvergnat.") 1/

One can follow themes of home ("and home no simple matter"— "Dislocations: Seven Scenarios"), innocence ("can I say it was not I listed as Innocence / betrayed you"— "Equinox"), and words ("the power to hurl words is a weapon," "a word can be crushed like a goblet underfoot"— "Transparencies") throughout *The School Among the Ruins*.

There are also themes of change ("and we remain or not but not remain / as now we think we are"— "As finally by wind or grass"), of self-criticism ("*Kid, you always / took yourself so hard!*"— "To Have Written the Truth"; "Cut the harping... / You're human, porous like all the rest"— "Tendril") and of old age ("Palms flung upward: 'What now?' / Hand slicing the air or across the throat. / A long wave to the departing"— "Screen Door"). The phrase "not here yet" repeats. There is a play on the etymology of the word "conversion": "You need to *turn yourself around* / face in another direction"— "Ritual Acts," my italics). The title poem is an extremely powerful statement of the immense human cost of bombing other countries ("One: I don't know where your mother / is Two: I don't know / why they are trying to hurt us"): "Great falling light of summer," Rich asks, "will you last / longer than schooltime?"

Perhaps the finest sequence of the volume—and the volume has far more "sequences" than it has "individual poems," the self as history asserting itself—is "USonian Journals 2000." The term "Usonian," Rich explains, is "the term used by Frank Lloyd Wright for his prairie-inspired architecture. Here, *of the United States of North America*." This section is in prose, but it is no less powerful for that. It touches on a subject dear to Rich's heart—the nature of the oral:

Imagine written language that walks away from human conversation. A written literature, back turned to oral traditions, estranged from music and body. So what might reanimate, rearticulate, becomes less and less available. 2/

In her attempt to write "the history of the dispossessed" ("Blood, Bread, and Poetry"), Adrienne Rich is not attempting a chronicle of events so much as she is attempting to transform the dispossessed: "We need to begin changing the questions," she writes ("Arts of the Possible"). *The School Among the Ruins* is a book full of questions, and it ends with still another question: "Not for her but still for someone?" The concluding stanza of "Tendril," the poem in which that line occurs, begins,

She had wanted to find meaning in the past but the future drove
a vagrant tank a rogue bulldozer

rearranging the past in a blip
coherence smashed into vestige

This experience of "coherence smashed," of "the broken," is a fundamental one for Adrienne Rich. She is fond of quoting a passage from James Baldwin: "Any real change implies the breakup of the world as one has always known it, the loss of all that gave one an identity, the end of safety." If chaos, incoherence, "the end of safety" is painful—the word Rich uses to describe her experience of it is "suffer"—it is also alive with possibilities. Her poetry is a constant affirmation of what Maria Mazziotti Gillan and Jennifer Gillan call "the unsettling of America": "the constant erecting, blurring, breaking, clarifying, and crossing of boundaries that are a consequence of the complex intersections among peoples, cultures, and languages within national borders, which themselves are revised constantly" (*Unsettling America*). The study of history is not the study of a series of events whose meanings are fixed by executive decree but the study of events whose intensity has erupted into possibility—

into *questions*. The capacity to write poetry, Rich says, is "the capacity to hook syllables together in a way that [heats] the blood." How does that heat—that alchemy—happen?

> one syllable then another
> gropes upward
> one stroke laid on another
> sound from one throat then another
> never in the making
> making beauty or sense
>
> always mis-taken, draft, roughed-in
> only to be struck out
> is blurt is roughed-up
> hot   keeps body
> in leaden hour
> simmering

("Tell Me")

Poetry is indeed "the school among the ruins" of Western history. (The word "school" conjures up Yeats, a favorite poet of Rich's and someone who also associates poetry with "school" and "schools.") But it is a school whose "teaching" is a curriculum of questions—and what is questioned is precisely the curriculum: "Can [I] say," Rich asks in one poem, "I was mistaken?" ("Equinox") The following beautiful lines, like Adrienne Rich's work as a whole, are this poet's answer to Robert Graves' famous assertion (made in his poem, "To Juan at the Winter Solstice" and echoing the scholarship of *The White Goddess*, 1947), "There is one story and one story only." Rich's lines are a miniature *ars poetica*:

> There is the story of the mind's
> temperature neither cold nor celibate
> Ardent   The story of
> not one thing only

("There is No One Story and One Story Only")

And again:

> No you can't go home yet
> but you aren't lost
> this is our school

("The School Among the Ruins")

Footnotes on following page

1.   I confess to being somewhat puzzled by Rich's assertion in *The School Among the Ruins* that "After Apollinaire & Brassens" is partly derived from Georges Brassens' song

"Le Pont des Arts." I'm familiar with Brassens' work but have no recollection of that title. There is "Le Vent," which has

Si par hasard,
Sur l' Pont des Arts
Tu crois's le vent, le vent fripon
Prudenc' prends garde à ton jupon.

and "Les Ricochets," which has

...On s'étonn'ra pas
Si mes premiers pas
Tous droit me menèrent
Au pont Mirabeau
Pour un coup d'chapeau
À l'Apollinaire
À l'Apollinaire

but I've been unable to find anything called "Le Pont des Arts."

2.   In "Blood, Bread, and Poetry" Rich writes, "I should add that I was easily entranced by pure sound and still am, no matter what it is saying; and any poet who mixes the poetry of the actual world with the poetry of sound interests and excites me more than I am able to say."

For the Shade of Joel E. Siegel,
My Classmate at Cornell (d. 2004)

Siegel you rat
After quarreling,
we didn't communicate in any way for over thirty years
and now you die. That
shows me.
Your obit's in the *New York Times*.
You cared for fame, I know.
        (The soul is eternally unslayable in the body of everyone, son of
Bharata...)
Your rhymes
never matched those of the great Porter or Hart
but your final
days were filled with spinal
meningitis and its aftermath:
death.
Your parents, whom you loved, survived you.
Dammit Seagull

(soul bird flying!)
I wanted one more chance to see talk
argue and reject you again. Dying
prevents that.
   (...*Therefore thou shouldst not mourn*)
You went from fumbling and boyish
to (your phrase) "mean and Jewish"—
arrogant, I thought.
Once, after you had insulted me in front of friends,
I said,
"The thing about Siegel is that
he's always wanted to be a New York Jew."
"That's not true!" you answered, proving my point. "I could have been
a New York Jew
lots of times."

   (*If the radiance of a thousand suns were to burst forth at once in
the sky, that would be   like the splendor of the Mighty One:Krishna*)
You settled for DC
and might have unknowingly seen my son
as each of you scampered around Georgetown.
Rest well, you bastard
I have put rhymes in this poem
not out of competition
but because you loved rhyme
You did something
with your life after all
despite my fussy disapproval
An obit in the *Times* and *Post* isn't exactly chopped liver, you know—
but I'm sad about your removal
   (*In some sort of crude sense which no vulgarity, no humor, no
overstatement can quite extinguish,* physicists have known sin; *and
this is a knowledge which they cannot   lose.*)
The memory of our brief friendship and our long enmity
still stands.
I'd have given you more life were such things in my hands.
   (*I am become death, the destroyer of worlds*)

Suzanne Frischkorn

Suzanne Frischkorn is the author of three chapbooks, most recently, _Red Paper Flower_, (Little Poem Press, 2004). Her poetry has appeared, or is forthcoming in _Poet Lore, JAMA, Pif, Mangrove, Paterson Literary Review, Wisconsin Review_ and elsewhere.

Youth Drowns in Housatonic River

> _Where were ye, nymphs, when the remorseless deep_
> _Closed o'er the head of your loved Lycidas?_
> _—Milton._

He swam across
the inlet near Beards' Island,

and I was lying in my river bed
watching light ripple the surface.

I saw him swim a straight line
through the sun. I had no choice

but to eat fish from the river,
and the soil, it finds its way into

my skin. I am the river and the river
is contaminated. The river is dying

and I am dying. His body was lean
and strong, yet the cold shut down

his circulation. His arms. His legs.
Please tell his mother I brushed

the hair from his forehead and sang
sweet songs until the divers came

a day later. Tell her, he swam a straight line.

Saltmarsh

It's spring tide—moon
    earth, and sun aligned—

a time when nests flood
    and eggs float away.

On a stalk of cord grass
    the sharp-tailed sparrow

begins his faint song.
    His mate filigrees twigs

and string. How easy they
    make it seem, to start over.

Naugatuck River Valley, Connecticut

*(The first dam was completed in 1706…by the 1950's, few living
organisms were present in the river's highly polluted water.)*

How long it takes the river to come clean—
to welcome fish back to its bed! Trout arrive
first, herring and lamprey still caught in a maze
of dams and passageways. Boys on the stony
bank throw back the day's catch, a sacrifice
to river god, lord of silt, prince of stone. Naugatuck
sleek under the rusty trestle, glistens and beckons
my eye. Over the starling's chatter
                I hear the hum of quiet machines.

Michael Graber

Michael Graber lives with his wife and three children in his native Memphis, TN. His first
poetry collection, *The Last Real Medicine Show*, is forthcoming from Turning Point. When not
writing, Michael plays mandolin with the Bluff City Backsliders.

Paris, Tennessee

Late that wet April Mom blew
out the backdoor, dress full
of steam like a lover in Chagall.

I followed the fragments
her shadow cast down through
the trees like specks of dust,

spied as she rooted herself
in the lumpy mattress of a trailer
park painter. He breathed loudly

in her ear: "I paint with my pecker."
Then shaved and stretched the goatskin
canvas he prepared from his pet,

and served its meat roasted as a snack.
Portrait finished, she cradled the piece
by the hairy edges over the threshold

of the prefab door. The grass
went flat under her feet, weighed down
by this rural Lautrec of her eating

roses. Still wet, thick paint dripped.
Showgirl-giddy, I swayed,
her son, her own confused creation.

A Fantasia for My Four Year Old Daughter, Mistakenly Given an Overdose of Demerol

The drugged hoods
you dance with
as gravity relaxes
    never asked my permission.
They sway the ballroom
so you know
only the low
    moan of the sea,
and flap
their dusty wings
and scratch their
    viol strings each time
I raise my voice
to keep you
from going faster
    into slow motion.
Water fills
your ears. Over
the pure music
    the nurse fights
with a machine
that breathes for you,
I call you home from the woods
    for dinner and a bath,
while the sick angels
rejoice when a child
cannot hear
    a father's plea.

Jealousy

The more you drink, the more my stinger grows
anxious to stun your wine-inspired nerve.
"Be with me. Your camera-ready curves..."
in your mouth his icy offer overflows.
His magic spell. His riding boots. The whoas
his saturated color and eye deserve.
Like light through frost, anger's blinding verve
obscures my better sense. I'm jealous, it shows.

I stab the shrimp, attack the artichoke,
scrape the hairy poison off the heart.
The table quivers—he smirks, you laugh—I can't
control my fork. Our marriage: a running joke
our friends follow like a game or work of art?
"My love," I request over roast and guests "don't pant."

Neile Graham

Neile Graham is Canadian by birth and inclination, but currently lives in Seattle. Her full-length collections are: *Seven Robins* (Penumbra Press 1983); *Spells for Clear Vision* (Brick Books 1994), and *Blood Memory* (BuschekBooks 2000). She is currently working on a series of poems about her travels in Scotland, two novels, and innumerable short stories.

Wearing Nothing but the Midnight Sun
—*Summer Solstice, Orkney*—

History is traditionally blind
to these movements of ordinary people
because it is dominated by culture and artifacts

I read these words on
the shortest night of the year

in a place where the sky never darkens but dims

we've spent this day circling the 30 remaining
stones standing to shape the Ring of Brodgar

learning the time-washed year-carved edges

of each stone
I showed you the Viking graffiti

we followed how sun's line

pierced the haze breaking
on cloud-washed stone

grey, grey-green, golden and whorled

now it's night but the dimming sunlight still
pours into the attic room we're given to sleep in

a room dressed mostly in pink

ruffled wherever a ruffle could go
our hostess named Venus truly for real

it's our anniversary it's the small dusky hours of solstice

your mouth on my mouth
my hand slides down the

primitive terrain of your back

we ring and circle each other
our purpose ancient, lost to history

mysterious as stone

tonight I see ghosts
lovers walking the Ring of Brodgar

learning the wear of each stone

while they lose themselves
in the silk of skin on earth on stone

and then on each other

tasting one another as we do
touch wakening the powers of the skin

the fingertip's whorls pressing

into the turf of each other's flesh
pulses beating in their ears

these movements of ordinary people

their cries like gulls
as lost in the instant they name each other

created anew by each other's fingers

bones and muscles lost to time
we name ourselves

The Walk She Takes

—Smailholm Tower, the Border Country—

Slow in the weight of the fog
on the rolling lands of the Merse—green, green
old hills—she hears the steps of ghost horses,
echoing hooves and rain.

In this distance where there is no distance
all horses are ghosts,
all wind the lament of the border widow,
she:
"I took his body on my back and whiles I gaed,
and whiles I sat, I digged a grave and laid him in
And happ'd him up with sod sae green."

Walking she traces the furrowed line
of a runrig—lines
that disappear underfoot. Lines
of cottage walls
leaning up against the laird's protection.
She can step right over the barmkin now, so little
of its height remains,

step in and out of strangers' lives: the old lord
who lost three brothers and a son at Flodden,
then the years after staggered by the reivers
stealing first 600 cattle then 123 then 60 then 6,
100 prisoners taken then 4.

It's here she finds her man leaning against a wall
of this tower brittle-patched with memories
patterned with blood and fear rising above the earth
into fog woven with wraiths and lamentations

crumbling alone. She's walking the borders,
she's out ghosting. She's getting used to harm.

Graves and Churchyards Cairns and Cairns

By whom the subterraneous vaults are peopled is now utterly unknown.
The graves are very numerous, and some of them undoubtedly contain
the remains of men, who did not expect to be so soon forgotten.

—from Samuel Johnson's
A Journey to the Western Isles of Scotland (1775)

the afterlife alive under stone
peopled by shadows skulls unruly dust
as we exploring exploit the world underground
tourists in cairns souterrains tombs

peopled by shadows skulls unruly dust
the bones of eagles deer and dogs
tourists in cairns souterrains tombs
their age measured in thousands of years

the bones of eagles deer and dogs
add fleetness to the weight of human remains
their age measured in thousands of years
counted in hundreds under the nearby church floor

add fleetness to the weight of human remains
the walls rise over them blocks of stone
counted in hundreds under the nearby church floor
someone rests beneath the stones beneath our feet

the walls rise over them blocks of stone
each bone placed by human hands
someone rests beneath the stones beneath our feet
and the flesh that nets our bones is thin

each bone placed by human hands
we are the gravid robbers of graves
and the flesh that nets our bones is thin
we belong here by our presence alone

we are the gravid robbers of graves
as we exploring exploit the world underground
we belong here by our presence alone
the afterlife alive under stone

Rafael Guillén

Rafael Guillén es español, nacido en Granada. Ha publicado más de veinte libros y figura en la Historia de la Literatura Española dentro de la llamada Generación del 50. En 1994 obtuvo el Premio Nacional de Literatura, tras ser finalista del Premio de la Crítica.

Rafael Guillén was born in Granada, Spain. He has published more than twenty books and is cited in the History of Spanish Literature as belonging to the so-called "50s Generation". In 1994 he was awarded the National Prize for Literature, having been a finalist for the Critics' Prize.

Translations by **Sandy McKinney**

Estoy Hablando

Estoy diciendo amor. Una muchacha
parte un bombón de menta con los dientes
y me da la mitad.

Estoy diciendo vida. Cien mil hombres
quedan roncos gritando
que no ha sido *penalty*.

Estoy diciendo madre. Una mujer,
cantándome una copla de otros tiempos,
me limpia las narices mientras lloro.

Estoy diciendo patria. Un hombre joven
tiene sangre en las manos estreabiertas
y dice que él no ha sido.

Estoy diciendo muerte. Alguien corre
por las calles desiertas, media noche,
en busca de un notario.

Esty diciendo fe. Un sacerdote
se descubre y eleva a Dios la vista
mientras pasa un entierro de primera.

Estoy diciendo Dios. Todas las cosas
me miran en silencio.

I'm Speaking

I'm saying love. A little girl
cracks a peppermint between her teeth
and gives me half.

I'm saying life. A hundred thousand men
go hoarse shouting it shouldn't
have been a penalty.

I'm saying mother. A woman,
singing me a song from long ago,
wipes my nose while I scream.

I'm saying my country. A young man
cups the blood in his outstretched hands
and says he didn't start it.

I'm saying death. Someone is running
through the empty streets at midnight,
looking for a notary.

I'm saying faith. A priest
bares his head and raises his eyes to God
as a first-class funeral passes.

I'm saying God. Everything
watches me in silence.

Apenas Si Recuerdo

Apenas si recuerdo tu voz, pero me dueles
en alguna parcela remota de la sangre.
Te llevo en mis abismos, enrededa en el limo,
como uno de esos cuerpos que la mar no devuelve.

Era un lugar perdido para el Sur. Una playa
sin barcas pescadoras, donde el sol se vendía.
Un litoral, ya selva de luces y de idiomas,
que desdeñó vencido su obligación de arena.

La noche de aquel día nos castigó a su antojo.
Te tenía tan cerca que era unútil mirarte.
El otoño blandía carcajadas y orquestas
y la mar se mesaba furiosa los balandros.

Tu mano equilibrada, con su calor opuesto,
la ondulante templanza del alcohol. Los jardines
me llegaban lejanos a través de tu falda.
Subía mi marea de nivel por tus pechos.

Alfombrados tentáculos por las escalinatas
atraían los pasos a las bocas del ruido.
Con luces y cortinas, más arriba del tedio,
hablaban las alcobas de los grandes hoteles.

Hay momentos oscuros en que nos vence el lastre
de tanto abatimiento. Son momentos, o siglos,
en que la carne asoma su desnudez y busca
la destrucción, bebiendo la vida de sí misma.

Yo palpaba tu abrazo por mis alrededores,
pero el amor no estaba donde estaba tu abrazo.
Yo sentía tus manos encima de mi pena,
pero la nada iba delante de tus manos.

Recorría, a lo largo, tu entrega desalmada,
por si había una cala donde tirar del copo,
por si acaso encontraba la voz del cenachero
aún mojada del brillo de los chanquetes vivos.

Era un lugar perdido para el Sur. El aroma
del moscatel tenía sinsabores de whisky.
Era un abrazo muerto, que llevo todavía

I Hardly Remember

I hardly remember your voice, but the pain of you
floats in some remote current of my blood.
I carry you in my depths, trapped in the sludge
like one of those corpses the sea refuses to give up.

It was a spoiled remnant of the South. A beach
without fishing boats, where the sun was for sale.
A stretch of shore, now a jungle of lights and languages
that grudgingly offered, defeated, its obligation of sand.

The night of that day punished us at its whim.
I held you so close I could barely see you.
Autumn was brandishing guffaws and dancebands
and the sea tore at the pleasure-boats in a frenzy.

Your hand balanced, with its steady heat,
the wavering tepidness of alcohol. The gardens
came at me from far away through your skirt.
My high-tide mark rose to the level of your breasts.

Carpets, like tentacles, wriggling down to the strand,
attracted passers-by to the mouth of the clamor.
With lights and curtains, above the tedium
the bedrooms murmured in the grand hotels.

There are dark moments when our ballast gives out
from so much banging around. Moments, or centuries,
when the flesh revels in its nakedness and reels
to its own destruction, sucking the life from itself.

I groped around me, trying on your embrace,
but love was not where your embrace was.
I felt your hands stroking that physical ache
but a great nothing went before your hands.

I searched down the length of your soulless surrender
for a calm bay where I could cast a net,
yearning to hear a trace of the vendor's voice
still wet with the glimmer of the flapping minnows.

It was a spoiled remnant of the South. The aroma
of muscatel was tainted with whiskey breath.
I carry that dead embrace inside me yet
like a foreign object the flesh tries to reject.

El Miedo, No

El miedo, no. Tal vez, alta calina,
la posibilidad del miedo, el muro
que puede derrumbarse, porque es cierto
que detrás está el mar.
El miedo, no. El miedo tiene rostro,
es exterior, concreto,
como un fusil, como una cerradura,
como un niño sufriendo,
como lo negro que se esconde en todas
las bocas de los hombres.
El miedo, no, Tal vez sólo el estigma
de los hijos del miedo.

Es una angosta calle interminable
con todas las ventanas apagadas.
Es una hilera de viscosas manos
amables, sí, no amigas.
Es una pesadilla
de espeluznantes y corteses ritos.
El miedo, no. El miedo es un portazo.
Estoy hablando aquí de un laberinto
de puertas entornadas, con supuestas
razones para ser, para no ser,
para clasificar la desventura,
o la ventura, el pan, o la mirada
— ternura y miedo y frío — por los hijos
que crecen. Y el silencio.
Y las ciudades rutilantes, huecas.
Y la mediocridad, como una lava
caliente, derramada
sobre el trigo, y la voz, y las ideas.

No es el miedo. Aún no ha llegado el miedo.
Pero vendrá. Es la conciencia doble
de que la paz también es movimiento.
Y lo digo en voz alta y receloso.
Y no es el miedo, no. Es la certeza
de que me estoy jugando, en una carta,
lo unico que pude,
tallo a tallo, hacinar para los hombres.

Not Fear

Not fear. Maybe, out there somewhere,
the possibility of fear; the wall
that might tumble down, because it's for sure
that behind it is the sea.
Not fear. Fear has a countenance;
it's external, concrete,
like a rifle, a shot bolt,
a suffering child,
like the darkness that's hidden
in every human mouth.
Not fear. Maybe only the brand
of the offspring of fear.

It's a narrow, interminable street
with all the windows darkened,
a thread spun out from a sticky hand,
friendly, yes, not a friend.
It's a nightmare
of polite ritual wearing a frightwig.
Not fear. Fear is a door slammed in your face.
I'm speaking here of a labyrinth
of doors already closed, with assumed
reasons for being, or not being,
for categorizing bad luck
or good, bread, or an expression
— tenderness and panic and frigidity - for the children
growing up. And the silence.
And the cities, sparkling, empty.
and the mediocrity, like a hot
lava, spewed out over
the grain, and the voice, and the idea.

It's not fear. The real fear hasn't come yet.
But it will. It's the doublethink
that believes peace is only another movement.
And I say it with suspicion, at the top of my lungs.
And it's not fear, no. It's the certainty
that I'm betting, on a single card,
the whole haystack I've piled up,
straw by straw, for my fellow man.

R.S. Gwynn

In 1997, **R.S. Gwynn** was named University Professor at Lamar University, Lamar's highest academic rank, and he has also been recognized as an outstanding teacher by Phi Kappa Phi, the national academic honor society, and as an outstanding scholar by the College of Arts and Sciences. His books inlcude *Bearing & Distance* (Cedar Rock Press, 1977), *The Narcissiad*, *The Drive-In* (winner of the Breakthrough Award from the University of Missouri Press in 1986) and . *No Word of Farewell: Poems 1970-2000* (Story Line Press, 2000.) He lives in Beaumont, Texas, with his wife, Donna. They have three sons and two grandchildren.

Ballade Beginning with a Line by Robert Bly
Poetry, February 2000

My heart is a calm potato by day.
My feet are three Belgian nuns by night.
My fingers are speed-bumps in my way
When I'm screwing onions in for light.
My tongue is a shoeless duck; my right
Elbow's a celibate tv star.
My navel's a stick of dynamite.
I don't know what my metaphors are.

My son is a half-eaten *creme brûlée*.
My daughters are all under copyright.
My wife's a convertible full of hay
In a small, abandoned nuclear site.
My father's a ten-round welterweight fight
With my mother, who isn't a Mason jar.
My family tree is a concrete kite.
I don't know what my metaphors are.

My books are chickens who kneel to pray
In a Unitarian solstice rite.
Each page is a prudish manta ray,
Each word an Arabian parasite,
Each letter an oyster-knife that might
Plunge fatally into a Hershey bar.
My poems are clocks with an appetite.
I don't know what my metaphors are.

Prince, pray for all those who have to write:
My brain is a clam's unlit cigar.
My ear is a cheese with an overbite.
I don't know what my metaphors are.

Ballade Toxique

"Got milk?" my mom would always say,
Pushing a plate of WonderBread—
Four basic food groups every day
With meat in every shade of red.
Thus swayed from looking underfed,
I grunt and strain to tie my shoe,
Sighing for braver times long fled
When men were men, and women too.

When brushing daily stopped decay
With Colgate squeezed from tubes of lead,
When kids were sent outside to play
With fireworks, pedaling bikes that sped
Into ravines, when Bubba's sled
Hit Dead Man's Turn and sailed on through,
Our world ran on a Firestone tread,
For men were men, and women too.

"Give up my cigarettes? No way!"
"No booze? Let's score some coke instead."
"Condoms? C'mon, man. *I*'m not gay.
Besides, there's only me, she said."
"Just go ask Alice: *Feed your head.*"
"That needle's used? It looks like new."
"What do you want—to die in bed?"
Ah, men were men, and women too.

Is our reward to live in dread?
Is nothing good now good for you?
Sooner or later, I'll be dead.
So will you men and women too.

Ubi Sunt? for the 70s

Where are the primetime Friars Club roasts?
Where are the lousy jokes they'd tell,
Slurred tributes mixed with sloppy toasts,
Canned laughs, and Dino's drunken yell?
Where's Tricky Dicky? Deep in hell
With all those creepy aides he had?
Do they, at long last, share a cell?
Where are the days that were so bad?

Where are the smarmy game-show hosts,
And where are Ali and Cosell,
The bad toupee, the endless boasts
Made good with every opening bell?
The ABA, the AFL,
Disaster flicks, the painted sad-
Eyed kids that K-Mart used to sell?
Where are the days that were so bad?

Where are you now, unquiet ghosts—
Hot pants, bad tie, cuff and lapel
So wide they seemed to span the coasts,
The teeming discos and the smell
Of smoke that Brut could not dispel?
Where is each crummy passing fad—
Mood ring, pet rock, or Weeble? Well?
Where are the days that were so bad?

Envoy
If fickle Taste has tolled the knell
Of parting for them all, be glad
For *temps jadis* where memories dwell,
Those yesterdays that were so bad.

Steve Harris

Steve Harris lives in Fredericksburg, Virginia, with his wife and three sons.
He is a two-time Pushcart nominee, and his poems and reviews have appeared
in numerous online and print journals.

Nightingales
(Latvia, 1919)

Everywhere sounds of cranes and geese
fill the air, while on roadsides magpies feed
on faces of the dead. We are in retreat,
passing fields of pale grass, grey willows,
and grey-green corn. Behind us are Riga
and the sea; before us a great forest.
Last night we burnt a village near a river,
tossed grenades through windows, dumped bodies
down wells. I saw my long-haired angel
from Bremen flail a blackened wall with a child.
I have forgotten how to pray. As our column
enters the forest we pass by birch and dark pine.
I hear larks and jays in the limbs above me,
and nightingales by the hundreds.

In the Circle

Our flight of Pintails darts and dances
between green mountains, then breaks apart
over the Red River. Beneath us orange tongues
and smoke erupt from Yen Bai; the canopy
shakes and my stick wobbles as fluid leaks.
I think of home, of Anne and Annapolis
and my too-distant son. I think of Paolo
and Francesca and Dear-Fucking-John.
Over Haiphong my mask cracks and hair
ignites. My faces blisters and grins. I wrap
myself in flame, amazed at the familiar flags
in the harbor below, the sheer distance of the sea.

Maces Spring, VA, 1927

(A.P. Carter)

He walked around the saw-mill just brought up
from North Carolina. One of the men
who helped him unload it said, "It'll rust
out here in this field." He looked out toward
Route 614, watching the slow uneven
crawl of a Model A rounding a curve.
In his mind he heard again Sara's Sunday
voice, not unlike her black curtain of hair –
somber, wistful, certain as grief. His mind
skipped to an ad he'd seen in the paper
by a man with the Victor Talking Machine
Company of New York. The blade on the saw
burned and gleamed in the late morning light.
He ran a thumb over one sharp tooth;
he remembered trying to sell fruit trees
to her uncle; how he'd stopped talking when
she began singing "Engine 143" from the porch.

To Her Son

(Kathe Kollwitz at Roggevelde, Belgium, 1932)

My son, my Peter, eighteen years and here we are,
Karl and I: blocks of stone, blocks of heart.
In this way I will honor God with my work.
I have felt you these many years, sensed you
as I sat alone in your room. How to make peace
with your pure heart? Your belief and my belief
in a Fatherland: how to be faithful? So here
I kneel with your father, forever on heavy knees,
my carved brow to feel, with you my boy,
the rain and sun and snow. On good days
we all will listen, here among the white rows
for the glad song of the lark; we will count
the tiny rows among the briars.

OxyContin

From this false shore I think I see differently,
in a new light that wavers in and out. I call
for Bird but hear nothing: I tap my blue arm
with its blue veins. I try to remember:
everyone is gone and outside the dog howls
at the trailer door. The poor, the suffering,
and messed-up women, this thought moves
through the butter-light and into my head.
Bird says that isn't in his red-letter edition.
Or does he? Bird walks now out of sight,
on his mountain top from where I've hurled
myself time and again. I say I'm sorry,
I say it to Bird, who's on the floor, a mound
of melting ice on his chest, his own blue arm
cast high, like Ahab on his whale: goodbye.
Again, I say I'm sorry and listen Bird, listen
to the winter wind in the trees – I look
into the night, through a cross-hatching
of branches: I see Jesus in the trees.

Lola Haskins

Lola Haskins' books include *Castings, Forty-Four Ambitions for the Piano, Hunger,* and *Extranjera.* A further collection, *Desire Lines, New and Selected Poems,* was recently published by BOA Editions

The Rim-Benders
-for Richard Eberhart

*Perhaps the most critical moment in the construction of a
grand piano is that in which the strip of wood which will be
the final casing of the instrument must be matched to
the curve of the frame.*

They have twelve minutes to marry
the thin edge to its curve.
There is great pressure. Fine wood
does not wish to bend. Let us
lean with them into this poem.

And if we fail, the set glue
leaves gaps, sharp mistakes
of air we will always see.
But how can we not try? These
are the twelve minutes of our lives.

Winnowing the True

Imitation pearls drawn across the teeth
feel smooth. Dyed fur resists when blown.
When out for butter, shun bright yellow.

A knot that moves on its branch is not a knot.
A word thrown over the shoulder is not a discussion.
A brick is not a personal flotation device.

A father will cover his sleeping son
but leave his dreams alone.
A jeweler will cut the extra face and risk the gem.
A Master will tell you he plays, a little.

Spell for a Poet Getting On

May your hipbones never die.
May you hear the ruckus of mountains
in the Kansas of your age, and when
you go deaf, may you go wildly deaf.

May the neighbors arrive, bringing entire aviaries.
When the last of your hair is gone, may families
lovelier than you can guess colonize
the balds of your head.

May your thumbstick grow leaves.
May the nipples of your breasts drip wine.
And when, leaning into the grass, you watch
        the inky sun vanish into the flat page

of the sea, may you join your lawn chair,
each of you content
that nothing is wise forever.

Django in Hang-Zhou

He is *waiguo ren*: foreigner. When he walks to
the market his dark head sees over theirs as if
he were a child, held on his father's shoulders.
They point at him and stare.
                    He is twenty-one,
and empty as a thousand-years old wine jug.
He is also in love, not with what is foreign
in Hang-Zhou, but with what is most himself—
the cold and ancient lake, the blue mountains,
and in spring with the puffs of dust that followed
the galloping carts of emperors.   I think he was
among the watchers that lined the streets when
these trees were small.
                    I asked him once,
Why is it that Mandarin's so easy for you?
Because I'm a musician, he said, which was
like the doll, that still has many dolls inside.

Matanzas

Matanzas Beach, near St. Augustine, was named to commemorate Pedro Menendez'1565 slaughter of Hugonaut settlers there.. Menendez justified the murders by saying it was not Frenchmen he had killed, but heretics.

A rod jammed into the sand
the thin line from its tip to the sea
relaxed

and him down the beach
picking up broken angels' wings
with a boy's faith

in what swims in deep water
when suddenly, raptly, his rod bends
and he pounds towards it,

pounds heart-footed
towards what is silver and struggles
in every boy and

flushed, he reels it in.
What next, he never thought. It leaps
and gasps in his hands.

For

For the daffodil's horn that blazes spring   For the hooting taxis
that don't give a damn whose door they crunch   For the Levis
of New York City, out at the knees

For the shadows between hardwoods that hint of zebras For
the zebra's yellow teeth that will bite if she can For the way
his stripey neck can twist itself towards your arm For other
beauties: the peacock and his unpleasant voice

For vivid violet lightning that won't stay put For the sound
thunder makes after love, the bang that makes you jump
no matter how you steel, no matter how you want the flash
to be enough

For the jittery innocence under the skins of rivers the clear
way they skip over rocks as though the rocks' indigestibility
were of no importance   For the stones women swallow
when they marry For the operation that removes the stones
so they can be kept as specimens or set in rings

For the way the birds do not realize they are flying   For
the baby who hums himself awake   For the cat in her
orange disregard For the moment just before we understand
what the promised little talk is all about

Against

Against gaud, the poet who slings words like drops of water the way
a dog shakes his fur, who slings so hard even fleas spin out
Against this: the dog who slings off all that is not-dog

Against dark, the reversion always to the easy choice, the one
dark glass every night always the dry, so careful never to choose
the sweet, what would they think

Against the unfaded rectangle of wall where I allowed the picture too long
until it burned its image there, peach rising, moon-fuzz over the lapping sea,
and how shall I cover that space, having no picture larger

Against the brain-coral, because it is no longer in the sea and is a lie,
because it gathers dust, my grandmother's body-dust who died
so many years before she died, against the black-red in me, my fury
like an angry horse at her going to bed to wait

Against the rough and pitted stone, because I hold a carnelian with its
blood lights year after year, because I polish it with a cloth whose emery
wears my hands away, because I passion this thing I do and you say
I should be satisfied, that I should not need you

Against my low and matted hair, my bitch-bones, against the food
I serve you raw, the fetching that I do   Against you

Jim Hayes

Jim Hayes has been a wheelbarrow maker, a draughtsman, a corporate vice president with Johnson Wax in the United States, a backpack designer and manufacturer and is now, in semi-retirement, a fly-fisherman, rare chess book auctioneer and shoe retailer. His poetry has been *Noted on The Gazebo,* published in *Susquehanna Quarterly*, *Melic Review* , *Electric Acorn*, *Buckeye*, and *Able Muse* on-line and print journals *Light, Iambs & Trochees,* and *The Best of Melic*.

The Auction

It's mostly junk in the auction hall
save lot 15, hung on the wall,

an antique fly rod with a reel.
It is, at any price, a steal!

He takes it down and dares not speak.
a split-cane Hardy!   How unique!

He feels the balance, its spring and heft,
And, swishing, casts it right and left.

The auction starts. Dismayed that plenty
of bidders are the cognoscenti,

he bids much higher than he ought
and wins - but with a nagging thought;

expensive rods that anglers swish
catch far more fishermen than fish.

The Merrow

Beware The Nore where merrow* dwell
ANON

From out the Devil's Bit a spring,
the river, deep and darkening,
wears limestone walls

down the Vale of Knockanaire;
then its tossing torrents tear
through Noreland Falls,

whence it flows sans foil or let
until beneath Mt. Juliet
it slows and stalls.

There nightly from a brooding pool,
wherein the pig-eyed merrow rule,
a merrow calls.

The men who hear the cry she makes,
human souls whom God forsakes,
the merrow takes.

*Merrow; water demons, the males are ugly and confrontational,
the females beautiful and charming.

The Man Who Used to Fish

For Wiley Clements

When younger, he went fishing every day.
His dinner over, he would pack his rod
and head down to the bank and there he'd flay
the water to a foam; and he would spray
the Nore from bank to bank with casts of flies.
When hope took luck in hand he caught a prize,
and then, as darkness fell, back home he trod
certain in his heart there was a God.

In time, he was a fisherman of skill,
casting thirty yards and more with ease
to drop a floating fly on to a rill.
If fish were there he seldom failed to fill
his creel and every season took a quota
of salmon from the Moy. In Minnesota
he even showed the Yanks his expertise.
Faith was with old women on their knees.

Now Time, the whelp of Death, has found his scent;
he hasn't dapped the may or tied a fly
in years nor stalked a bank as night-time lent
its cover to his singular intent.
And though the hour has come for giving thanks
for time spent fishing on so many banks,
he's lost the way and doesn't want to try
and doubts that even God can fathom why.

M.E. Hope

M.E. Hope grew up in rural eastern Oregon, went on to join the Navy and see the world. She has a small portfolio of works published on line and in print and was a 2001 Fishtrap Fellow. She currently lives in Southern Oregon with her husband of 18 years, 2 above average children and 5 cats.

A Poem for Timothy McVeigh — *April 26, 2001*

Timothy, what I want for you is not a grave;
a place for the other mis-martyered to come
and seek your counsel.
For you I want a dark corner of concrete
where all day, like prayer,
some one will speak the names of those
you buried.
A tone just outside your door
in a voice lower than a whisper,
like the scraping of a fingernail
against the wall.
The type of near silence your bomb routed to life.
When you close your eyes I will introduce light
the way a child opens the eyelid of a sleeping parent
asking if anyone is home.
This light will look for life inside your eyes.
But what I want for you most is a weight
for the end of time, like the load a parent
of a dead child drags through their days
waiting for peace.
And this, Timothy, I want you to carry forever.

Thoughts on fog

1. Magic

An odd shadow tricks the eye
trees are running. They tumble down
the hill and where road slices fog
a flash of dun falls from gray

      — now you see deer
           now you don't —

loping into the curtain of juniper
                  roots loop behind.

2. Fruit

In the dead pine
cormorants huddle

dark plums   awaiting harvest.

3. Snake

No stranger here, fog arrives
to hunt the lake's shore.
Tasting sunrise

with a tongue's quick flick,
he rolls through the reeds
and swallows dawn.

4. Land mass

In this fog the stand of trees seems
a lonely outlet on the island.
Gray and black, in the gray,
the surrounding pond a dull pewter:
simple shadows on the horizon.

Like me the trees are wavering
longing to break earth's hold
and wander off

leaving behind the empty cavity of root beds
destroyed in flight.

Andrew Hudgins

Andrew Hudgins, born in 1951, has won numerous awards for *After the Lost War* and its predecessor, *Saints and Strangers*. His latest book, *Ecstatic in the Poison*, was published by Overlook Press. At present he teaches at the University of Ohio.

The Tooth Fairy

Each time another tooth falls out,
I yearn to learn the truth
about what kind of crazy thief
swaps cash for my old tooth.

I'd like to catch her by surprise
when she flies near my bed.
If I could hold her in my hands,
I'd squeeze her tiny head

between my finger and my thumb
and ask her just one time
why Jason Farber gets a buck.
I only get a dime.

His Imaginary Friend

I meet her twice a day for tea.
We talk about the weather,
her dolls, my love for her, her dolls,
and how we're good together.

We smile. I take her dainty hand
and beg a little kiss,
and then I peck her on the lips
and linger in the bliss.

I whisper to my fantasy,
"I want to more than kiss you"—
before I consummate my love
in Kleenex facial tissue.

Had it Coming

Hush now—don't cry, my wayward son.
You couldn't see you were becoming
someone who'd study "Manual Arts"—
rough carpentry, not even plumbing.

Mother smelled, and Father too,
the cigarettes that you've been bumming.
We searched beneath your bed and found
the dirty books that you've been thumbing.

And what about your so-called friends,
the criminals and thugs you're chumming
around with at the Mini-mart?
They hang with you and think they're slumming.

And as we yelled, you sighed and snorted,
eyeballs rolling, fingers drumming.
You snorted, picked up your guitar,
tuned, retuned it, started strumming.

Your father cursed, and slammed the door.
I slapped you till your head was humming.
Hush now—don't cry, my wayward son.
You little shit—you had it coming.

Our Neighbor's Little Yappy Dog

Our neighbor's little yappy dog
yaps all day long on their front lawn.
At dusk he takes a little nap
so he can yap, yap, yap till dawn—

and even turn the volume up.
At breakfast, sleepless, we discuss
if we should talk to them again,
and maybe, this time, end the fuss.

But soon the talk gets serious.
Mom says she simply wants to shoot him
while Dad thinks that's not good enough.
He wants to snatch the brute and boot him

over the phone and power lines.
He'd raise his arms and make the call:
Field goal! Three points! We win the game.
And then of course he'd spike the ball.

But in the end we all agree
their ways are good, but mine is better.
I want to feed him—tail-first, slowly—
into the yard man's chipper-shredder.

The Circus in the Trees

I love to watch the gray squirrels leap
from limb to leafy limb,
tumbling like furry acrobats—
and every tree their gym.

The oak limbs are their trampoline,
and their trapeze the pines.
They stroll, like tightrope walkers, up
the looping power lines—

and sometimes they gnaw through a line,
exploding as it arcs,
and lighting up the evening sky,
cascading down as sparks.

Amy Crane Johnson

Amy Crane Johnson has been published in several anthologies including *Words That Hold the Weight of Bone*, and *Crossing the Rubicon*. Periodical and online credits include the *Wisconsin Academy Review*, *The Alsop Review* and *Eclectica*. Amy lives and works in Green Bay, Wisconsin, her native birthplace.

A Reminder to Read Latin

If your head hurts
from not writing
and piles of words
grow unruly,
scatter into thin air,
escape like the Latin
you used to be able to read—

it's time to unexcuse yourself,
no more polite guest
at your own dinner table. Forget the
"I'm too busy.
My husband hates art.
Poetry doesn't pay the rent.
It's a dead language,"
excuses
and get on with it.

If a wayward leaf of a word
flies by,
open your mouth,
clamp down,
chew, taste and swallow.
Yes, I said swallow.

Do not ignore those damnable dreams
where words
weave themselves into poems
and you have to get up
and write them down
because you can't get back to sleep
anyway

so you might as well get up
and write them down.

Get up! Get up!

Soon it will be another winter
of naked trees,
your head just another empty jug
unless you save
these oranges, reds and yellows
commit
them to memory
with the blackest ink,
drop everything
to press them
into the creamiest
sheets, use
those twisting words
before they fade to ash,
before you forget
you once knew
how to read Latin.

Mary

I've given up a son.
all I can do is weep
and drone
about coming storms and
God blessing America.

I sit here, unpatriotic,
sip a mild arabica brew,
oppose the war
in a country where
I'm free to oppose a war.

Only a mother,
I hunt words
to hurl, words to expose
how deep a hole
a holy war can make.

Sleeping in a War Zone

Let's bed down—
you hug Atlantic; I'll go Pacific,
your side/my side.

Before sunrise, someone will
retreat
to another room, a shredded couch, a lover.

A vague full moon does its slow
glide as our bodies
remember nightspooning,

tangled limbs, thrilled skin.
Here we lie, separate
slivers of memory, shrapnel kisses.

Night falls as the dog sleeps
near the edge
of one bed or another.

Mia L. Jones

The editor of *Tryst*, **Mia Jones** was born in Korea. She has been publishing her work since 1984. Most recently her work can be found online at *Ariga, 3rd Muse, Mentress Moon, MiPo, Lotus Blooms, Paumanok Review, Pixiport, Three Candles, Wired Hearts* and others.

Corinthians 13:4-8

Love is patient, love is kind
love endures all manner of things.
Love swallows. Love believes
'til death do us part. Oh Lord,
when will it, will it ever end?

Love like this can never win:
Give her the moon, her cycle
her spoon, her midnight rounds;
love, the minion, brightened eyes
evening wears her best disguise.

Should a pair of mourning doves
alight the Joshua tree, lovers
do not mistaken this for a good sign;
'tis easy to read intimacy like theirs
through the leaves, such gentle cooing.
Love bears all things in the Kingdom.

But of the affairs of man, the sermon goes:
Love the self, love the fish (as leavened loaves).
Love lorn love, the handmaid's tale, a stitch
in pillow, stitched in red, love worn out
'twill not last, whilst true love often dies.

Love, the naïve, love, the fool, love you,
love you not, never again. Oh love
miserable love, you lied.

Bad Kitty

The cat wants a squirrel
but she can't see the fence for the lawn—
the neighbor's yard poses a problem. Big
fat, juicy squirrels jauntier, quarrel, chew on
real estate and barter with the sun. Their kingdom
all the way to the street, only place off limits
except for the dead ones.

The cat is synonymous with carpet
table, chaise lounge. Dressed-up doll, so much so,
her face doesn't even register feline. She
inveigles bacon in the morning, sashimi for lunch
lean chicken cut up finely. This is her domain
which would be acceptable if there weren't
mice hooplas in the kitchen every night. The one
and only one hope when a mouse darted
between her toes, she scuttled it across the floor
then lay next to it and licked its fur as if
she had given birth.

Concierto de Aranjuez after Lorca*

Grass once verdant, once moist
velvet shorn to its roots and brittle
spikes thrusting through the soil
swallowed the sword of the ancient prophet
split wide-open its belly

so earth could purge the secrets
of its prized son; where his body lay
buried in an unmarked grave.

Body of the beautiful balladeer
overcast eyes and shadowy hands,
stringed heart of astral origins
one who rolled glass marbles
between his assured lips.

Those same lips now spewing forth
rivulets of blood, black and sluggish
salted his tongue whitish-gray;
the smell of black dahlias in his hair.

So earth covered him in a shroud of rain, gauze and linen
sent his corpse floating on the back of the weary tortoise
where it turned up in Granada, in Canaan
there! in the streets of Gaza, where

it was torn to pieces by a pack of wild dogs
fighting for his liver, his lanced ribs, palms
pierced by bullets and taste of the inner thigh.

The wind pacing back and forth
to hear the news, sent word
to his mother who wept; cursed
in Hebrew, in Arabic, in Gaelic,
in Basque....Castilian. What did it matter?
sorrow dug its claws in deeper, ripped
away the soft lining of her throat

while villagers celebrated el Dia de la Muerte
in a slow procession of assumed penitence
brought to their knees with self-flagellation
tied to crudely-made X's, trying to understand
the souvenirs of pain.

Love Poem to Her Lover

I repeat, my love, I am ruined, ruined
for the captive wife. I was meant to be
bedded having practiced all my life
for this mattress, supine. I don't mind
the occasional ball, the whip, ceiling cage
but not the chain. Pardon me
if I decline, though I have loved
the animal, not so, the dead skin—
having brought my own. Behind
the smile, more teeth. The tongue
attached to ancient rhythms of its own
and the need to know: The difference between
fear and desire, sweat and heat. The arcane
made beautiful when darkness sheds its light
and I allow naked torsos of men loosed
into that stream of lurid dreaming. I am not,
I repeat, not cheating on you. But for you,
for you, I would do anything, even if it means
I must cut off my breasts, shore my hair
and bind them to my feet.

Richard Jordan

Richard Jordan is a PhD research mathematician who lives in Western Massachusetts. He is also currently enrolled in the Stonecoast Low-Residency MFA program at University of Southern Maine. A Pushcart nominee, his poems have appeared recently, or a forthcoming in *Concho River Review*, *The Pacific Review*, *Harpur Palate*, *Cranky*, *The Chiron Review*, *The Adirondack Review* and *Redactions*.

Through the Ice

I wanted to imagine fish asleep
below thick ice, with black eyes lidded, fins
slowly twitching in dreams where they slip
away from predators, buffered by current.

I didn't want to drop a leaded minnow,
pierced only millimeters from the spine,
through the jagged hole. But as it tumbled
out of sight, I couldn't look away.

I wanted to believe my father when
he explained that fish—especially bass—can't feel
a swallowed hook. He told me this because
I was seven, and the heavy largemouth

I didn't want to hold was spilling blood
and flopping on the snow. My father clubbed it
with the blunt end of a hatchet, had me kneel
beside it for a photo. A rumble echoed across
the lake—ice settling, like the smile on my face.

One Way to Go

I asked him one time, "How did Grandma die?"
and Grandpa said, "Well, blame the goddamn cats."
He claimed that one had crawled up Grandma's chest
while she was sleeping, glued its mouth to hers,
and sucked out all her breath. But, still, I knew
he must have taken in a dozen more
after Grandma passed away. He swore
the coeds dumped them in his yard before
graduation. "Like abortions. Christ,
I don't need another pissing flea
hotel," he bitched, while warming buttermilk.
"So why then, Grandpa? I mean if Grandma..." "Shush,"
he cut me short and gave the pot a stir.
"Look, kid," he said. "There are worse ways to go."

Whenever Light Arcs

Danny's gone and my wife saw a shooting star just around the time he passed. She insists that every time she sees one someone dies. She means someone she knows, of course. Statistically speaking, it's a near certainty a stranger is dying whenever light arcs across the night sky. I never tell my wife that some must be satellites, that space hardware probably shouldn't count.

I put greater faith in the vocalizations of canines—Baxter for example. He bayed the whole night my mother died, got worked up while she was still on life support. And he paced and whimpered for days when the neighbor girl went missing. My son likes to tell of a chorus of howls on the evening we made the humane choice for Baxter. Dogs know. That's the only explanation.

But look, I've told you nothing about Danny. He was sixteen and drunk. Fell into a river.

Bait

I've always hated this old photograph:
my dad so proud, so confident, alive.
He hoists a stringer—Brookies lured with worms.
The purest way to go, he always claimed;
but I insisted sportsmen fish with flies.

To spite the bastard, I learned how to tie
my own from scratch and taught myself to cast.
I even caught a few trout now and then,
and when my balls had grown to twice their size,
I asked my dad to come along with me.

He laughed and spat at my new graphite rod.
"The only thing you'll catch with that is shit."
"Up yours, old man!" I said. He wouldn't bite.
Instead he watched me deftly hook an oak,
then pissed a perfect arc into the brook.

Alex Keegan

Crime and Mystery writer **Alex Keegan** is the author of five novels and numerous prize-winning short stories. He lives in England with his wife, Debbie and two children.

This Will Not Be Easy

This will not be easy. It involves socks, underwear, what we choose, the pain of a lunchtime pizza, Alice Munro, a fisherman dying, a student, two; and money, art, the menopause.

It came to him as he bathed this morning, as he washed his feet; to be precise, as he washed his toes; to be *exact*, as he rediscovered the space between the big toe on his left foot and the second toe on his left foot, slightly sudded, faintly pink, touch of eczema.

Why it, this, the toe mattered, why the moment came back, has to do with the sock-drawer, the drawer that holds his underwear, (and Alice Munro and Saul Bellow), (and people will think this is a narrative error) but in this morning bath, alone, he was suddenly in another bath, alone, a bewildered bath, the white telephone on an extension, perched on the corner of the bath in the hope – he is alone – that it would ring, bring, so loudly, six hours after thirty-five deaths and him bloody, faintly heroic, and now pathetic, discovering his feet, marveling at his skin.

He had arrived home, (a Samaritan, then a frightening slow clank from a little station – they still didn't know how many had died) made tea, sweet tea, too strong, so strong, so sugared that the spoon could stand upright; and into it, this healthy eater, this *athlete*, dipped bread and butter and sucked the concoction, not knowing he was back in his father's kitchen (then it was Echo margarine) and missing his mother.

Now, he is in a bath, out of the bath dried, and here at the computer, and still in that kitchen, globules of margarine emerging, amber circles in the mug, floating, molecules, pustules. He is bare-chested at his computer, and dressed for a trip to town, he is home later, he is dressing, he is not.

His father is here and he is not, and he is a father, a son and he is not, and now, if he wasn't about to finish dressing he might go through to the kitchen, make builder's tea, take bread, a knife, and begin buttering.

And what has brought this on? What trivial event? Choosing a pair of underpants!

He had opened the drawer of drawers (not a long way) and taken a pair, any pair, from the front. He had taken the pants from the front, and tomorrow, washed, dried, pants would be pushed *into* the drawer at the front and the next day, from the drawer, he would take –

Socks (from the front of the draw too, the rest mysterious, rejected) they too meant. The longer socks left marks, his calves swollen, (he sits too long) and he would think of heart failure, his heart failing, of old men, and old women outside bingo halls with rolls of obscene fat around their ankles. So he selected ankle-length wear, and his heart would be better.

And the pizza.

When she rings, and her lunch is cancelled after all and she'll be home, he grunts and then, on automatic, he says we could meet in town for something (he was dripping, rushed, his dark feet-marks on the stairs and the sock drawer thing had not then struck him) and she says yes, and it is then that things come to him. This is why he mentions pain because he does not want to eat a pizza, he does not want to meet in town, but the part of him which talks on the phone pretends too well.

It is like love; he means like unlove; he means not love; and yet this is something he says almost every day, "I love you." He has never meant it. Not from the first date, through marriage, the children. "I love you," means "Thank-you. I am not alone. Thank-you, I am not alone. I am not alone, and for this, sometimes, I give thanks."

Appreciate, all these things flash through him or sail in parallel with other, more mundane things, or circle his thoughts, weave in and out of the ordinary, that which is presented. For like a man will talk to you of home-extensions, astrophysics or the declination of a verb, understand that he is all the time and none of the time, contemplating your sex. He is not undressing you for you begin naked.

So like this, like the man does so ordinarily, so matter-of-factly, so trivially and so automatically, so does the man, even as he sees this woman, wife (she wears a red leather top and is desperate to be thirty-five again) and grins, and kisses her cheek and jokes, "This is like a date!" he is thinking, "What is all this, and what does she think, of whom does she think, since I know she does not love *me*."

It is not pizza he orders, but risotto, chicken, and mushrooms, tasty enough. He tells her of a little money he has earned, a small story sale, and they successfully moan about people being like sheep even though the place is packed, they bleat too, and this farmer charges.

He tells her, asks her about underwear and drawers, and he knows, even as he asks, that not only will she shatter his metaphor but she will say things which remind him how gossamer-thin all this is, that they are held together only by light, sound and various overlappings.

"Of course, I *choose,* " she says, and then she hesitates, and it's these split moments that drive thunderous black wartrucks through all he has concocted and called a life. His why is in the air, though he manages not to utter it (he sips his Nasturo beer like someone smug on University Challenge, but here it is to hide what otherwise might quiver) until, at last, her voice a different voice, and looking for the collie-dog black-and-white waiter, she says, slowly, "To match my outfit," and he pretends this is so silly, a woman thing and smiles. He doubts it is a pretty smile.

"I *mean*," he says that people, *people,* take their lives from the front of the drawer. It's all this week's thinking, last week's ideas. They don't rustle round, they don't go deep." And she tells him about the swimming club committee meeting on Friday and he thinks about the bill.

They part, still in town. She goes to buy dye, he goes to a bookshop and forgets to get the milk he promised to pick up. He buys, *"Quantum: A Guide For the Perplexed."*

On the way home so many things rush into him, through him, but, unlike neutrinos, these invisible things, impact and shock. To the core.

He thinks of some digital photography he did recently, young women, impossibly optimistic, impossibly beautiful, and how, when he blew up their images to remove a blemish, to correct red-eye, he felt *guilty* that he could be so close, could touch their hearts, their bodies, while brushing a pimple, making an eye gleam.

A building sign, too red, too bright, a man walking wearing his firm's plastic dog-tags and grinning while admitting, "I am owned". The car fan too loud, too insistent, but when it's off, the road screams instead, the sign, the dumb robot with his tags, all those things over lunch (we are omitting the fear) and no paper, only hope, but a single telephone call, or a red light, and what will be will be something else.

He is almost home when he sees his wife coming the other way (they are in each other's car so recognize car rather than driver). He lifts a palm towards the windscreen acknowledging, then realizes they could be two couriers for Parcel-Line, two engine drivers, grimacing, holding their dead man's handle, rattlety-crap, rattlety-crap, en route to London.

And now he's here, the man, this man. And he knows that what was to be (before the pizza) and what could have been (after the pizza) and what will now be, are utterly different. He hopes only that some *essence* is within, some small him-dom, some faint reflected glimmer of the desperate screaming dark he looks out from.

It's now he thinks of *A Silver Dish*, of a son climbing into the bed of his rampant, dying father, of a pre-lunch abortionist with egg and cress sandwiches in a brown paper bag, of a fisherman, his drowning son on his shoulders, of the way the world aches, a beautiful ache, one that words can only dance around, perhaps glow lightly to illuminate.

Oh, and there is a darkness. There is a wholeness, a separateness; there is a one-ness from where we must surely wish to scream and say, "No, it isn't like that, I am not that. I am not me, and I know you are not you."

They called him a hero. Thirty-six died. The truth? The truth was he couldn't and wouldn't stay on the train. He wanted to *act*, to be, to do, to be moving, motive. He was too scared to obey the little fat man who cried out, "Stay on the train! Stay on the train!" He had not an ounce of courage, bravery wasn't an issue. He simply wanted to execute.

The carnage was still invisible to him. The locomotive up on the embankment was ludicrous (it would not strike him fully for weeks). His damaged carriage, the fourth – he always sat in the second but had lost his seat to someone now dead – was in a concrete gully, and to jump out and up onto the white-frosted wall was dangerous and difficult, but this was not brave, just something to do. Unless he wanted to stay on the train, baaaa, stay on the train, baaaa, stay on the train.

Here is some more of the darkness. It was so beautiful, the blood running down his face, the day (it was gloriously winter, frosten, silver, sharp, alive, alight) the *event*. He was immaculately dressed (a computer consultant in the city then), fit, a young 41, a runner, hard-bodied, used to doing, being, going, surviving, running *past* fat spectators. And he wasn't going to be one now. You see, dark, confessional. He did all that for *him*.

He actually did a good job. The other side of the spiked railings, two black teenagers responded to his orders. Sure they could divert the traffic, sure Mister, do you know you're bleeding?

Yeah, yeah (but I'm feeling heroic) but they are going to want to bring ambulances here, fire trucks.

OK Mister.

And he sent white faces to telephone. When they said but someone already – he *ordered them* and said *do it again* and this time tell them the name of this street. Tell them to come *here*. Tell them to come *here*.

And he turned round. Here is something from the inside. This is something the hero doesn't mention in the interviews.

The loco was too big, too cold, too massively above him, and there were bushes, thorns; he felt surrounded, no way forward. He went to the train. Perhaps, though he was not in khaki or wearing a hat, perhaps some might come with him?

How far is – what's the drop that side?

Same as this side, someone said.

And in that moment life changes, becomes darker, lives are lost. Someone mutters "John bloody Wayne" and this man, no hero, embarrassed, and nothing more than embarrassed does not jump back on the train, and does not jump out, down the other side, does not go forward, does not step into the hell to care. He *avoids further embarrassment*, he avoids the blush, he avoids, the coward, the cute remark from a simpleton, a fat sheep.

That is just one darkness. Now, rewinding, he imagines a greater heroism, shoving aside the flaccid, bleating commuter with disgust (but it's too late, too late) but do not think in his dreams these things do not recur, even if he has the press-cuttings – "The scarred and bloody face of a hero" – or likes to talk about that day, the time (08:12) and how it was such a beautiful day and he felt so alive.

Ask, him, he opens a drawer. Just inside are bright moments, the frost, his athletic jump, the blood, the almost-good things, the cameras, the moments in the round-walled pub, how that night, sore, he went out and jogged and felt the wind passing over him, through his fingers.

This bit, near the front of the drawer. The old man (broken wrist) that he got out through a roof and down a ladder. The man he got up the bank, rotten with footfalls by now, so rotten there was a rope to pull up, and how he threw some bleater, eighteen, from the ambulance and sent him to get teas. Let someone *injured* sit down.

Nearby, still near the front, hear the onset of Post Traumatic Stress Syndrome (impressive, huh?) and when he talks about the business that crumbled he will be sure to tell you how good it was *before* (for hadn't he built it?) and how the girlfriend he lost was, of course, gorgeous, the love of his life, what else, and, of course, a wonderful fuck.

He's a man, a dirty man, layer upon layer of untruth. His problem is he sees these things and feels these things (and pretends to write about these things). He sees posters that are too red, robots walking and the world fills him up, it rushes him, it rushes into him.

And he, the sane, regurgitates; he returns the compliment, he writes. Those who vomit life back they call insane, and those who do it a little more slowly they sometimes call hero.

Rose Kelleher

Rose Kelleher is a computer programmer who lives in Maryland. She's had several poems accepted by *Anon*, *Worm*, and *Light Quarterly*.

Evolution Fruit

"Unto the woman he said, I will greatly multiply thy sorrow and thy
conception; in sorrow thou shalt bring forth children..."
—*Genesis 3:16 KJ*

The blackest plums were clustered at the crown,
swollen with sun. A female was the first
to try it: standing upright, spurred by thirst,
she stretched a furry arm and plucked one down.
Her brothers caught on quick, and soon the ground
was littered with pits and pulp, and juice that burst
from purple mandibles to wet the earth.
Such bliss! They hardly thought to look around.

Sated, the creatures found that when they stood
on just two legs instead of four, they saw
above the brush, much farther than before;
and what they learned was not all for the good.

Our bones have shifted since, and birth's become
a trial — hard labor for a stolen plum.

Sole Searching

Comfy pumps and soggy sneaks,
snappy straps with piggy peeks,
butchy boots that weigh a ton,
sequinned sandals just for fun,
frumpy flats for work-a-day,
all revealing, in their way;
but those that speak the loudest are
the ones I left in Kelly's bar.

Rosa Rugosa

Rugosas bloom in a mess of bramble,
scourged with salt on a burning dune;
cans and bottles roll where humble
Rugosas bloom.

A ship was wrecked and seeds were strewn
along the shore; now roses ramble
amid New England sand and foam.

Tough and teeming still, a symbol
of our roots in shallow loam,
at home in the coastal rough-and-tumble,
Rugosas bloom.

The Rectangle

A jungle gym, a see-saw, and a patch
of sand have snipped a corner from St. Paul's
parking lot. The wheelchair ramp is new;
phlox now crowds the walk. Behind a yawn
of double doors, the floors are fresh-swept green;

thrown out, the squares of burgundy and tan
scuffed up by hundreds of schoolchildren's shoes
in lines of two. In this fluorescent light,
the Virgin Mary with her chipped half-smile
looks out of place, like a museum piece.

A sense of something missing haunts the hall.
It throws a shadow, though it has no mass—
its presence real, its color black, its shape
rectangular, behind the trophy case,
where Father Geoghan's portrait used to hang.

Koko Taylor, ca. 1987

She thrilled an all-white audience that night
in Boston: glorious, with gleaming gold
eyeteeth, the Queen of Blues, a woman bold
enough to make a pit bull fear her bite.
She roared; the chandelier shook, shedding light
in nervous splinters down the walls; she rolled
her fifty-something hips, and with controlled
fury, whupped each song with all her might.

My boyfriend sat transfixed, ignoring me,
in awe of Lady Earthquake. It was odd,
she didn't look like women on TV,
she didn't bother with a coy façade,
she didn't need a man to tell her she
was beautiful, for she was loved, by God.

Jesse Lee Kercheval

Jesse Lee Kercheval was born in France and raised in Florida. Her second poetry book, *Dog Angel,* has just been published the University of Pittsburgh Press. Her poetry appears in recent issues of such magazines as *Poetry London, London Magazine, Poetry Wales, Poetry Ireland Review, Poetry New Zealand, Prairie Schooner, Field,* and the *Virginia Quarterly Review* among others.

Hototogisu: The Cuckoo

"Namiko is happily married to Takeo, but when she contracts tuberculosis her mother-in-law forces her to divorce him. Deep in despair, she dies a tragic death."
Le Giornate del Cinema Muto catalogue

Picture a girl sliced, a clean break in the femur of her life, an interruption in the signal between her nerves and certain cells.

Imagine, too, a beach becoming seashore. Rocks, white and geometric. Schools of nervous fish, also white.

Now the girl walks into the waves. See the water broken by her body? Fish just outside the net often turn as one for flight.

This girl does not turn,

her life a rounded stone, the moon a whitefish, the shore a shining bone.

Picture a girl.

Familiarity, My Husband

One morning in
the small Italian town
where we're staying,
you discover the church door open.
Inside we find the body
of Saint Gregory,
his bones dressed
in embroidered satin
& we can't help comparing him
to other the saints
we've seen in our travels:
Santa Lucia with her heap
of eyeglasses in Venice,
Mother Cabrini marooned
in the upper reaches of Manhattan,
St. Boniface, unfamous
apostle to the Germans.

Like the explorer
Sir Richard Burton—
we take ourselves with us
everywhere we go.
He traveled
all five continents,
learned a hundred languages.
By the time he wrote
his final book on Iceland
every rock he saw
was the shadow of a dozen others,
every word
had ten synonyms
in his cacophony of language.

In the end,
no one could understand
a thing he said.
—not his most ardent reader.
—not his wife Isabel who rarely traveled.

No one except God. One can always
hope for God.

&—I count my blessings—

I have you, too.

At least for this life;
at least for now.

Ein Werktag

"[This early Swiss film depicts] human destinies caught up in the realities of life . . . a truck driver and a shop girl face long working hours, exhausting labor, low salaries, and the constant threat of unemployment." *Le Giornate del Cinema Muto catalogue*

Do you remember? How despite

the shuttered window
the closed and mended curtains
the smell of mountains   was in every corner

was all the breath there was?
We were without experience   were novices
at love.

The mountains!
To smell them in the middle of city
trucks grinding by outside

was to be blessed
though we ached from foot to head
with this love

which was clearly not   *agape.*
A man walks this earth
in his tight skin

in rain
and drought   with nothing much
to fear from either

but love
the world's incisor
gnawed us to the bone.

Still   there were mountains
beyond the curtain.
Do you remember?

The smell of snow in every room.

Peter Krok

Peter Krok is the editor of the *Schuylkill Valley Journal*, a journal of the arts of the Manayunk Art Center and the Humanities/Poetry director of the Manayunk Art Center His poems have appeared in the *Yearbook of American Poetry*, *Midwest Quarterly*, *Poet Lore*, *Negative Capability*, *Mid-America Poetry Review*, *Blue Unicorn*, *New Zoo Review*, *Poem*, *Potomac Review*, *Connecticut Review*, *Octavo* (on-line journal), and numerous other publications.

Hands of a Ball-Bearing Worker

Those powerful hands,
Scarred, nicked and thick
Like stubs of piecework formed
Out of a machinist's labor.

Those hands knew the certainty
Of the lathe and brutal steel
And warmth of small hands
Holding a dog's leash in the park.

Those hands worked the second shift,
Late hours when all the world was turning in.
The house in its vigil rested on its paws
Awaiting familiar sounds in the darkness.

A stir. And steps. The doorknob turned.
Barks would bang up the walls and stairs.
Those laboring hands would greet
The living room with light and a biscuit.

His coming would close the evening;
The house could ease until tomorrow.
So night and day would go on, go on;
Those hands knew what was required.

How Do You Explain It?

"What have you done?
What do you want to do
with your life? If you
have asked these questions,
then you are interested
in contacting J. P. Morgan
& Co. We have a combined
experience of 160 years
in the banking business."

Here on my way to work,
a radio announces the questions
I keep asking myself.
A voice inside goes on,
"What have you done?
What do you want to do
with your life? If you
have asked those questions, then . . ."
You got to be kidding I tell myself.
Who would believe that? Even if
you do, how do you explain it?

Driving on the Boulevard I think
of "Asphodel: That Greeny Flower."
It is difficult to get the news
from poems . . . That red wheel
barrow glazed with rain water.
A host of golden daffodils. A sprig of lilac.
Auden wrote, *Poetry makes*
nothing happen, but there're times
I read this stuff I feel mighty
as a sparrow.

Desire

Sometimes parting is so wide,
you can not get across it.
Sometimes the desire will not go.
The shadow keeps returning.

You hear a knock on the door
A whisper   She calls your name
You let her in   She enters the room
dressed only in sable   Smiles
Lets down her hair   Unwraps her body
Comes beside you   Invites your arms
You follow her into the night
Your lips hum to her scented skin

Her breath is with you still
You see her under the stars
on Lemon Hill when you gaze
at the silver night and white eyes
of headlights passing along the river
You see her in the moonlight
when you walked along the whispering wall
and lay by the sycamore and her white shoulders

Her parting eats at you
like the fox that gnaws
the child in the Greek fable.
The parting still goes on,
a wound of desire
that will not close.

Andrew Lam

Andrew Lam is an associate editor with the Pacific News Service, a short story writer, and and a regular commentator on NPR. Lam was born in Saigon, Vietnam and came to the U.S. when he was eleven years old. His awards include the Society of Professional Journalist Outstanding Young Journalist Award (1993), The Media Alliance Meritorious Awards, The World Affairs Council's Excellence in International Journalism Award (1992), the Rockefeller Fellowship in UCLA (1992), and the Asian American Journalist Association National Award (1993; 1995). He was honored and profiled on KQED television in May, 1996 during Asian American heritage month

Pho

A bright Saigon morning in March, 1975. At Mrs. Tran's restaurant on Pasteur Street and bad news came blaring on the radio. Da Nang was under attack. Two Russian MIGs had flown all the way from Hanoi to the central highlands without ARVN resistance. Bombarded by VC mortar, the city was veiled in black smoke.

Everyone—customers, waiters, a dozen passers-by, even Mrs. Tran's mangy, flea bitten German shepherd—all held their breath and listened. The plump and sturdy matron, too, stayed her cleaver on the large chopping block where she'd been slicing beef tripe. With closed eyes she listened. Her husband, a captain in the Marines, was stationed north of Da Nang. Since mid-February she had no news of him.

Customers broke out in gossip when the special news report ended, some openly wept over their uneaten soup, others, their faces ashen, pushed their chairs and stood up and left without paying. Mrs. Tran didn't care. She began to remove her jade bracelet, gold Buddha necklace and two ruby earrings, then wrapped them in a white handkerchief. She handed the tiny bundle to her daughter, Nga, the dreamy-eyed teenager who was busy staring at the bright street outside, where flame trees bloomed red and orange, and where people rushed here and there in a state of panic.

"Stop day-dreaming, my child," Mrs. Tran scolded her, "put this away and write this down. Get pen and paper. You should have memorized it by now, the way you devour poetry, but I know you haven't. And may Lady Buddha Quan Yin protect us all."

Allow the oxtail and marrow bones to unleash their flavor, and the star anise and cloves to permeate thoroughly, making it a worthy base for the delicate rice noodles, which are, as you know, freshly cooked for each bowl.

In 1964, in the middle of the monsoon season, 50 South Vietnamese soldiers with northern accents and ancestry, in a program concocted by the CIA, parachuted back into northern territories to act as spies. Of the 50, Mr. Chi Nguyen was the only one who managed to elude capture and to blend in with the general populace.

Now in Sacramento, California, a wizened old man with a toothless grin and a throaty voice, Mr. Nguyen told his story to a pot-bellied reporter from the *Sacramento Bee*. Having infiltrated Hanoi, he ordered *pho* in a well-known restaurant near Hoan Kiem lake. In the middle of eating his soup he spotted Vu, his best friend and comrade in espionage, sitting at another table. They made eye contact but did not dare talk. Mr. Nguyen desperately wanted to warn Toan to stop slurping so loudly, as he was attracting attention. But before he could gesture or say a word, Vu already made a second mistake, which proved fatal: He ordered a second bowl.

Customers and waiters gasped. Heads turned. For it was a time of ration and of self-sacrifice, a time of anti-bourgeois behaviors, and no one, not even Uncle Ho himself, especially him, ever ordered a second bowl. Eat a second bowl and you'd have committed an anti-revolutionary act. Eat too much and you'd have shown your true bourgeois colors. Eat more than your share and you'd never survive the communist paradise.

Vu never did. Like the others from the group, he was promptly arrested, tortured, then, four months later, executed on espionage charges. Mr. Nguyen himself survived by sheer luck: he had a small stomach and, besides, had never forgotten the unforgiving nature of the north.

After the war ended he left the country on a boat with his wife and children. The wife, a peasant, did not know that he was a spy for the South until they reached the United States. The children, too busy becoming Americans, didn't care. But it was not his story of espionage that Mr. Nguyen recalled now with fondness. It was his first bowl of soup in Hanoi. "You know what," he said to the reporter in a voice now tinged with longings, "it was the best bowl of *pho* I ever had. Simple, but delicious. No garnish, just a squeeze of lime on a few pieces of raw beef the size of your fingernail, and the broth—oh la la, it smelled distinctly of star anise and charred onion."

"I was hungry with my eyes and nose even if my stomach couldn't hold," said Mr. Nguyen. "If I could have eaten like Vu, poor bastard, I probably would have, at the risk of death and destruction, ordered another bowl." Then at the thought of his own death and destruction the old man fell into a laughing fit that almost killed him, his eyes, tearing, disappeared under wrinkling epicanthic folds.

Mr. Nguyen grew five kinds of basil all in his garden in Sacramento, plus a few other herbs, like Vietnamese coriander, lemongrass, mint, and many bushes of star anise flowers and some parsnip. "So where is home now for you, Mr. Nguyen?" asked the *Bee* reporter. Home, he said, is his pungent garden, home is the hot summer breeze in which herbal aromas waft and fold. Home is what you run away from in your youth, only to be trapped again in longing for it in your old age. Faraway restaurants are known to order his anise and coriander. "Smell this," he said as he mashed a dark green basil leaf between his tobacco-stained fingers and held its fragrant juice against the reporter's nose. "Smell good, yes, yes? This smell, it makes me remember, it takes me all the way back."

To make pho be of many minds. The side dishes alone can distract you from the main broth. The broth demands constant care, for without it, my dear, you have nothing.

Late afternoon of the last day of April in 1975, the sun burned like a piece of coal overhead, an eerie silence reigned over the entire city, and communists tanks crashed through the gilded gates of an empty Independence Palace. Inside, a fat president named Big Minh, who had been president for a day, sat waiting to surrender. The city had fallen, and young Viet-Congs sat on rusty mud-caked trucks and rusty tanks with awe and bewilderment on their sunburnt faces. Saigon was beautiful, rich beyond their imagination, not the poor, wretched place suffering under imperial powers their leaders had filled their heads with all those years in the jungle. Already some began to ponder that question that is still argued to this day: who's liberating whom?

From behind curtains and over red and purple bougainvillea-veiled walls, or hidden behind tamarind and flame trees, well-fed, discreet Saigonese stole glimpses at their emaciated conquerors, though a few of their rowdier children climbed the walls, and, thinking it was yet another military parade, hollered and waved.

At the dock, it was another story. Thousands had gathered and were jostling each other onto the planks of waiting ships. Nga herself boarded a crowded boat with her younger brother. Their aunt was with them. Nga's mother had accompanied the three to the dock but decided to stay and wait for news of her husband. Her aged parents, besides, needed her back in Quang Ngai province, if they'd survived. But even if they hadn't, she needed to fulfill her filial duties and bury them properly. With hoarse, weeping voices, Nga, her little brother, and their young aunt all begged Mrs. Tran to come along—"Please, sister, I beg you, think of the children!"; "Oh mother, how can you possibly not come?"; "Ma, I'm so scared!" But Mrs. Tran was adamant. "Go! Go with my blessing. And you, take care of my children like your own," she ordered her younger sister, and hastily stuffed all the gold and dollars she had traded earlier that morning into her sister's and daughter's outreached hands. She imagined herself giving away dowry at her daughter's wedding, which she, in flash of prescience, saw as taking place on a kept lawn and beside a lake dotted with sailboats. She even saw the groom's face, a smiling, blue eyed stranger who was now lifting her daughter's pearl-studded veil to kiss her.

The ship engine rumbled, the smell of diesel assaulted the air, her children called out desperately for their mother, but Mrs. Tran kept walking. She willed herself not to look back, not even once. On the streets and sidewalks near the dock, motorbikes and cars and army jeeps and suitcases and clothes were left abandoned. And in the air Vietnamese *dong*— green, red, and orange—fluttered like butterflies. This colorful South Vietnamese currency had lost all its value that morning and was now worth only as much as the paper mock offerings one burned for the dead. However, the street urchins did not know this. A band of them, wearing new clothes that were too big for them, were amassing the notes they had coveted for so long, singing gleefully their prophetic ditty of what was to come, "Oh we're paupers who turned into princes and kings, and we'll run the world with our ding-a-lings."

In the dying light of April, Mrs. Tran mumbled her Buddhist prayers while clutching her rosary made of black bodhi seeds, which were shiny from years of use. She kept on walking. Behind her one ship after another left the harbor.

A bowl of pho with marrow served on the side is treasure. A dish of oxtail bone to accompany it, sprinkled with green onion, black pepper and freshly chopped chili, is love.

A windy autumn morning in the mid 1960s, the sky a benevolently blue, the war undecided, a handsome young man named Quang set sail. Long before leaving was thought possible, before the word *vuot-bien*—to cross the border—was to become a household word, Quang alone had already seen the seven seas. A genius with pipes and propellers, a doctor of ailing engines, he could hear their unquiet murmurs and name their ailments without fail. He would then set out to fix them and made himself indispensable to the Golden Seahorse shipping line from Hong Kong, who paid a small fortune to the foreign department in Saigon to purchase his exit visa and, in doing so, gave him the world.

The night before he left, his mother, pricking her thigh with a small hairpin under the table so that she wouldn't have to pay attention to the real pain of losing her only son, said in a stern voice: "Go! Please go! I'd rather have you alive in Morocco than coming back to me in a body bag from the DMZ. Go! Save yourself. And listen to me, unless there is real peace, don't you dare come back."

So, there was a war and he was sailing far away from it. There was a war and he didn't sleep well in any port or on any ocean. Tet offensive and he was in Madagascar. His mother's death and he wept all the way to Iceland. His best friend mortally wounded in Dalak and he watched a gorgeous sunset from Sydney with a Chivas Regal bottle as his companion.

When the war ended and the communists won, he couldn't come home. He kept his promise to his mother and kept going, though Quang kept dreaming of his homeland and everyone he knew there. His yearning over time made him at once handsome yet impossibly aloof. He had no friends and his lovers were fleeting and far between. Always, he dreamed of his mother's house, his little hamlet on the outskirts of Saigon by the river, and, of course, his sweetheart who had long ago married and was already a mother of three. In dreams, in reveries, Quang stepped off his ship with gifts in hand and shouted out to all the people he knew and loved, but, in reality, the gifts, bought and wrapped, stayed locked in his cabinet, and, since there was no real peace, he never returned.

On a beach in Reunion one day, a lush green island with waterfalls and gentle luring waves, though he was already late and should have been heading back to his ship, Quang kept on walking. Far down the beach, Quang saw a little makeshift restaurant with coconut trees and thatched roof and, though he really should have been getting back, he headed for it. A dark-skinned, elegant-looking mademoiselle greeted him with a bright smile and gave him the menu. Conch and fish he had plenty but as Quang scanned the menu with the boredom of someone who had eaten too many exotic meals, he saw at the bottom of the page a word that caused him to sit up and stare: "Fo."

Remember, you have to learn to be patient. It takes cooking all night for a broth to be ready in the morning. Skim the surface for scum that boiled to the top, make sure the broth is perfectly clear, yet its taste should linger.

Dawn in her memories: she stretches like a kitten on her bed next to the large French window on the second floor. It looks out to other balconies, eight houses in all that share a leafy and mildewed courtyard. She hears the solemn sounds of Buddhist chanting from Old Lady Muoi who lives across the way. In her memories the wind is always cool and supple, and her curtains would sway just so, and the smell of sandal wood incense, fragrant and holy, along with her mother's complex aromatic broth from the restaurant downstairs, would fill her nostrils.

On the balcony to the right Toan, a boy her age, is already up, diligently practicing his martial arts. She can hear the dull, thudding sounds from the impact his feet and fists make against the sandbag that hangs from the eave of his roof. If she peeks, she can see the beads of sweat on his bare shoulders, his stomach rippling with abdominal muscles in the early light. Sometimes their eyes meet for half a second, and it would be enough for the boy to be completely disarmed. He would turn as red as a firecracker and the sandbag would suffer more assaults than usual, and she would hide behind the curtain, her hand on her mouth to stifle a giggle.

Other times, Nga remembers this: wild parrots squabbling over the ripened fruits on the single mangosteen tree in the middle of the courtyard, and Mai, the servant next door, singing a song from her favorite Cai Luong opera while doing the laundry, her voice sad and mournful; the heat rising.

Downstairs, in the restaurant kitchen, her mother, who had risen hours before dawn, is already preparing the day's fare with the help of her two servants. Soon the noise of the wooden chairs being dragged on the tile floor, of chatting customers, of motorcycle mufflers, of children on their way to school, will rule the world. But not now. Not yet. Now there is only a stillness in the salty dawn.

Nga will always associate this moment with home, a sweetness in the world so rare that it can now only be had in the recalling. She can feel it still, hear it perhaps with more clarity because of her unfulfilled longings, and the years. Her mother humming softly, ladles against the pots and pans, and the steady chopping sound of the cleaver on the worn wooden block, Old Lady Muoi's pious chanting, Toan's sandbag being pummeled, his roan back, and Mai's lovely and sad voice .

All this—her unhurried lullaby, what insulates and owns her still, even now, from an unfathomable distance.

The bowl comes to you hot, extremely. That's how the aroma reaches the diner. Imagine dropping freshly cut onions into a bowl of cold soup—you will smell nothing, a waste of all the efforts.

A hot August day in San Jose at the turn of the millennium, Kevin Pham, a boyish 24-year-old electrical and computer engineer working for Hewlett Packard, entered "pho soup" in his favorite search engine. The number of hits that came back was staggering: 2883. Kevin wasn't sure exactly why he entered "pho." He could easily have entered "manga" or "kung fu movies" or a dozen other things that always lurked at the edge of his pop culture-flooded mind. But it was near lunch time, and as he later wrote to Bernard, his wealthy ex-dorm-mate from U.C. Berkeley now living in Brussels, "I suppose I was both hungry and missing my mom's cooking." It was a fateful choice. For then, almost as a joke, he began a website called whatpho?.com, a popular site that rated various *pho* restaurants in California and had 10,000 hits daily. Five bowls for the best. Two for mediocre ones, and bad ones, really bad ones, got a pair of broken chopsticks.

A few months after he built his site Bernard sent him a cryptic email:

"Dearest K.,

If you want to eat the best pho in Europe come to Belgium. Your homeland's exquisite broth travels—to mine. Stay with me as long as you like and we can make many an excursion. Besides, I promised you 'moules et frites.' Just tell me when and I'll send tix.

Tu me manques,

Bernard"

So Kevin came to Belgium on a culinary quest—and found himself driving up a country road one sunny afternoon with an enigmatic but beaming Bernard who intermittently stole glimpses at his profile as they drove, their black Porsche zooming down country lanes stirring up afternoon dust.

Soon they came to a small forest, then an impressive medieval castle that loomed over the hedges. "Are you sure, Bernard?" Kevin said. "It's private property."

"Just relax and enjoy the ride, would you, babe," Bernard said. "I have a surprise for you." At the moat, standing on the drawbridge, Kevin stopped. And sniffed. He had expected it, but it still shocked him. It was unmistakable. There it was, that complex aroma wafting in the air—cinnamon and cloves and ginger and fish sauce and star anise and beef broth. Someone was making *pho*.

Bernard steered him down a dark staircase toward an enormous kitchen, the kind that could cater to 300 people, or a hunting party of yore. In the middle of it stood an elegant Asian woman in her mid-30s, two little mixed-race children, a boy of 4 and a girl of 7, playing on a slide next to her. At the far corner, a blond maid was skimming the soup. The Asian woman greeted Bernard with kisses and then she turned warmly and addressed Kevin in Vietnamese. "Here you are. I've been waiting for a long time. I thought you both got lost in the woods." Then she kissed him on both cheeks. "Bernard spoke so often about you that I started to miss you too."

The shank and oxtail bone, pick them carefully. Make sure there's plenty of marrow inside the shanks and, as for the oxtail, don't buy those that are too large, or they can't fit in the bowl for a side dish, and can often overwhelm the diner.

"Fo" was once *pho*, after many generations, so Quang found out on that beach in Reunion. Still, who would complain about spellings when the broth simmered in the kitchen? There was no rice noodle in what survived, no star anise smell, not even fish sauce. The mademoiselle with a slender figure and a bright smile made noodle out of tapioca. She rubbed it into uneven strings between her dexterous fingers, then boiled it.

Yet it was "*un plat Vietnamien*," as she insisted when he asked about its origin. Some green onion was sprinkled on the soup and a waft of ginger was enough to tell him *quelque chose de son pays* had indeed survived. When he asked her how a Vietnamese-like dish ended up here, she shrugged and said "*Mais Monsieur, moi aussi, je suis Vietnamienne*"— But sir, I'm also Vietnamese.

But how? Impossible!

"Si, si. Depuis cinq générations, mais Vietnamienne quand même. C'était mon ancêtre qui me lassait cette recipe," she said with seriousness.

Five generations ago! Quang searched his high-school memories and a piece of history made itself clear through the monotonous voice of a flint skinned, bespectacled teacher who smoked while he lectured. *In 1888, the French exiled King Ham Nghi and his entourage when they refused to follow French rules . . .*

To who knows where.

. . . Then Prince Thanh Thai and his entourage who conspired against the French in 1907 met a similar fate . . .

How many rebellious Vietnamese ended up here and never came back, Quang wondered? He heard the distinct whistle of his ship from a distance, but he couldn't get himself to leave. In the kitchen the refrigerator sputtered; it needed fixing. He squinted his eyes and stared at the young restaurant owner, trying to imagine her in a conical hat and a white *ao dai* dress. This mademoiselle, she grew familiar in his eyes, and Quang had to fight very hard to suppress a profound desire to reach out and caress her kinky hair.

As in all kinds of serious cooking, making pho depends on intuition, feeling, and taste. The garnish must have it all to wake up taste buds: fresh basil and bean sprout and three kinds of chili, and wedges of lime and coriander leaves. And plum sauce for those who like it sweet.

In Ubud, Bali, Vietnamese pho had taken on a delicate taste. Served with fresh snow peas and a wedge of lime and no other garnish to speak of, except a sprig of amazingly spicy basil, it's a delight to the visitor, especially when the waitress blesses the soup with a white orchid to enhance the spirit of the broth.

In Buenos Aires, an Argentine who had been to Vietnam years ago as a doctor and knew the recipe, nursed her ailing husband who suffered from multiple sclerosis back to health solely on *pho* broth. She told the Buenos Aires *Herald* that it was a miracle cure, "but you have to cook it with absolute devotion and love and say your prayers repeatedly as the broth simmers."

In Nargakot, Nepal, high above the clouds, an Indian hotel owner whose grandfather used to live in Saigon working as a tailor, is known to serve *pho* to celebrate Vishnu every month. Though, as in India, beef is not available in Nepal and oxen meat is used as a substitute, it doesn't detract from the taste. "The meat is only a little bit more chewy, but just as good," he claims. "Plus up here, with such clear air and strong wind, everyone, the tourists, the people in town, everyone knows when my wife and I are making *pho*. Even the bloody yetis."

The lime, especially, you will pick with care, the thin-skinned ones tend to be full of juice but they rot easily. Yet nothing's more irritating than squeezing a dried-up, thick-skinned lime over a bowl of pho. Whereas a juicy, fragrant piece of lime in its prime is heaven.

The Vietnamese woman living in a Belgian castle was now a baroness, so Kevin learned. Once a high school teacher, she fled after the war ended. With a few gold *taels* in her pocket, she said good-bye to her mother and father and younger brother and made her way to Vung Tau and bought a seat on a crowded boat. In the dark of night, they set sail. A week or so later they ran out of food and water. A few vessels passed them by, none stopped. Some people died. Though she didn't believe in God or Buddha, the high school teacher prayed and prayed. Then a miracle: a Belgian merchant vessel took pity on their ragged S.O.S. flag and picked them up. The high school teacher was brought back to Belgium where, owning nothing, she resorted to living in the basement of a church.

She was poor, she was wretched, an exile, but she was finally free. And she was not unhappy. She did menial labor and helped clean houses and gathered wheat crops to get by. But life is strange when you cast yourself away from what you know, and who could guess what fortune would befall you from unexpected sources, especially when you are free and open to the world?

Nearby there lived a baron, a devout Catholic and a bachelor in his mid fifties. He had wanted to be a priest but because he was the last of his line his family insisted he remain a layman. Still, he stayed pious and a bachelor. One day, while the baron was praying, kneeling at the front pew and staring up at the Madonna and child, the high school teacher emerged from the stairwell of the church and, well, the sunlight streaming through the stained glass window must have made her glow with a certain aura. And the baron lowered his gaze and followed her down the aisle and out of the stale church. They married. Now the mother of two children of noble blood, she would sometimes catch glimpses of herself as she glided past the gilded mirrors along the old castle's corridors and shudder, wondering, who is that? Is that me? Other times, when entertaining European royalty, she felt as if she was on a movie set and kept waiting for the director to yell: "Cut!"

When her maid brought out the steaming bowl of *pho* and as Kevin's face expressed awe and amusement, she said, "Eat, eat," and continued to tell more of her fairy-tale adventures. Wise now to love's variations and strange destinations and its endless hunger, the baroness was not unaware that another romance was about to unfold under her table: While Kevin ate, Benard's hand was inching across that short yet impossible distance toward his ex-roommate's thigh.

When ready to serve, bring the bowls out steaming with aroma. Watch the faces of the diners: their eyes squint with anticipation, lips curve into smiles. Their delight; your reward.

On the wall of his office overlooking the Duc-Ba Cathedral in the first district, Saigon, Toan keeps a framed article he found in a fashion magazine a few years back. Among the carved jade and gold plaques that he collected over the years, it stands alone, a treasure.

The article has a catchy riddle for a title: "Where's the Most Remote Restaurant in the World?" But it is not the answer that thrills him. No, it's the photo of a Vietnamese woman who stares past camera with dreamy eyes to the world—the face of his true love.

Once upon a time she lived next door to him. Her bedroom he could see clearly from his balcony each morning when the curtain was pulled back, or when the wind lifted it for a second or two so as to reveal his love reading or combing her hair. Toan had recovered from the devastation of war, its horrid aftermath, had rebuilt his life after coming back from the New Economic Zone, had married, found success, but he had never recovered from a broken heart. What, after all, are ideological struggles compared to love? Perhaps it is fitting that she should come back smiling to him from a black and white photograph, after all the years. But where was this restaurant? In a scientists' colony at the edge of Antarctica. The article told him that Nga had married, that her husband was a famous scientist, and that among glaciers and tundras and chatty penguins she grew bored. While her husband studied magnetic fields, to amuse herself, Nga made *pho*. But it had gotten so good—everyone could smell it in the colony, how could they not?—Nga ended up selling the soup as a way to buy ingredients from South America and to make more *pho*—not to make a profit, mind you, only to keep everyone around her warm and happy against the bitter cold.

Sometimes, in a whimsical mood, Toan looks at the photo and imagines himself flying over a sea of ice to see her. Just thinking about it makes his heart palpitate.

What would he say to her? Everything. A million things. Like how he ran out after her that day the communist tanks rolled into the city but he was too late: her ship had already sailed and the world as he knew it shattered. How he would have hopped on the next ship to go after her if it hadn't been for his family, his younger, helpless siblings. How he'd never had the chance to tell her how much he'd loved her. How he'd carved her initial and his on the mangosteen tree after she was gone and punched it so hard that his blood stained them forever, and that those initials have risen higher than his head. And how, despite everything, despite the changes and the years, his love for her hasn't changed.

Nga, the soup restaurant on Pasteur Street closed after your mother retired and went back to her province. A family moved in from Hanoi where you used to live and after *perestroika*, after the Cold War ended, they turned it into video parlor and it is full of kids playing those noisy electronic games. And now, last time I drove by, it's also a cyber-cafe full of smelly foreign backpackers.

The neighborhood has changed so much you wouldn't recognize it if you returned. I don't recognize it myself and I live here in Saigon. But you'll never come back, I know you. Only a handful ever return to where they used to live, and then only to look and cry a little at how the old place has fallen apart or changed, and then again they take leave.

Nga, remember those mornings when the borders were still real and even talking across the clotheslines or the courtyard was as treacherous as crossing the ocean? Yet how I long for that world! How I long for the smallness of things. Everyone knew each other then, and leaving was only for the few, not the many.

Everything has changed, Nga. Everything turned upside down. I changed. I'm a father of three, a vice president of an insurance company, the first in the country. Imagine that! I insure people against tragedy, in a country built on it.

But some things never change. I think of you. I think of you all the time. I imagine you among the howling winds. What I would give to see your face again. See how you try to guess who I could possibly be, a familiar-looking stranger standing there in front of you at the far end of the world.

But if you don't remember, if you can't recall, then I will tell you. I will remind you where we used to live, the old neighborhood, the mildewed courtyard with the mangosteen tree, and the wild parrots that fought for every fruit. Maybe you would remember. Maybe you would offer me a steaming bowl of *pho* while it is snowing outside. And I would be ravenous. I would eat like a mad man starving for decades, and you, you with your eyes always dreaming of some faraway place, would look on with amusement and approval.

And Nga, it will be the sweetest bowl of *pho* soup I'll ever taste.

Dorianne Laux

Dorianne Laux is the author of three collections of poetry from BOA Editions, *Awake* (1990), introduced by Philip Levine, *What We Carry* (1994), finalist for the National Book Critics Circle Award, and *Smoke* (2000). She is also co-author, with Kim Addonizio, of *The Poet's Companion: A Guide to the Pleasures of Writing Poetry* (W.W. Norton, 1997). Recent work has appeared in *The Best American Poetry, The American Poetry Review, Shenandoah, Ploughshares Barrow Street* and *Five Points*. Among her awards are a *Pushcart Prize* for poetry, two fellowships from *The National Endowment for the Arts* and a *Guggenheim Fellowship*. Laux is an Associate Professor and works at the University of Oregon's Creative Writing Program.

Trying to Raise the Dead

Look at me. I'm standing on a deck
in the middle of Oregon. There are
friends inside the house. It's not my

house, you don't know them.
They're drinking and singing
and playing guitars. You love

this song, remember, "Ophelia,"
Boards on the windows, mail
by the door. I'm whispering

so they won't think I'm crazy.
They don't know me that well,
Where are you now? I feel stupid.

I'm talking to trees, to leaves
swarming on the black air, stars
blinking in and out of heart-

shaped shadows, to the moon, half-
lit and barren, stuck like an ax
between the branches. What are you

now? Air? Mist? Dust? Light?
What? Give me something. I have
to know where to send my voice.

A direction. An object. My love, it needs
a place to rest. Say anything. I'm listening.
I'm ready to believe. Even lies, I don't care.

Say burning bush. Say stone. They've
stopped singing now and I really should go.
So tell me, quickly. It's April. I'm

on Spring Street. That's my gray car
in the driveway. They're laughing
and dancing. Someone's bound

to show up soon. I'm waving.

Give me a sign if you can see me.
I'm the only one here on my knees.

Ghosts

It's midnight and a light rain falls.
I sit on the front stoop to smoke.
Across the street a lit window, filled
with a ladder on which a young man stands.
His head dips into the frame each time
he sinks his brush in the paint.

He's painting his kitchen white, patiently
covering the faded yellow with long strokes.
He leans into his work like a lover, risks
losing his balance, returns gracefully
to the precise middle of the step to dip
and start again

A woman appears beneath his feet, borrows
paint, takes it onto her thin brush
like a tongue. Her sweater is the color
of tender lemons. This is the beginning
of their love, bare and simple
as that wet room.

My hip aches against the damp cement,
I take it inside, punch up a pillow

for it to nest in. I'm getting too old
to sit on the porch in the rain,
to stay up all night, watch morning
rise over rooftops.

Too old to dance
circles in dirty bars, a man's hands
laced at the small of my spine, pink
slingbacks hung from limp fingers. Love,
I'm too old for that, the foreign tongues
loose in my mouth, teeth that rang
my breasts by the nipples like soft bells.

I want it back. The red earrings and blue
slips. Lips alive with spit. Muscles
twisting like boatropes in a hard wind.
Bellies for pillows. Not this ache in my hip.

I want the girl who cut through blue poolrooms
of smoke and golden beers, stepping out alone
into a summer fog to stand beneath a streetlamp's
amber halo, her blue palms cupped
around the flare of a match.

She could have had so many lives. Gone off
with a boy to Arizona, lived on a ranch
under waves of carved rock, her hands turned
the color of flat red sands. Could have said
yes to a woman with fingers tapered as candles,
or a man who slept in a canvas tepee, who pulled
her down on his mattress of grass where she made
herself as empty as the gutted fire.

Oklahoma.
I could be there now, spinning corn from dry cobs,
working fat tomatoes into mason jars.
The rain has stopped. For blocks the houses
drip like ticking clocks. I turn off lights
and feel my way to the bedroom, slip cold
toes between flowered sheets, nest my chest
into the back of a man who sleeps in fits,
his suits hung stiff in the closet, his racked
shoes tipped toward the ceiling.

This man loves me for my wit, my nerve,
for the way my long legs fall from hemmed skirts.
When he rolls his body against mine, I know
he feels someone else. There's no blame.
I love him, even as I remember a man with cane-
brown hands, palms pink as blossoms opening
over my breasts.

And he holds me,
even with all those other fingers wrestling
inside me, even with all those other shoulders
wedged above his own like wings.

Sunday

We sit on the lawn, an igloo
cooler between us. So hot, the sky
is white. Above gravel rooftops
a spire, a shimmering cross.

You pick up the swollen hose, press
your thick thumb into the silver nozzle.
A fan of water sprays rainbows
over the dying lawn. Hummingbirds

sparkle green. Bellies powdered
with pollen from the bottle-brush tree.
The bells of twelve o'clock.
Our neighbors return from church.

I bow my head as they ease
clean cars into neat garages, file
through screen doors in lace gloves,
white hats, Bible-black suits.
The smell of barbeque rises, hellish
thick and sweet. I envy their weekly
peace of mind. They know
where they're going when they die.

Charcoal fluid cans contract in the sun.
I want to be Catholic. A Jew. Maybe

a Methodist. I want to kneel
for days on rough wood.

Their kids appear in bright shorts,
bathing suits, their rubber thongs
flapping down the hot cement.
They could be anyone's children;

they have God inside their tiny bodies.
My god, look how they float, like birds
through the scissor-scissor-scissor
of lawn sprinklers.

Down the street, a tinny radio bleats.
The sun bulges above our house
like an eye. I don't want to die.
I never want to leave this block.

I envy everything, all of it. I know
it's a sin. I love how you can shift
in your chair, take a deep drink
of gold beer, curl your toes under, and hum.

Frances Leviston

Frances Leviston graduated from Oxford in 2003 and is now completing her MA in Writing at Sheffield Hallam University, England. A short pamphlet of her work will be published by Hallam's Mews Press in autumn 2004.

Pitt Rivers *

All I've said on regret,
its notion that *now* could be anything other
than wearing a worn shirt
and always thirsty, still stands
at the roadside, waving me through
with a hand so gentle
you'd think it knows what I know,
that inside the pain of his finger
too hard on my sex
was the pleasure the dumb find, dark
as the heart of a candle flame,
and that suffering is lifted
with something like pride
in the long shadow of the museum
where children pace a furrow in the grass
and throw a rubber ball against the building.
One day it won't bounce back.
They will creep, then, under the awning,
through the turnstile, into their inheritance
of wooden masks, torn canoes, a century
of arrow-heads that can't be un-invented,
and under a sheet the only possible future,
which is a history, fixed, lamented.

*   *The Pitt Rivers is an anthropological museum in Oxford.*

On His Mother's Birthday

By dusk it's clear
he will not say
the words she wants to hear
from him, the words we deem today
demands – that no beribboned
thoughtful box
will happen in his hand.

The shops have shut.
He's chatty over tea
as if to salt his slight with what
could pass for normalcy,
and there it hangs – a nothing
in the air above their table,

the many open wounds of speech
outdone by one who's chosen
not to speak when he is able.

A Razor Shell

I know he's down there,
variegated,
fooling the birds
with his breathing pipe.

He drowns twice a day
and each day survives—
bubble, bubble,
grow another stripe.

I kneel in the sand,
slide him from his sheath,
with a bread knife
break the hasp, and peach

that pale engineer
inside his machine,
powerlessly
curling in the breach.

RoseMarie London

RoseMarie London is a 2000 Fellow of the Ucross Foundation in Clearmont, Wyoming. Originally from New York City, RoseMarie lives in Wyoming where she is working on a novel. An excerpt of her book, *What Jim Recommends*, was anthologized in "Dry Ground: Writing the Desert Southwest", edited by Annette Chaudet.

In Ranch Country Men are Valued by Their Ability With Horses

Scree \ n [of Scand. origin] : an accumulation of stones or rocky debris lying on a slope or at the base of a hill or cliff

I'm not too sure what made me agree to have a drink in town with Chad, exactly. Company most likely. I'd summarily rejected any prospect of companionship at the Owl Hoot Artists Residency where I was a third through my stay, though the residency director insisted that part of the criteria for acceptance is the individuals probability of providing a well-rounded artistic experience to the rest of the mix. I was not an unpleasant guest. I was willing, though not anxious to make friends. Dinners ended early. No one lingered. It was still day when I went into my room to change my clothes for drinks.

Curiosity had made me go back to the ranch for another trail ride and ostensibly my first lesson from Chad on what a real cowboy is as opposed to a fake. That afternoon, Chad had taken me out behind the ranch buildings, again through the swift moving Piney Creek and up the jagged edge of a bluff to show me some Crow teepee rings hidden in the brome. In the end, I'd agreed to the drink, I think, because I didn't want to disappoint the ranch owner, Jeb, who was standing beside the corral when Chad and I came off the prairie soaked to the bone.

The sky held no grudge against the mid-afternoon storm and streaks of bright sunlight crossed the quilt on my bed. Eventide, I thought. An archaic word, however appropriate here.

He'd put me back on Sparky who was slightly more resigned though still none too happy about the weight of my ass on his back, especially when someone let the herd out to pasture and my horse saw his friends flashing colors through the cotton woods. Sparky tossed his head high, and impossibly tried to turn around. His shoes clacked on loose rock and occasionally his knees buckled.

Chad kicked his horse up to the top of the bluff. "We're here." Chad was seated in his saddle right; knees perfectly straight. The reins were slack in his hand, and he guided his horse with a subtle shifting of his thighs. His horse stepped delicately, tracing the two hundred year old tee-pee and fire rings just about invisible in the grass to someone level with the ground. Chad pointed his hat down left and then right over each shoulder, and told me the story of the lichen covered rocks as he no doubt had heard it being told. I only heard some things. I was too busy feeling the dance that Sparky had decided to do. "Makes sense,"

• 174 •

Chad went on. "We're about five hundred feet above the valley. You can see the whole plain from here. There's Owl Hoot, over there. Young Crow, on the lookout for hostile New Yorkers," he said.

Sparky cut his circles tighter. I felt his increasing agitation. Chad stopped his horse suddenly and looked at the sky. Sparky refused to stand still, but there was a lot more room up on the bluff and so I didn't care. "What?" I asked, the tableau spinning. That's when the hail began.

I was laughing at first. Sparky did not agree with the humor and then I was horizontal like a bronc rider. Sparky came down hard and I slid against the saddle horn. There was half a breath before Sparky took off, running like he meant it with another square state on his mind. I smelled leather and what was the straining engine of my determined horse. Ice hammered my head and stung where there was bare skin. My hands were slick but when I had the courage to look the reins were still there. My hair was wet and heavy and slapped me in the back while Sparky was kicking up the earth, trying to run away from the weather. I had no idea how far we were from Chad and what might happen when we ran out of flat. Chad was nowhere. I had no technique but neither was I hanging off the saddle. I pulled on Sparky's reins but he didn't seem to mind the poor aerodynamics of racing with his head in the air.

Chad came up on us, riding with just his legs and grabbed at what he expected to be runaway reins. For a while the animals were in perfect sync and it was beautiful. At once, Chad's horse broke away and the wrangler had Sparky by the throat. I waited for Chad to tell me what to do. The dark of my horse's eyes had disappeared, but he slowed enough for Chad's feet to get hold of the dirt.

In the storm, Chad shouted for me to step off. "Get down," he said with a seriousness that made me hurry. "We're going to do this the cowboy way. Chad held Sparky's bridle while the animal heaved between them. "Hold on to him while I go and get mine."

I wondered what made Chad choose Sparky out of all the other horses in the barn as my match. The hail was evenly mixed with rain. Chad walked his horse around so that he and I could stand pressed between the two animals to wait out the storm. He closed the open end of the triangle with his back. I could smell the minerals rising in the steam off the ground, the simmering panic in the skittish horses and the loam of Chad's drooping hat.

"Lesson one," Chad said. "This is why most don't like cowboying in the winter." Ice clattered in the brim of his hat. There was that and the noise of breathing.

"This is winter?"

"Just about."

I liked it here because unlike in the Big Stinky, people take their cues from instinct, weather, large things, not trends or Simon Says. No one asks too many questions here. No one really cares where you came from, or which direction you're headed when you leave. Just about the job you do, that you do it well, and respect the men who've taught you how. For this reason, I like it here very much—the honesty of hard work and all that. Blue collar attraction, firemen, cops, steel-workers...cowboys. Chad's accused me of being on the run, in between. I don't mind so much this qualifier; it's what he can see, there's no way he can know the rest.

"And are you most?" I said.

"Haven't decided. Probably."

I called out to Jeb as Chad and I took a short cut through the parking area toward the barn, "I'm thinking this is a good look for me." Conversation kept my teeth from chattering.

"Aw, you're pretty any which way," Jeb said. "My wrangler here would own you a shot or two if he were old enough to buy 'em." The old man slapped Chad on the ass the way he did his favorite head of stock. Laughing out the side of his mouth, Jeb walked away, missing every mud filled puddle, not giving much thought to the facility provided by his bowleggedness.

Without being told, I brought Sparky to the barn door. "How old are you?"

"Twenty this past July." Chad nodded at my horse. "You can give him to me." Chad took the reins out of my hand. "Oh, come on," Chad said. "What does it matter?" I watched him disappear into the shadows; I waited for something else, but heard only the clacking of the horses' feet on dirt so dry and compact it's like concrete.

It is a Browning .30-.06 in the rack, Chad told me when I asked. He pulled against the curb, close, two tires in the gutter. I told him I knew the landmark neon of the Stove-Up Saloon from before I ever thought twice about the square state. I had to laugh a little that I was back in the Stove up two nights in a row, walking around with someone named Chad, who holds open the door.

We settled in at the end of the bar. Across from the juke box. I hooked my heels over the brass and leaned over the lip of the bar that's been smoothed by the underside of generations of forearms. Janis nodded at me and then raised an eyebrow at Chad who had his head down. Janis was deep in conversation with a narrow man in a J.B. Hunt baseball cap. I hadn't noticed the string of amber lights that outlined a Peterbilt across the street. Janis leaned in, flicked her long dark hair over her shoulder, rapt until the man finished his yarn, even while he took long drags off a Camel where all the commas are.

Chad played with his dingy belt buckle.

"Where'd you get that anyway?" I asked.

Chad scooted back, away from where I'd reached. "The usual way. I won it."

"Doing what?"

"Shoveling horse-shit."

"Be that way," I said looking again down the length of the bar. "I'm parched, aren't you?"

"Riding bulls," Chad answered finally. "Made a mess of my bladder. You'll see, I have to piss every—"

"Eight seconds?" I laughed.

"You're funny, Katy."

Janis came over wiping her hands on a rag. "What can I get you?" She had a look like she'd set up a joke and was ready to be amused. From under his misshapen hat, Chad said, "Bud Light."

"I'll have a double Beam and Coke, short."

Janis reached for a glass. Filled it with ice and said, "Hey cowboy, I'll need to see some ID."

Chad patted himself all the places where his wallet might have been. A bottle of Beam hovered longingly over my glass and Janis holds her other hand on her hip.

"I must have left my wallet in my work truck," Chad said.

Janis looked out the window. "And what would you call that thing you've got outside?"

"Would you like to see mine?" I said, hoping to draw attention away.

"Sure," Janis said. "New Yawk City!" Janis announced. A couple of people near the front window acknowledged the occasion. It took Janis a moment to find my birth date. "Lord girl," Janis whooped. "You're older than I am."

I held out a hand for either my license or my drink, I didn't care which. Janis, genuinely curious turned the card over the examine the other side before she handed it back.

"Thanks," I said. Janis slid me my drink, reached into a cooler and yanked back the top of Chad's beer. She was still holding it when she said laughing, "So tell me. How does a kid like you find a gal from New York Citeee?"

With a little bit of knowing in his voice, Chad said, "I work at a guest ranch."

"Well here cowboy." Janis passed him the can and before walking away said, "I wouldn't want to be the one to deny either of you the experience."

"I don't know how I feel about that remark," I said.

"I'm all right with it." Chad said tipping his head back. The beer did not wash away the bit of chew caught near his gum line.

"No wallet. I guess to keep up the charade I'll have to pay your tab," I said.

"I'll buy you breakfast someday."

I got up and loaded the jukebox with Marshall Tucker and Chris LeDoux. "You know, I've been thinking," I said leaning on the lighted glass. I'm pretty sure I lost my virginity the year you were born."

Chad sat perfectly still. "So did my mother. You know," Chad said. "I've been thinkin', you should get yourself a pair of Rockies. You've got the best kind of ass for jeans with no hip pockets."

"Haven't any of your friends warned you that someday someone might make you put your money where your mouth is?"

"I've got a leg up on my friends. It's just been my mother, my sister and me. I've spent my whole life around the habits of two crazy women. I know when to duck."

"The real secret, Chad. Is to not be so cocky about it."

Wick broke through the murk back by the pool table. "Yeah, Chad," Wick drawled. "Better do what the lady tells ya." Wick positioned himself between Chad and me to drain the last of a Coors. His forearms were a canvas of hand-poked tattoos depicting poorly rendered skulls and rattle snakes. The barbed wire that wrapped from shoulder to wrist had been beaten to a sea-slime green by his proximity to the sun. Wick put his beer down. "See ya later Miss Janis."

"See ya around, Wick," Janis answered also checking the level of my drink. "Friend of yours," Janis asked Chad.

"Same ranch," Chad said.

"Small town," I said. In a minute I asked, "Hey Chad, I have a question. I hear in ranch country the men are valued most for their ability with horses. Who were you saving this afternoon?"

"Well, it wouldn't be right coming back with just one of you. It would take a mighty long time to pay the ranch back for a lame horse on six dollars an hour."

Fred Longworth

Fred Longworth has had his poems published in numerous journals including
*Rattapallax, Melic Review, California Quarterly, Spillway, Pearl,
Poetic Voices, Kimera, & miller's pond.*

After the Animal Show Filed Bankruptcy

The dancing bears still had a job,
the lion act still roared,
the seal show barked on, and leap-
ing dolphins were adored.

These other creatures hired on
at Vargas, Disneyland,
and Barnum – critters glamorous!
Poor Octopus was canned.

By day he hid in toilet bowls,
by night he shambled streets,
a little, tarnished piece of eight
in search of friends and eats.

His tentacles grew thin as strings,
eight shoulders stooped in shrugs.
He found no clams in garbage cans,
instead he dined on bugs.

And yet, despite his woeful luck
and shriveled eight-legged bod,
he stumbled to celebrity!
A famed cephalopod!

In search of roaches, worms and flies,
he crossed the freeways fast.
A tractor trailer squashed him flat –
eight-pointed star at last!

Workshopped to Death

By the condition of the corpse,
there's no doubt whatsoever.
It's another poem snatched from exuberance
and workshopped to death –
syntax perforated by firing squads
of constructive criticism,
red pencil bleeding out of every line,
images so mangled with ambiguity
even literati scratch their pompous heads.

Before the police arrive and cordon off the area,
I press my hand against the executed lines
and feel the fleeting heat of life just taken.
I scrape the poem into a plastic bag
and shove the bag into a cooler full of ice.
I rush the victim home.

Thousands of frail and sickly verses
sit anxiously by the phone, waiting for the call
that says a transplant has been found.
Perhaps I can salvage a liver,
a kidney, an eye, a length of gut,
a fragment of a heart once rich and sure

Stillness

The silence has the quality of expert masonry,
each quietude pressed against its neighbors
seamlessly, so that a cough, a shuffling of feet,
a creaking of the wooden floor, a slap
of branches against the window glass,
sets no tremors, carries no rattle or resonance,
like a prickly pear dropping to the desert sand.

Here, an invocation needn't shout.
A whisper finds its Ear surely as a dew drop
gathered at the corner of a leaf lets go
and finds its earth.

Heather Simeny MacLeod

Heather Simeney MacLeod's first book of poems *My Flesh the Sound of Rain* (Coteau Books) was published in 1998, *Shapes of Orion* (Smoking Lung Press) was released in 2000, *The North Woods* (Artesian Press, Australia) co-authored with Coral Hull is forthcoming as is *The Burden of Snow* (Turnstone Press). Heather's poetry has also appeared in a number of anthologies including *Breathing Fire* as well as *Re:Verse!*. Her poetry and short-fiction have been in most major Canadian literary journals as well as appearing in reviews and journals in the United Kingdom, New Zealand, Australia, Israel and the United States. Heather's plays have won awards through magazines and honorable mentions through the annual Alaska Playwrighting Contest. She lives in the interior of British Columbia and is currently at work on a novel.

Your Voice

It was your voice I heard long ago amid the crowds, heard it through caverns, heard it in the long forgetfulness of other lives when you and I lived in the dark, blankness of short days in damp caves, and painted with charcoal from the fire your first desires of fish and sea. And when I saw you, two years ago, in brown corduroy and a plaid, short-sleeved, cotton shirt with small, delicate, egg-like buttons I *made myself* look away. I remembered you from those other days and thought in the back of myself, hidden from light and knowing, *This is what they mean when they say love at first sight,* that loving at first sight is a remembering. Love at first sight is a kind of haunting, distant lullaby, and when you spoke pieces of me splintered and a section of who I am ran to your side and another fled from the room and I stayed in my chair pretending I didn't know you, pretending I did not remember your voice, the sound of your timbre, the clearing of your throat, the moan of your desire. Pretending I didn't remember.

Yes

Yes, I say, yes to Bach and no to Beethoven.
Yes to Pearl Jam and no to Celine Dion,
but who could really compare the two, really?
I say, yes to hips and breasts and flesh
and knee high socks, and I say, no
to the barefooted, no to the zucchini eaters.
No, I say, no to zucchini and not just no
to those crazy enough to eat zucchini.
I also say, no to cilantro, but yes to the sound
of the word: cilantro.
    Cilantro.
I say yes to the beautiful, dark crown of your head.
I say yes to pink. Yes to Electric Pink,
yes to Paradise Plum, yes to the frost of Ice Blue Pink
lipsticks. Yes to lavender and lime green underwear,
but no to wearing them together. Yes to underwire bras.
Yes to cotton, no to polyester. Yes to flannel pajamas
and bedding and no to percale. Yes to kilims and sumaks
and no to wall to wall carpets. Yes to espresso
and French Press and no to cone and flat bottomed filters.

Yes, I say, yes to God the Father, the Son
and the Holy Spirit, and no, I say, no
to the inherent loneliness of atheism.
I say, yes to freckles and bruises against
alabaster skin and no to the burnt almond,
buttery blonde, Toast of New York
(Revlon lipstick'd) had too many Mai Tais,
light my cigarette bitch who looks like a long,
drink of (what was said in that Tarantino film?)
cocksucker. Ya, that was it: *cocksucker.*
I say, yes to Tarantino and no to Oliver Stone.
Yes to Jack Gilbert and no to Paul Dugan.
Yes to Salma Hayek and no to Jennifer Lopez.
Yes to Saint Michael and no to the bringer of light.
I say, yes to piercing the eyebrow and no to piercing
the tongue. Yes to popcorn and no to chips.
Yes to raspberry jam and no to marmalade.
Yes to you and no to every other man because
I want   I want   you, I want.

Yes, I say, yes to pale, but no to chalky.
I say, yes to cats and no to dogs. I say,
yes to God, yes to the Holy Church of Rome,
yes to the Fourteen Holy Helpers, yes
to the blesseds, yes to all the other saints,
arch angels, seraphims, and I say, yes to body,
yes to affection, passion and desire. I say,
yes to sex and no to chastity. Yes
to the Eucharist, yes to the flesh
and the blood of God inside my mouth.
I say, yes to limbs parted. Yes to the building
of my body from your rib. Do you hear me?
I was made from your rib, and can't you feel
the way I complete you, the way I count
and stroke your ribs, kiss your flesh, pull you
apart with my teeth. The way I say,
yes to you. I say, yes and I am afraid,
I am afraid you will say *No*

My Voice

after Patsy Alford's poem, Warning

My voice is the screech,
the howl of Lilith
as she moves
through the garden.
My voice is the dandelion,
the spot of yellow,
gracing your front lawn.
My voice is the whine,
the break-neck spin
of tires along Fortune Drive.
My voice,
my voice,
my voice
is weeping.

My voice is the twang
of Alison Krauss
and the rough Birch bark
cackle of Kris Delmhorst.
My voice is a CRF450 Honda,

and riding it is like wrestling
a rhinoceros in the grasslands
of the Thompson River.
My voice is Muddy Waters' blues guitar.
My voice is Minny Mouse
when she's had too many
Bloody Marys and is standing
on the table inhaling helium
from birthday balloons.
My voice is drunk
and out of control.
My voice is weeping.

My voice is the spire
of the Space Needle,
the docks of Ballard,
the waves of Vashon,
the Bainbridge Ferry
moving past Little New York.
My voice is a broke down
Volvo on the I-5.
My voice is weeping.

My voice is a tart, sour candy.
My voice is a strand
of red hair being carried
off in the beak of a crow.
My voice burns all bridges.
My voice is an accident
waiting to happen.
My voice is an arsonist
and has left a wasteland in its wake.
My voice is weeping.

My voice makes mistakes
as if they're valued commodities.
My voice is a thief
in the broadness of daylight,
sunshine on the dark,
punk crown of her head
and her bag from Value Village
stuffed to bursting.

My voice renounces,
It redeems,
it massages,
it desires.
My voice is the quilt
made for my grandmother's wedding day.
My voice is weeping.

My voice is the door slamming,
it's the shadow against the sand,
it's the bells ringing on Sunday morning,
it's beckoning. My voice is beckoning,
my voice is calling, my voice is wanting,
my voice is imploring, *imploring,* beckoning,
my voice
is in love.
My voice is in love
with you.
My voice is in love,
and it's weeping.

My voice,
my voice
is weeping.

Frank Matagrano

Frank Matagrano, born in New York, has had poems in Many Mountains Moving, Another Chicago Magazine (ACM), Chiron Review, Exquisite Corpse, Flint Hills Review, Cimarron Review and Roanoke Review, among others.

Throwing a Shoe at the Branch

My last ditch effort is to throw a shoe
at the branch before having to choose
whether to walk away in grief or climb
the tree and try to separate the tangled knot
by force from the rest. There will be a loss
of thread either way. If I leave now, I will need
to adjust my memory so that the kite comes off
as the last great image willing to make any risk

to live, even if for just a minute, so that when I return
to Astoria and sift for an hour in the thrift
shop a few blocks from Steinway for the right
pair of reading glasses to go with my unshaven chin,
I can let the acrylic pipes and pocket flasks on display
along the counter have their way with me without fear
of being watched. Everything that has made me will be
on display here, even the baseball cap and thumb
ring, and I will be so overwhelmed by all

of this latitude that I won't notice which parts
of me have been wrapped in a paper bag and taken
away, not until I have returned home at least
a hundred more times with a little change, a pack
of matches and the front page folded under my arm;
not until I am doing the dishes before bed, slowing
my breath, making far-flung connections with a reel
of string, remembering how the spine and spar joined
in the shape of a cross, looking up, hearing the wind.

Waiting With Alexandria for Her Mom

I didn't take the bus to Blooming Glen, Pennsylvania and sit
with Alexandria in a booth at Ruby Red's for nothing.
She had no idea how much I adored the ride — I carried
two books with me, one of them a dictionary, I didn't check
a word in it. I recited Lincoln. Of everyone that passed,
the kid in a mini-van made a point; with a finger he told me

to fuck myself. I think the white collar and the blue
tie pissed him off. I was trying to give one life a rest
and resume the other one, my top button was undone,
there's a start. I didn't understand how to open the window
in case of an emergency. I followed the lines along my palm,
one went back to New York, God knows where

the rest went. The other book had everything I needed
to know about protest — one man stitched his lips shut,
another tried to drive a nail through his own palm;
they were heading to ministry; no one there could be reached
for comment. I want to describe the mouth as "tender,"
I mean well, there aren't too many other ways

to explain the white sores along the gum that come
with a denture, my Four score and seven years slurred,
the tongue caught in a small nitch between the plate
and the roof whenever it shifted to roll an "r." I loved
one phrase in particular, I was attached.

Driving Down Route 80 Without a Radio

                              I couldn't bring Pavarotti
even if I wanted to. There isn't enough room in the front seat
for his lung, whether it be the one from 1961 doing Rodolfo
at Reggio Emilia, or the one from '72 that hit nine high Cs
at the Met, changing our lives forever. I sign my own version
of *Luisa Miller* to get through Columbus, Ohio without losing
my mind from too much thought. I begin at the village green
mourning the end of my spoony youth. I play Elvino,
taking the ring back from Amina. I play Louisa, lovesick
for Walter's son. I play her father, dragged to jail for execution.
I do Carlo, reading a letter in the garden, breaking everything
down to life or death, looking for happiness in either one.

Sandy McKinney

Sandy McKinney has been writing poetry for fifty years and translating Spanish poetry for forty or so of them. In 1979 she met Rafael Guillén in Granada, Spain, and their literary partnership has persisted ever since. The proudest moment of her life so far was when *I'm Speaking*, a bilingual edition of 28 of Rafael Guillén's poems with her translations, was presented by Northwestern University Press in the Spring of 2001.

Fishing Off San Blas

The guide put out for Guano Rock at dawn
just as the shrimping fleet came in,
trailing flocks of gulls that flapped
and dipped along the nets,
skimming the wake with a sad cry.

You can smell the rock a mile away.
We must have circled it a dozen times,
half-blinded by that jut of dazzling white
where a gang of boobies screeched their crazy tune
and the sun beat like a blowtorch on the waves.

We caught a shark and bashed its head against
the seat before we threw it overboard
and headed back past islands where the rare
green turtle leaves her eggs, and when they hatch,
the frigate bird, that split-tail skydiver,
spears the new life as it waddles toward the sea.

New Mexico Quincentennial

The Conquistadores came, bringing guns,
    helmets, horses, plagues, priests and nuns
    and a stark medieval tradition.

Nothing remains
    but a few adobe churches,
    some rusty ironwork rotting in the desert
    and their names.

Epifanio, Tranquilino, Celestino,
the missions have melted away. Your names
are the ghosts.

    We want you in cassock and surplice,
     blessing the young lieutenant as he rides in
           bloody from pillage,
    capturing heathens
    for the One True Faith and
        chinga
    the pagan heresies of spiders and eagles
    and the sacredness of the young corn.
          Instead
    you do small farming or auto mechanics
    and drink up your welfare check
    on the way home from the bank

Candelaria, Encarnación,
    an Irish priest confesses you
    in a corner of the stone cathedral raised
    on the legend you wear
    as casually as your shoes, Concepción
          Reina, Inmaculada
               Ascención.

Rosa, Dolorosa, heirs of Espinosa,
march out to bring their warriors home
and find them routed by cheap
California wine, slumped
against the lampposts in the plaza,
a bicycle chain
the only weapon left to their battalion.

Nancy, Kevin, and Cherie
have come from the University
to take over "Collections" at the museum.
Porfirio Reyes Griego
watches them as he sweeps.

Agapita, Carmelita, Mercedita all work
at Sears Roebuck, wearing mini skirts,
and a Texaco star adorns the breast
of Jesús Gonzales.

A Fear of Landing

Is that the Southern Cross, that almost random
collection of unfamiliar lights? Time ago, someone
must have named it something else, volumes
of prehistory before the Greeks and Romans
put chariots in the sky. But I'm hunting for something
that can't be named, so all the things with names
go on hiding from me, or becoming invisible
by virtue of being familiar. Whatever we find
is never what we were looking for.
Tonight, while the hunter in me still resonates
to the shock of distance, I take heart
from those millions of the nameless who
could walk across the whole flat face of Australia
squeezing frogs for water, learning grubs from stones.

If I could see what I'm looking at, I could speak
to those magpies in their own language, could understand
how that celestial song can pour from the throat
of a crow spattered with whitewash.
But even here, where the world
is upside down, I'm drawn to the love
and the lust I left behind by the pure
soles of my feet, and my head hangs into a blue sky
stained with the furious rust of sunset.
This is what I want: to know one single
thing entire, to let it exist without naming it,
or just drop off and float until I see the round fact
of this planet in space, the way we pick up what must be
the whirling dance of Venus, as a mere point of light.
And going back with neither this nor that, I'll scan
the wing of a plane that's more alive than I am, dead metal
that can mime a feathered thing and hurl itself at the sky
like a yowling beast crazed with the notion of flight.

At twenty thousand I'll believe we're headed straight
for the heart of the sun, a wish as reckless as the one
that strains my face against the window, coming in
along the coast at night, and imagines diving straight into
the water, its scarcely wavering, its dark beauty.
But no. I clutch the harbor lights and choose
to stay suspended there, in the perilous moment
before commitment, of what I'm willing
to promise, to be promised. Whatever
we find is never what we were looking for.

Chelle Miko

Chelle Miko is a former "military brat" She and her husband reside in the Finger Lakes region of New York. Her poetry credits include *Poet Lore, Nimrod, Rhino, 32 Poems Magazine, Anon, Valparaiso Poetry Review, Eclectica, The Paumanok Review, The Poet's Canvas, Caveat Lector, Snow Monkey, The Mid-America Poetry Review, The North American Review, River King Poetry Supplement, an upcoming anthology edited by Virgil Suarez and Ryan G. Van Cleave: Red, White, and Blues: Poetic Vistas on the Promise of America, can we have our ball back?,* and others.

In The Habu Hour

Katsue separates lettuce leaves
of confusion and curls,
shapes my sister's stubborn strands
pulled taut to her baby head
in a bun chopped with sticks.

Katsue murmurs gentle Japanese
while Mother gestures southern courtesies
poured from her lips like green tea
sweetened with Okinawan sugar cane.
My sister crawls, tells stories
with her tears swimming
laps from her lids.

Boulders of a creek challenge my brothers
with their scope: they unzip boasts
like pants and lean a little too far
making a stream a tub
full of big words and piss.

Dusk is a race against Habu time.

In the dark, Katsue unravels
green silken Kimona, sashed
with long silk like blades
of grass, supine secrets.
My sister's tresses spring free
like coiled snakes
from the silence of meadows.

Appraisal, 1973

In Father's workshop, I perched on a stool,
my attention buried in a book. I'd become oblivious
to the hostile ticking of a dozen clocks
when his *What the hell?* pulled me back to listen.
Father didn't know he'd been scraping red layers of war
from a wall clock—almost nicking its secret
shell: mother-of-pearl. He traded his knife for a cloth
and worked into the night, littering the floor
as he exhumed each iridescent songbird.

At dawn, Mother brewed green tea, and I tiptoed in,
slipper deep in the night's debris,
just as Father opened the glass face and set one hand
to the hour. He fit the brass key then let me gently wind
the movement. He whispered, *Imagine. For thirty years*
the South Koreans hid this beauty from the Japanese.

I had been with him in Etaewon, in a narrow shop
dimly lit and lined with the argument of clocks,
a frantic chorus, when Father bargained Mr. Kim down
for the music of this one's chimes.

More time passed.
My sister said, *What a great conversation piece.*

She nailed it to her wall in Pittsburgh.

How To Make An Agnostic A Martyr

First you match your moon to his sun
and all the shades of light between, but you forget

to ask the question. (This is your sin.)
When you remember, you beg him

for the clarity of repetition, pressing the point
with fingers curled like question marks

into his skin; but his doubt is reasonable,
so you pound fists into midnight soil instead.

Eventually, your palms assume the hue
of burnt offerings, as if you've buried something

there. You glance at a lit firmament, and ask God
not to drop a star on your head; then you dash under a slab

of stone—which is fitting—and beguile this man to lie
down and make gentle lamb sounds. Raking your nails

across his skull, you picture him shorn; but he just yawns,
wants to know what you mean by *sacrifice*.

You confess, *It means to be alone*; and you don't care
who witnesses you running after him—but God knows

it's not Isaac you've chased but the ram, and yes,
you must give him back.

Then (as if you are faithless) your teeth
hammer a nail to its bed—and you mourn.

Kei Miller

Kei Miller has been a visiting writer at York
University in Canada and the Department of Library
Services in the British Virgin Islands. His collection
of short fiction *The Fear of Stones* is due out by
Macmillan in 2005. His poetry collection, *Kingdom of
Empty Bellies*, is also forthcoming.

Church Women: Shekinah

Even when the sermon grows
past mid-day and 90 degrees
the men, cool as iron,
will not flinch or loosen
their ties or uncross their legs
to let the bronze breathe
from their pants.

But women fan themselves
frantic, as silver melts
from behind their eyes, rolling
out; gold travels up through pores
and spreads itself across their skin

where it glows Shekinah,
catching the magpie eyes of Jehovah.

Church Women: Marching

It is more than the fear of whale bellies
that keeps her walking.

Give honour to the woman who marches
around Kingston, bearing her banner,

a stout witness: REPENT JESUS SOON COME.
Give honor for the role she played

marching behind Carnival drums,
her own slow time and tune;

for each mile surrendered
as a widow's mite; for her starched dress –

who knew the armour of God was cotton and light?
For the Holy Ghost, Paul Bogle's ghost,

and all the freedom spirits inside her;
for faith which can stand the bruising

weight of sun, which stretches
longer than roads. Each dawn

the woman wields a marker, brightens
the letters on the placard she will raise

like a chorus, like a shout. She is saving
her voice for Jericho.

Church Women: Psychopath

you will not suspect her —
lazy eyes, a soft equator
of waist and the peach floral dress
which like a miracle contains it.
She does not seem the type
to put her mouth on wounds
and suck-

Yet how serenely she speaks
or crushed bodies, plucked beards
and catonines - how sweetly
she sings of a fountain filled
with blood.

Church Women: Communion

for whoever eateth and drinketh unworthily, eateth and drinketh
damnation to himself - 1 Cor. 11:29

This morning, Geraldine must repent;
a root of bitterness has been spreading
in her heart. Sunday after Sunday, no one
has said Amen to her precise arrangements
of spathodia and daisies. Even the Easter bouquet,
sunflower rising tall from a crowd
of aralia, more poignant than any resurrection
sermon, did not draw the Hallelujahs
she expected. Kneeling for bread,
she must let the anger fall away like yellow
leaves. Geraldine looks beyond the parson,
to the red flowers laid at the altar
and imagines her sweet Rose of Sharon,
Lily of the Valley, beautiful crown
of Bougainvillea thorns in his head;
how he too sweated blood in the Garden
and all through history people just have
no appreciation! Geraldine swallows, repents.

Steve Mueske

Steve Mueske holds an MFA in Writing from Hamline University and has published poems and short stories in Water-Stone, The American Poetry Journal, Redactions, 88, Typo Magazine, The Drunken Boat, Blaze, The Wisconsin Review, The South Dakota Review, Redactions, Diner, ArtWord Quarterly and others, and in the anthology Hymns to the Outrageous: an American Poetry Sampler. Editor of the online literary arts journal three candles, he was a recent Pushcart Prize nominee and a runner up in the Winnow Press First Book Prize and the Poetry West / Eleventh Muse chapbook prize. His first chapbook is *Whatever the Story* Requires (2004, Pudding House Press)

After Reading of an Amazing New Device That Brings Back the Dead in Lifelike Holographic Images
— *Weekly World News, 7/15/2003*

Someone has left the box on again, and there Aunt Mertle
bends to the bright task of baking rhubarb pies. She wipes a hand
on her apron, looks toward the stairs where those still alive

have dropped anchor, their little dream boats afloat
in the wide lake of sleep. And soon Uncle Fred,
dead these seventeen years, is done splitting wood for the fire,

hands folded over the ax-head in that momentfollowing work when the
muscles still sing
and the mind is freed from the habit of motion.

How young these habitués of the laser look, how comforting
and familiar. Here cousin Matthew will never know
the slice of a boat propeller, and Anne can safely ignore

those pricks of pain in her arm. After two weeks at the lake,
he's mowing the lawn's shaggy hair, and she's sitting
at her desk overlooking the wildflowers,

organizing a protest to save the city's trees. Meanwhile,
the stars of another decade swing round the house
and slowly disappear in the orange flame of early light.

Another Kind of Resurrection

I remember how your long white hair
flowed like water

down to your waist, rivulets
over the bed of a beaten leather jacket.

I thought you must be some kind of river god,
not a guitar player

or a hard drinking Norwegian
who loved Jesus and a good fight.

It didn't help much that I was only seventeen,
face blistered with pimples.

My arms and legs were like nervy ganglions
I could barely control.

I saw how easily girls came to you,
how you would cast them off with a boyish shrug.

I wondered why they forgave you
and kept coming back.

So I learned to play. Really play.
Cloistered in my room with books

splayed out on the bed,
I learned the caged system, and the Segovian,

the augmented and diminished scales,
pentatonic and blues. I drew

time-lapse pictures of my hair growing —
three-months, six months, two years —

while time folded itself
into the sound of a crowd,

that murmuring gathering of water you can hear
from backstage.

I say this now because you've been gone
for fifteen years, and I've been thinking about the angel

holding the scepter of fire over your head,
the angel you talked about that night

at the Blackbridge Bar as we knocked back
burning shots of Yukon Jack and Rumpleminze,

in a contest to see who would last the longest.
Sometime after midnight, you pulled me close and told me

you were called by God
to raise a band with spiritual powers.

You wanted to heal the sick,
have the power to raise the dead.

But you were a man, and even then
you were already dying.

When you pulled out from the stop sign that May,
did you sense the nearness of death

behind the wheel of the drunken dermatologist's Ford?
Did you look out the car window

and think, *Shit I'm going to die
just like my old man*. I'd like to believe you laughed

at the fucking irony of it, the flick
of a second before impact.

While this is not exactly a scepter of fire,
know that this small wraith of flame

is raised in your honor, blue
at the core, like water.

At the Lightning Strike Survivor's Support Group

Who could believe such dumb luck
as to hear *Agnus Dei* after the white clutch releases,
when you are face down in the culvert,
cold rain muzzling your neck,
air pricked with the scent of — what is it? dog lips?
You stand up on dead, stone-ancient legs,
soaked clothes seeped to skin,
and walk the three miles home. It is dark,
colder than obsidian. The moon is
nowhere to be found. Who would believe
such a story, the odds of being struck
by a million-watt nerve hammer?
Or later: the muse of muscles
and lesser viscera slowly letting go
it's cellular charge: your hand
become thing, heart the accordianist
of the *Sagra della Bistecca*
that year you fell in love with
a green-eyed girl from the vineyards.
Now you're gathered in the YMCA
with those few who understand that twinning
sense of luck and loss,
death come and averted, the rushing itch
of ignition. *I was pinning laundry when*,
the woman from South Dakota says,
and touches the pinkish scar
that travels ear to ankle like a testament
of chance, alchemic burn of circumstance.
You want to talk about your arm
as *that arm*, how it dangles
like a washrag, how on some days
you'd rather just cut it off
and be done with it. But you stare
out the window at the rain, struck
by a vision of loneliness: minutemen sleeping
in their silos, each wearing
a ninety-ton night cap of concrete.
You think about the air command's
symbol of hands holding lightning: *deterrence*
through strength. Was it easier to sleep

knowing the ruin of the world
was in someone else's hands? Imagine
the isolation of two soldiers
ensconced in an underground room,
their every move a trained stop gap for liftoff —
that 65,000 pound hammer, bleeding
fire, headed toward some nexus of unmaking
on the other side of the world, warhead
singing like that otherworldly turn
one minute and twenty-four seconds
into Barber's song.

Ginger Murchison

Ginger Murchison assists Thomas Lux in the direction of POETRY at TECH of the Georgia Institute of Technology and Associate Managing Editor of The Cortland Review. A 2003 Pushcart nominee, she has published poetry in many magazines and journals, including, most recently, *Atlanta Review*, and more than a dozen anthologies.

Burger King Birthday

August ripe-thick on Interstate 75,
where metal is muscled from one 99-cent meal
to another, the day and the year
begin dying in the sickening heat.

Inside, six crooked hopefuls—
the van says Haven of Hope—lean
polyester and print into a scant celebration
like dusty flowers tossed in a common grave.

No one looks at the empty chair;
no one sings Happy Birthday,
and the Bible, open at some unread verse,
does its best to impress, but no spring
rains promised there encourage
vomit-pale plastic vines to climb,
like veins under transparent skin,
windows opaque with stain.

Candles crowd the cake, make
a brave flare, giving the collapsed faces
all there is to look at and count on.

Small Craft Advisory

—*to my son Jason after reading* Huckleberry Finn *chapter by chapter*

It takes serendipitous, found things to make a raft,
some nailed-together boards, maybe an old wooden door.

You'll need a steering oar, but mostly trust
the raft to find a current, dangle your feet, and drift

where drifting never was a dirty word. Those ragged holes
where the water's thick are mink and muskrat homes. If

you're quick, you'll see a snake slice the brackish water for a meal
of frog or fish or salamander. Lie face up, imagine

you're another Galileo. The compass, microscope, and telescope are his,
as is the law of pendulum. That's how he learned, you know,

counting with his heartbeat, that Copernicus was right,
the world *was* round, but he couldn't say so—

stubborn men make stubborn laws. Take some water, too,
some apples, bread and honey and, especially, a friend.

It will take both of you to untie the language
and discover the insignificance of speech.

Vocabulary

The first thing I remember being dead
was my grandfather, lying there
as if a prairie wind had blown him down.
His 90 pounds, skin taut
on long and angled bone, was all
the cancer left: his face, plains dust;
lips cracked by cold; stiff
Sunday shirt a contradiction
to his hands—fingers dried
corn stalks in August, folded
in unfamiliar ease. They came
by ones, as if there'd been an ad—
an opportunity to see a neighbor sleeping
in his dining room. Hoping not to see
more than they wanted to, carved faces
looked at him, then off
to flowers on the wall, brown,
dead as he was. Pretending immortality,
sons in suspenders on the back porch,
squinted at cigarettes smoked too far down
and pulled at ties like boys caught telling lies.
Homemade bread rose in the kitchen
with choruses of *Inka Dinka Do*
and *Won't You Come Home, Bill Bailey*,
my own mother (who'd slap me
for giggling in church) louder than the rest.
Even the priest who bowed his head
beside the body had a beer. I couldn't tell
where death began and ended,
but that whole farmhouse tilted
toward the casket with the weight
of my new word.

Joyce Nower

Joyce Nower's first book of poems, *Year of the Fires*, was published in 1983. More recently, in 2001, *Column of Silence* was published by Avranches Press and, in July, 2003, Avranches Press published her *Qin Warriors and Other Poems*.

Private Parts: Erotic Poetry by Women

Explicit sex had not been, until the 1960's, in the literary arsenal of most Western writers, and women poets in particular. The usual perspective, even in love poems, had been psychological or spiritual, in the *romantic* love tradition as, for example, in the love sonnets of Elizabeth Barrett Browning or those of Christina Rossetti. And even where there is a recognition of the fact that, after all, people do sleep together as, say, in the poems of Edna St. Vincent Millay, there is still little or no reference to the mechanics of sexual intimacy. Neither male nor female genitals are ever mentioned, although there is an occasional reference to the female breast.

The reasons for the historic female silence on the subject of sexuality lie, of course, as much in the condition of women under patriarchy as in the conventions of the Western poetic tradition itself, with its ideological origins in the mores of a Judeo-Christian, or Christianized, ethos.

By contrast, some ancient pagan poetry deals with explicit sexuality in a quite open manner. In the Latin poet Catullus (84B.C. – 54 B.C.), for example, one finds a full array of voices on sexuality. (1) They range from poems on sex-for-sale (#110: "an honest girl, Aufilene, an artist at her trade of love..."), to casual liaisons (#25: "O mellow, sweet, delicious little/piece, my Ipsithilla..."), to humorously boastful multiple homosexual encounters (#37: "Come now, line up,/ bent double in a circle, a hundred of you, or two hundred,/ come, do you think I am not able to take on/two hundred of you in one grand bout of pederasty?"), to the famous sequence of heterosexual love poems to Lesbia. In the Lesbia poems, Catullus traced what, in later centuries, became accepted as the conventional route of love: love-at-a-distance-for-a-married-woman (#2), the call-to-love (#6), impatience (#7), love-to-lust (#72), idealization of the Beloved (86), and love's-eternal-torment (#85). Strangely enough, in the midst of the often sordid reality described so brilliantly in these poems is a paean of praise to marriage, virginity, truth, fidelity, monogamy, and children (#61). In this epithalamion, lust is reconciled with "the higher virtues," including procreation. It is a poem of transcendence in which the crassness of human interaction has been reconciled – at least for the time being – by monogamous marriage. One discerns in Catullus the sexual neurosis of some men: the separation of love and sex which becomes, at best, only partially resolved in an *idealized* monogamous marriage!

But while in Catullus' poetry women appear in various conditions – debased, exalted, on level ground – they are not stereotyped. It is post-pagan Christianity that did that, via the mythic figures of Eve and the Virgin Mary. Medieval courtly poetry, for example, developed the perspective of a romantic love, in which the Beloved is perceived as an idealized human version of the Virgin Mary, and participates through her virtues in the spiritual transformation of the Lover. Dante's Beatrice and Petrarch's Laura exemplify this attitude. (This attitude persisted in poetry throughout the Thirteenth Century, even though by then male scholars and saints began to view Woman as a *source of danger* to Man's soul.) Thus, as a result of the tradition of romantic love, Idealized Woman is robbed of her sexuality. (2)

We are, by now, familiar with the constraints on the mind and behavior of women resulting from female roles. In <u>The Death of the Moth and other Essays</u>, for example, Virginia Woolf refers to our inhibitors as the "Angel in the House" and the "internalized Man." In the "Angel in the House" are our traditional virtues of sympathy, charm, unselfishness, self-sacrifice, and purity. It is just these "virtues," Woolf observes, that have kept us from making decisive appropriations of the events of the world. The "Internalized Man," on the other hand, is our inability to write about the experience of our bodies – being imbued with the social definition of what is an appropriate subject matter.

Whereas the first wave of the Women's Movement (1848-1920) initiated the struggle against the "Angel in the House" stereotype, the Second Wave, in the Sixties, took on the "internalized Man" – one of the last psychological stumbling blocks to women's defining themselves in accordance with their own experience. Consequently, since the rise of the Second Wave, women poets began to write more and more freely about the experience of their bodies. (It is important to note at this point that the Fifties and the Sixties also saw the loosening of sexual taboos in male writing, especially after the free-speech legal victories over the works of James Joyce and Henry Miller and the rise of the San Francisco Beat Movement – all of which clearly had an impact on women's writing.)

So what have women poets been saying throughout these long centuries of patriarchal hegemony? (3) There are known to us only a few female voices from the Western classical period, and the fragments of their poetry are insufficient to lead us to any conclusion regarding their views of the world, society, and themselves. The earliest voice, that of Sappho (b. 612 B.C. , a poet, teacher, and choral leader from the island of Lesbos), tells us of her own loves, jealousies, and rivalries, as well as those of the young women who apprenticed to her poetic and musical skills; but whether or not she wrote erotic poetry, we'll never know. All we have left are fragments based on hearsay, and truncated lines on strips of papyrus found in Egypt in mummified crocodiles. The Greek poet Nossis, a later example (c. 290 B.C.), was also reputed to be passionate, but we have no examples of that passion either!

Marie de France, one of the best known women poets between pagan and Renaissance times, wrote love poems in which love takes on the twin burdens of fostering self-awareness and of providing a vehicle for overcoming the sorrows of the world. No eroticism here, however.

As far as English literature is concerned, we have to wait until the late seventeenth century for our first example of erotic poetry by a woman, Aphra Benn (1640-89). In her poem "The Disappointment," the classical pursuit of Lysander after Cloris ends in a "lone Thicket made for Love." After Lysander strokes the "snowy Brest" of Cloris – she lies panting in his arms – he, emboldened, now moves his hand to her genitals, that "Altar.../Where Gods of Love do sacrifice:/ That Awful Throne, that Paradice/

Where Rage is calm'd, and Anger pleas'd;/That Fountain where Delight still flows,/And gives the Universal World Repose" (The World Split Open, Ed. Louise Bernikow, Vintage Books, 1974). Unfortunately for Lysander, however, his agitation has become so great that his penis won't stiffen. Cloris, still panting, gives him a hand – literally:

Her timorous Hand, she gently laid
Upon that Fabulous Priapus,
The potent God, ...

Thus does a woman poet write the first western burlesque of the sex act in which the male proves unequal to the task: "... *the o'er Ravish'd Shepherd lies/Unable to perform the Sacrifice.*" (The "Sacrifice" is her eagerly anticipated loss of virginity.) Cloris, disdainful and resentful, flees the scene, still a virgin. And "that Fabulous Priapus"? It certainly did not perform up to its lineage. Priapus, a Latin word for penis, is, in classical lore, the god of male procreation, son of Dionysus and Aphrodite.

If you thumb through the Penguin Book of Women Poets, you'll find several women from the eastern half of the world who wrote poems that either infer sexuality, or are sexually explicit. The Chinese poet Huango O (1498-1569) is an example of both types:

If you don't know how, why pretend?
Maybe you can fool some girls,
But you can't fool Heaven.
I'd dreamed you'd play with the
Locust blossom under my green jacket,
Like a eunuch with a courtesan.

But lo and behold
All you can do is mumble.
You've made me all wet and slippery,
but no matter how hard you try
Nothing happens. So stop.
Go and make somebody else
Unsatisfied.

These few courageous pioneer women poets of the erotic were quite isolated because of the social milieu in which they wrote. We have to wait for the American poet Edna St. Vincent Millay (1892-1950), writing in the Twenties, Thirties, and Forties of the Twentieth Century, to find a pioneer who, as the result of political changes in women's status, was able to insist on eroticism as a valid female theme - and to actually push the theme of female eroticism towards the mainstream — although her eroticism itself seems moderate in comparison with some of the earlier examples. (See Collected Poems of Edna St. Vincent Millay, Harper & Row, 1956.) In love, she insists on her right to inconstancy ("Oh, think not I am faithful to a vow"), thus flaunting the double standard criticism of the fickle woman – and striking a blow against both ghosts described by Virginia Woolf. She refers to the body as a "temple of delight" in the poem "As to some lovely temple tenantless," and mentions the lover's weight upon her breast in "I, being born a woman and distressed." She even mentions sleeping with her lover in "What lips my lips have kissed." And, finally, in the most blatant statement of all, she writes a sonnet addressed to "almighty Sex,' which concludes with the line 'And lust is there, and nights not spent alone."

But the first attempt by an American woman poet at *explicit* eroticism seems to be Lenore Kandel's "holy/erotic" poems in The Love Book (Stolen Paper Review, San Francisco, 1966). Innovative and daring, the book, unfortunately, reads with all of the awkwardness of someone writing in an unfamiliar language: a few heretofore "forbidden" nouns and verbs are held onto for dear life! This poetry comes out of the heady post-World War II poetry renaissance, inaugurated by the group of poets who circulated mainly between San Francisco, Berkeley, Black Mountain college, and New York City. It comes out of the confluence of post-war alienation, Southern civil rights sit-ins, protests against the House Un—American Activities Committee, the Berkeley Free-Speech Movement, the Black Movement, the Anti-War Movement, the influx of Eastern religion, self-imposed semi-nomadic life styles, rock and soul music, and so on. These liberating movements, trends, and protests were created by those segments of the population who looked for a basic reorientation of American society. One aspect of this total reorientation was a challenge to traditional mores, including conventional language and sexuality.

Into the lexicon of this rebellious generation stormed the so-called "street language": "cock," "fuck," "cunt," "shit," and so on – the four-letter words traditionally shunned by "polite" society. The more crucial fact about this language was, however, that it often implied the threat of masculine violence! This was not understood until the Women's Movement in the late Sixties created a general heightened awareness, and an awareness of language in particular. But at first the scene was a heady one, and male – as well as several women – poets incorporated this new language into a poetry that called for, and practiced, greater freedom of expression. One of these women poets, probably the first, was Lenore Kandel.

The Love Book, subtitled "To Fuck with Love," is an historically interesting book of poems; aesthetically, it is a five-page example of unimaginative verbal overkill. Within this brief space, we can find each of the following words at least once: "fuck," "cock," "cock-god," "suckfucing," "cuntdeity," "cocksucker," "cunt," "love-fuck," and "cuntmouth." The acts described range from caressing the penis to copulation to oral sex, interspersed with a putatively intoxicating brew of juices and smells. But, of course, such a collection of nouns and verbs is no substitute for poetry; yet it paved the way for genuine erotic poetry by proclaiming that women are erotic beings who enjoy sex. (4)

Eventually, bonafide erotic poetry did enter through the doors forced open by the rapidly changing times, exemplified by these pioneers as well as the Feminist Movement. One of the crucial results of the Movement was the emphasis on revealing the *real* responses and experiences of women. A corollary to this was getting to know and understand how the female body really works. Movement creations – such as CR (consciousness raising) groups, the Self-Help Health Movement, feminist counseling, etc. – gave rise to a psychological and verbal environment in which reliance on street language was no longer necessary or appropriate. What was created instead was a much fresher and precise sexual language, both connotative and denotative; and the search for egalitarian relationships in which the keynotes of communication and honesty were emphasized, created, with much struggle, a framework in which both heterosexual and lesbian relationships were variously validated in the arts. The upshot of all this was the rooting out, to a significant extent, the second inhibitor described by Virginia Woolf as the "Internalized Man."

Since the 1960's, the output of erotic poetry by women has increased manyfold. One might almost be lead to guess that every poet writing since that time wrote at least one erotic poem. (5)

Nikki Giovanni's "Seduction" (Black Feelings, Black Talk, Nikki Giovanni, Broadside Press, 1968) taps into the humorous side of eros. The poem presents a man and a woman at cross-purposes with each other: the man discusses some abstract revolution while the woman tries to shift his attention to making love. Ellen Bass's "In Celebration" (No More Masks, eds. Howe and Bass, Anchor Press, 1973) is a robust and humorous cataloging of metaphors for an erection. The penis is compared to 1) bread baking, 2) a helium balloon, 3) a soufflé, 4) the head of a turtle, 5) an accordion, 6) an expandable drinking glass, 7) a lollipop, 8) a plum, 9) a mitten, 10) a cup, 11) vintage wine, and a few other items on a gourmet menu.

Maxine Kumin's "Together," dated as early as 1970, (No More Masks), describes sex thus: :

Now we are new round
mouths and no spines
letting the water cover.
It happens over
and over, me in
your body and you
in mine.

Two well-known poets who come readily to mind are Carolyn Forche and Adrienne Rich. Forche's poem "Kalaloch" (Gathering the Tribes, Yale University Press, 1976) is as much about nature as it is about a sexual moment between two women, two women who are living and working together in a natural setting. Here the arousal mechanism of the clitoris is referred to as the "clit,' an informal form of the word, forced in part by the rhythm of the surrounding words. Oral sex is described realistically, and with pleasure; there is nowhere any reliance on ideology, on idealization, or on dehumanization:

A woman's mouth
is not different, sand moved
wild beneath me, her long
hair wiped my legs, with
women there is sucking, the
water slops our bodies. We
come clean, out clits beating
like twins to the loons rising
up.

And in Rich's "Unnumbered Floating Poem" (<u>The Dream of a Common Language</u>, W.W. Norton & Co., 1978), a sexual moment is all but one aspect of a longer relationship between two women. The "thighs," "fingers," "tongue," and "nipples" are the named parts used in lovemaking, and the word "come" has the standard meaning of "arrive' as well as "achieve orgasm." An accurate and original metaphor for the vagina is used: the "rose-wet cave," and its use extends the meaning of the poem to the psychic lair of woman-ness. Here again we find a direct sexual statement without the use of such overused commonplaces as "fuck" and "cunt," words which have been so demeaned that the possibility of their reclamation in the foreseeable future is doubtful. Here are the last four lines of the poem:

your touch on me, firm protective,
searching me out, your strong tongue
and slender fingers reaching where I
had been waiting years for you in my
rose-wet cave – whatever happens, this
is.

Marilyn Hacker is another one of our pioneers. In "Alba: March " (<u>Separations</u>, Knopf, 1976), the poet refers to lovemaking the night before, including a specific reference to oral sex. Here the male penis is referred to as a flower: *"I kissed his knees, ate honey from the flower between his thighs, and felt it rise with sap against my tongue."* In other poems – "Chagrin D'Amour," "Two Farewells," and "Return" are good examples – she makes explicit sexual references, but always within the context of a relationship.

This observation also applies to the wonderfully erotic poems of Olga Broumas. Broumas's poems in <u>Beginning with O</u> (Yale University Press, 1977) differ, however, in that over the dozen or so erotic poems the sexual partner changes more frequently. In fact, the poems seem to commemorate the various partners. So how can we tell if the relationships extend beyond the sex act itself? I take clues from the evidence of tones of tenderness, biographical data, and the camaraderies evident in the work. In "Amazon Twins," for example, the title itself is a sign of camaraderie. In this poem, the poet and her lover are described as "crustacean-like" from the dried sweat of their love-making.

Everything live
(tongue, clitoris, lip and lip)
swells in its moist shell. I
remember the light
warped, round our bodies
finally
crustal, striated with sweat.

This observation is at once new and accurate. Again, the poet relies on the evocative nature of words, and on precise description, rather than on stock clichés whose only power is to evoke a stock response.

In "Love Lines," the speaker remembers a man whom she had loved, and a moment of love marred by her inability to reveal a secret. The word "cock" is appropriate because it is used as an instrument of passion, and not as a word selected merely to titillate.

love orbits
us, all night
long, your cock is an instrument
in my palm to gauge by, at break-
fast you pour

the coffee, I hold
my tongue, what I keep from you
keeps me from you, the ship

is fading like sunlit frost, silver
gleams on our table, mugs shine
red as cranberries, blue as frostbite,
I want

to hold
on, not back, brave
morning's fierce tangibility
tell you

And again in "Four Beginnings/For Kyra," the eroticism is conveyed through an accurate yet dense image:

I take your hand
hesitant still with regret
into that milky landscape, where
Braille is a tongue for lovers,
where tongue, fingers, lips
share a lidless eye.

In this poem, the relationship extends to concerns about the wounds the lover had acquired on her journey to that new moment. Sex and love are certainly close companions here.

It seems clear so far that, where contemporary erotic poetry by women is concerned, there is usually the intimation of a relationship extending beyond the physical one; but not in the sense that the sexual component is of lesser importance, to be gotten beyond because it is less worthy. No. The earmark of female erotic poetry, at least so far, is that sex exists as a component co-equal, in most instances, with other components of the relationship. This means not only that sex and love, or at least companionable feeling, are not divorced as, say, in Catullus, but also that sex is a pleasurable activity not to be "spiritualized out" of the female personality. In general, women's erotic poetry seems practical, realistic, self-aware, sensual, and embedded in the meaning of unique relationships. This is an important tradition to be yet firmly established. For in order to expunge completely Virginia Woolf's inhibitors – the "Angel in the House" and the "Internalized Man" – women artists must chart in precise detail an ever-growing psychological independence from a world that has distorted our image.

(1) The Poems of Catullus, tr. by Horace Gregory, Grove Press, 1956. The only known Latin female poet, Sulpicia (c. 20 B.C.) is reputed to have been a skilled writer of love poems. Unfortunately, there is only one tame poem by her extant.

(2) For an exciting and scholarly analysis of courtly love literature, see Joan Ferrante's Woman as Image in Medieval Literature, Columbia University Press, 1975.

(3) Two good sources are The Penguin Book of Women Poets, Eds. Cosman, Keefe, & Weaver, Penguin Books Ltd., 1978 and The World Split Open, Ed. Louise Bernikow, Vintage Books, 1974.

(4) A case could be made for pioneer status for African American female blues singers. "If you don't like my ocean/Don't fish in my sea," lamented "Ma" Rainey. And Memphis Minnie tells us: "Baby drives so easy/I can't turn him down." Is it poetry? This question will not be answered here.

(5) Possibly the shortest erotic poem on record, called "Gardening," was written by the author: "Everything grows lush within your sight:/ You look at me – my breasts rise up a nipple's height."

Shann Palmer

Shann Palmer, a teacher and musician, serves as Vice-President Central and Student Contest Coordinator for the Poetry Society of Virginia. She hosts readings and workshops in the Richmond area. A calendar can be found at her website, also photos and links to her online and print publications including *Eclectica, Melic Review*, and more. Pending publications include the 2004 Austin International *Poetry Festival Anthology Di-Verse City, the Wicked Alice Print Annual* and *Gin Bender*. Palmer's webpage:http://groups.msn.com/FlashpPaperPoetry

Picture Perfect

I've been framed flat,
run over by fate's big black Buick,
9 by 12'ved behind glass
so thick I can't breathe.

Frozen in a grimace of a grin,
on a face the camera never loved,
there's a stranger at four a.m.
looking back in the bathroom mirror.

The older we get, the more invisible
we become, even people we love forget
the need to pay attention to us, don't see
past the snap-shots they hold in their heads

Once upon a time I was twenty-five
and beautiful but I didn't have the sense
to take care of myself, to floss,
to put out bridge fire's, shut my big mouth.

Now, I'm set apart from you, still
in the picture, though our storyline's dropped
we've blended into the background- neutral
shades in Kodachrome, process out of date.

When I heard you were getting married,
it was as if I misplaced a box of photographs,
paper images of a trip to Seneca Rocks,
a waterfall there as long as I remember.

Bread 'n butter pickles

make or break a sandwich
(she'd say), you got to have
beef bologna and American cheese,
summer tomatoes and salad greens,
(jabbing the knife for emphasis)
two slices of meat.

She always cried
if it was right before her period,
telling anyone who'd listen
how she'd never had two slices
on a sandwich until she was grown.

If she'd had a wine cooler
it'd be the tuna fish tale, too,
making lunch for seven people
out of one six ounce can
and half a jar of relish.

(he wanted to say)
Just shut up about it.
You have what you need now,
but he'd grunt and nod–
no use in begging trouble.

She could always suck him up,
had a way of sticking her fork in,
twirling him like spaghetti;
before he could untangle
she'd have him in her mouth.

Comfortable there, familiar
warmth between two people
who might've have done better.

The Nature of Belief

(Inspired by "Larry the Liar" - Philip Levine)

He loved liars,
clever ones
those who chew words
into new shapes
spitting them at his feet
like a proud pet
bringing trophy catches.

This is not a lie:
to say you went to Spain
when you visited Portugal,
that is only misdirection.
Better to say:

*"I was followed by a bald man
wearing red suspenders."*

Shut the drapes, walk to the wall,
ask if there is any horseradish.
Absurd behavior encourages assumptions.

When she left him the last time,
he was honored by her story.
A tribute to love, misplaced
somewhere in the linen drawer.
Unused, with salt cellars
seafood forks, and brocade napkins.

She told him her brother was missing.
Only she would be able to save him,
she knew he was in the Lost City.

"Of gold?" he was intrigued already.

"I cannot say," she answered.

Later, in the slanting light falling
across the unmade bed,
he held her pillow to his chest and slept.

Christine Potter

Christine Potter is a poet who lives in Rockland
County, New York with her husband, Ken, and two
spoiled half-Siamese cats, Desmond and Molly. She has
worked as a writing teacher, a chef, and a bell
ringer. Recent publications include *Redactions, three
candles, miller's pond,* and *Eclectica*.

Tolling Thirty-Three

Sometimes I fear all I have done
is not enough, that I have to be truthful besides,
and wise as the end of time. This morning
I drove to work, and the sky to the northwest
grew darker instead of more brilliant,

the traffic signal at my corner a green sun
on the wet slate behind it. Light
flowed backwards until eight o'clock,
when a freshman boy in first period asked me why.
I said a storm was coming, which was probable
but wrong. It passed. I longed for lightning
and extremity as day began itself again,
twenty minutes later.

I thought of ringing church bells on Good Friday,
how I climbed tower stairs fixed on the number
thirty-three. I wanted to toll the bourdon evenly
as each year's passage, to wait for one note to waver
into silence, to sound the next as the first
slipped away, counting out a grave, ancient frequency
in a slow shimmer of overtones, grateful
when the wild bird of it lit on my outstretched hand

It was more than enough to say thirty-three
that way, marking the gift in iron to the troubled
sky
that offered it. And to know this truth:
there is nothing to fear in any morning's
odd darkness, even without
the proof of thunder and bells,
even without wisdom.

For My Husband

(Who Dreamed of Tidal Waves as His Father Was Dying)

I think of your father born, instead,
in a hospital I have never visited:
bright high windows, sun drifting
across iron beds painted white.
Bulbous black telephones, their cords covered
in brown cloth. Someone typing echoes
down a green linoleum hall.

Or born in a farmhouse near an uphill road.
Bitter nightshade strings tiny red berries
onto the front porch. Your grandmother
sleeps after the delivery; the family
walks uneven floorboards outside her room.

Listen to me. No matter how well you remember
an Indiana sky, you cannot say for certain
whether God's hands were closed
or remained open. That's why we come to doubt
that sky can reveal the secret of any birth.
So it all tumbles apart after an hour or two
of watching: splashes of blue tangled in clouds,
noontime sun beyond white, the stars

bleached out, hidden under day, invisible
as inner rooms of a neighbor's house.
Everything but light lies.
And what I am telling you is absolutely still,
too brilliant for easy revelation.
It is all we have. It is rest after labor,
the Ohio River wrinkling silver
under the splintery wooden prow
of a tied-up boat. You and I have not arrived, yet.
Your father has just been born, and the story
of what will happen next is taking a breath
before it can go on.

And what happens in the end
is no tidal wave: the sun goes down. Your father
moves to Florida. Suddenly, there is less traffic
on the street outside. The roof line
of your grandparents' house fades to cobalt,
to indigo, and disappears in the night
like a round stone dropped in deep water.

You need not know this story to tell it,
and it is not even secret:
the stars are back again,
silent as new ice and perfect, perfect—
the pin-pricks of a million questions and answers
the huge, white blossoming of time.

A Hard Rain Falls

A hard rain falls on maples
that hold light within themselves,
where their leaves have changed color.
There is a rush of rain; clouds streak overhead;
the air is heavy and cold.

It grows darker. Yellow leaves move
like guttering flames. Tonight smells of clay
and wet ash. When I close the window,
all that's left is light we direct onto
green dinner plates, candles simmering
behind glasses of white wine.

Except when we talk to each other,
when we touch each other,
what lost part of light is that?
Is this what leaves remember
or what we remember of leaves?
And what should we call our prudent
selection of tasks, our quiet meals?

We descend into sleep. Closed windows muffle
the sound of rain falling from a closed sky.
Maybe there is something the cold changes
that is the better for it.

There is always relief in darkness,
in silence unquestioned.
It will probably rain all night, but there is always
the tilt of your shoulder towards me
under the white comforter,
in the slender, grey line of light
left where the curtains have parted.

Jennifer Reeser

Jennifer Reeser is the author of An Alabaster Flask, winner of the 2003 Word Press First Book Prize. Her poems, translations and articles have appeared or are forthcoming in such journals as *Salt* (Austr.), *The Dark Horse* (Scot.), *The Formalist, The New Laurel Review, Louisiana Literature* and *Pivot*, as well as the anthology *Rising Phoenix*.

Why It Wasn't You

So tender were you in the love you made
to me, so slow against that chilly piece
of midnight — all the house at rest, afraid
to sigh or settle, lest your patience cease —
the walls themselves continued up, without
the slightest tremor at your gentle hand,
and no such fate as may squeeze faith from doubt
could hear those words you breathed, or understand.
So tender were you in your love to me,
but so inured was I to indiscretion,
outside, the rousing remnants of the sea
drowned out its cry, and I its soft confession,
even as your selfless body drowned the skin
that housed my heart, and whose love hid within.

The Fall

As I came down on wings between the blue
requirements of the wind and green grass, crisp
with frost - despair consorting with a wisp
of flesh - I prayed for soft, forgiving dew.

The ground received me gently, while throughout
my body, sleep, embroidered in a blend
of lethargy and faith, came to extend
my hands to hymns, my eyes and ears devout.

But He stood aft aloofly, catching air
before it could encase me in its cold,
as though I were too delicate to hold
by other than the answer to my prayer.

Miscarriage

Fold this, our daughter's grave,
and seal it with your kiss.
For all the love I gave,
you owe me this.

Inside of me, she had
your lips and tongue, my air
of grimness, thin and sad,
with your thick hair.

Inside of you, I trust,
she was a simple mesh
of need and paper, lust -
potential flesh.

And there was such pure song
in life begun from you,
I held the dead too long,
as women do,

but leaving like you did,
when only I could feel
the biding, body, bid
of what was real,

she's put out with the cur,
the garbage, heartache, cat.
Promise you'll sing to her.
You owe me that.

Robert Riche

In addition to *What Are We Doing in Latin America? (A Novel About Connecticut)* **Robert Riche**'s short stories have appeared in *Commentary* and a number of literary magazines. His plays have been performed off-off Broadway in New York, and in regional theaters in Berkeley, Washington, Atlanta, and in Bristol, England. He has co-authored one self-help book entitled *The Ten Most Troublesome Teen-Age Problems (And How to Solve Them)*, and he has had numerous comedy television assignments. He writes periodically on food, wine and travel subjects.

The Theft

My thoughts are turned to my prepubescent dog
due for a "surgical procedure" next week.
They plan to snip his little balls
hardly visible yet.
Under anesthesia, he will feel no pain,
nor in weeks to come will he miss them much.
He'll lick himself, as he does now,
and sniff at the saltier parts of his kind,
not just females, but males as well,
and jump on their backs and roll around.
Will he ever know that for the common good
something precious was stolen from him,
two little gems
pride of beggars as well as kings?
My wife scoffs at such sentimental nonsense,
tells me to feed him, take him for a walk.
Bark, little puppy, sing with the *castrati*
of splendrous medieval choirs.
I, your master,
am the thief of nature's grand design.

My Hometown

My hometown –

Host to the nineteenth century literary pantheon –
Longfellow, Hawthorne, Melville, Holmes –
Magnet to the nation's iron dynasties –
Morgan, Vanderbilt, Harriman, and Schwab,
whose stolid pleasure domes were cast
in the sylvan bowl, heart of the surrounding Berkshire hills.
Hotbed of freedom's volunteers
who joined the Green Mountain Boys
at Bennington, Troy and Ticonderoga.
Proud to accommodate American industry –
riches tumbling from textile, paper, plastics mills.

My hometown –

Pittsfield, incorporated in Massachusetts,
named to honor William Pitt,
Parliament's voice for liberty.
City renowned for its gracious elms,
sanctuary for the avant-garde –
Jacob's Pillow, where bare-chested men
danced together their arabesques,
and Tanglewood concerts floating magic
over manicured lawns under the moon.
City with vision to encourage local art,
the stern simplicity of the Shakers' hand.
Blessed with nature's multiple treasures,
Onota and Pontoosuc lakes,
teeming with bass, and pickerel, and yellow perch.
Wahconah Park where hopeful ball players
displayed their skills under electric lights.
Those names! — Wahconah, Onota, Pontoosuc —
due respect to the Mohawk tribe
that once dwelled beside
the pristine Housatonic's leisurely flow.

My hometown –

Proud I was to be from there
until the mills began to close.
One by one
they slipped away, seeking lower wages to pay,
leaving behind in the pristine river
a poisonous slime of a century's spoils,
reflection of a city's despondent soul.
One by one
the stately mansions, no longer fashionable,
sold to firetrap nursing homes,
or sometimes bed-and-breakfast lodges,
where city folk pass through (quickly) every fall
to view the sugar maples' changing hews,
the elms long ago having succumbed to disease,
chopped to the ground as during a plague,
the streets an empty shelf of bleak abandoned stores.

My hometown –

Once so proud, barren now,
host to junkies, panderers and thieves
who never heard
of Longfellow, Hawthorne, Melville, Holmes.
They scrounge the bottom of the valley bowl,
chew on the remains of this heart of the Berkshires,
surrounded by the everlasting beautiful hills.

New Year's Eve

In years past, on New Year's eve,
we blew brazen horns, donned silly hats,
celebrated midnight, as arms on the clock
embraced the new arrival. No
thoughts of the old man
who would knock on the door later and
steal away with our precious time.
The future was the present. Oh,
perhaps we made a resolution or two
to throw out with the Christmas tree.
We danced and laughed
at fortune's plans. We put on masks,
drank "to our health", sang
"For Auld Lang Syne."

The bells are ringing. The ball
drops. The sirens wail.
"Another year," my wife intones.
"It could be great," is my response.
Frayed vocal chords twang, my
mask this year a wrinkled palm
to hide a cough that mimes a
faint but husky horn.
I raise a mottled hand
dry as the skin a snake has shed,
try not to tip my champagne glass,
a kiss at midnight, a reassuring smile
that wavers on my lips like a faded flag
fluttering on a battered hulk.

Miriam Sagan

Miriam Sagan is the author of over a dozen books and her work has appeared internationally in some two hundred magazines. Her non-fiction appears in *The New Mexican, Albuquerque Journal, New Mexico Magazine* (Bimonthly Book Shelf Column), *The Santa Fean, Crosswinds* and *Sage Magazine*. She has held residency grants at Yaddo and MacDowell, and is the recipient of a grant from The Barbara Deming Foundation/Money for Women.

Writing on the Body

After Shirin Neshat, artist, Iran/USA

Beneath the veil
A script of Farsi, or Arabic
Written on skin
Nose, cheeks, forehead, chin
In an alphabet that sheds vowels
A dot, a dash, an umlaut,
Your tongue on mine.

It is too late to be unwritten
As if breath had tattooed from within
There is no paper on the ward, in prison
Or in the white-walled room that once schooled girls
Only the words
Written on the wrist
Like hospital tag, or silver bracelets
Or what the suicide will slit,
Your own name—lest you forget.

Enveloped in latex like a caul
The nude is struggling to be born
The holy book is black fire on white fire
That's obvious, a dominant script
God writes on the blank
But the void itself
Writes on our hearts' silence
White fire of emptiness.

Jizo Statue, Art Institute

How Japanese
To catalogue
Attributes of compassion
This young monk
Serves as protector
To women, children, travellers, soldiers, monks
Also to waterbabies
Miscarried, and aborted.
Isn't it kinder
To care for
What we couldn't bear
Than forget completely?
Maybe that's why
I'm in tears
In front of this statue in the museum
Thinking of you
With your shaved head
Even though you died
So long ago
And I grieve for us
As much as if we'd never been born.

Tea Room

In this winter's light
I might be sitting and waiting
Anywhere in the past
For you to arrive and order oolong tea
This might be San Francisco, or Boston
And you—a woman in a dark scarf
Or any man I loved
Turning his hat to the wind.

Every story has its variant
Donkeyskin who flees her fatherâ ™s love"With a magic trunk of gold
and silver gowns"Might be some other girl I knew"In her plaid school
uniform, gray blazer."And even Beauty, who goes almost willingly"To the
Beast's elaborate castle"Well, there must be something"She is glad to be
quit of.

I sit at the small table
In the adobe teahouse,
snow threatens, then falls.
It's too high, and wrong continent
To grow tea. What is my nostalgia for
Now that I'm fifty
Lips I neglected to kiss
Or the lips I did?

P-town, Bayside.

Towards mid-summer, late afternoon
Where sky and sea
Merge in a haze of light
Like some New York abstract expressionist painting
Just before it completely transcends the figurative
That's when we chat pleasantly to each other
With an "I hope you didn't forget
The beach umbrella"
The one with color blocks
Green, blue, yellow, red
Next to the lime green
Hull of the sailboat
Beached, bare mast
Looking like a French Impressionist
Painting just before
It completely loses the narrative in mist
And something towards the horizon
A dirigible? A parachute?
And the P-town Pilgrim Tower
On the promontory curving around to the right hand corner of the view
And people I don't know playing on the sand
And the sea's debris, like a cast away dream...

Lighthouse, Cabrillo Point.

What once was remote—
Coast in fog, sweep
Of mountains into Mexico
Now lets tourists pass
White lighthouse with its small rooms
Victorian and cosy,
Pictures in decorative frames
Composed of tiny seashells, dried weed,
A sailor's valentine.
Kichen garden for parsly, lettuce, any fresh green
In what was once two days from town.
The assistant in his own little house
Invited to dinner—
But think of the loneliness
Even for the keeper's wife, the keeper, the children
In their tower rooms
Curved, as light is curved.

Paul J. Sampson

Paul J. Sampson has been a professional writer and editor for more than 30 years. He lives with his wife, the artist Marti Fellhauer-Sampson, near Terrell, Texas.

Funeral March

Make flutes of my long bones,
dice of my knuckles
and play against all odds

Drum bony finger solos on my skull
scrub out a rhythm on my washboard ribs
and play a dirge to dance to

in a major key

Choosing My Grave-Goods

If Death should open up his fist and let us go,
a little breathless at our long confinement,
what should we have taken with us?
Too late then to stock up on supplies.

Well-provided for forever will I wend,
dowered for death with golden grave-goods:
Weapons, food, gifts for whatever gods I meet,
(three puppy treats for Cerberus, of course);
trophies to prove my prowess (my Collected Works,
all in ASCII format on a single floppy disk),
maybe some random crap from the top drawer
of the old teak desk, to fool some scholar yet unborn
whose theory of paperclips and orphaned keys,
a stapler and some pencils, gleaned from my grave,
will earn him tenure for his monograph.

Wake the Dead

When I was "old enough", some four or five,
my parents let me tag along at wakes,
kneel briefly at the box, peer up the empty nose
of some dead neighbor, see his hands,
waxy with makeup, handcuffed with a rosary,
and say my little prayers from memory:
"...and let perpetual light shine upon him."
(The temporal light came from pinkish baby floodlights in the ceiling.)

The undertaker, who looked pink-lit himself,
whose name was Leo, listened modestly
as grownups praised his work: "So natural.
You musta had a job, bad as he looked at the end."
Leo murmured thanks; he'd do as much
for each of us
When The Time Came.

As it did come, time and time again,
Time for Grandma, Grandpa, Dad and Mom,
interspersed with lesser deaths: uncles, aunts,
old family friends, the grief attenuating
with distance out along the social web.
And each time someone thanked the modest craftsman
in his beautiful grey suit: "So natural."

So, naturally, I searched each pink-lit effigy
for any sign of nature. There was none,
mercifully; who could have borne
the negligent sprawl of actual death?

Nursery Rhyme

Madman, madman, have you any sheep?
Yes ma'am, yes ma'am, marching into sleep.
One for my body, one for my mind
One for the little boy I have to leave behind.

Madman, madman, have you any dreams?
Yes ma'am, yes ma'am, can't you hear the screams?
Dreams that are strangers, dreams that I know.
I used to dream of falling, but now it's letting go.

Madman, madman, have you any sperm?
Yes ma'am, yes ma'am, see how they squirm.
Some for my self and some for my spouse
And a little bit left over just to keep around the house.

Madman, madman, having any fun?
Yes ma'am, yes ma'am, just had one.
One in the bird and one in the bush
And one where we thought we'd have to stand outside and push.

Madman, madman, have you any fear?
Yes ma'am, yes ma'am, singing in my ear.
Fear of my death and fear for my life
And lots of fear left over to share with my poor wife.

Madman, madman, feeling any guilt?
Yes ma'am, yes ma'am, right up to the hilt.
Some of it's wide open, some it is hidden,
Some for what I did and more for what I didn't.

Madman, madman, have you any dope?
Yes ma'am, yes ma'am, it fills my soul with hope.
Every day the doctor brings the medication 'round
And when we take our medicine, it calms us down and down.

Madman, madman, where does it all end?
Don't know, Sir or Madame, but I think I see a trend:
The onwarder we go, the less it seems like fun;
When all the fun is over, then I guess the game is done.

Sue Scalf

Named Alabama's Poet of the Year in 1992, **Sue Scalf** has received over 100 awards for her poetry including recent awards by the National Federation of State Poetry Societies. She has also received four Hackney awards, Alabama's most prestigious prize. She has published four books of poetry and has appeared in a half-dozen anthologies. Sue's work has appeared in publications such as *America, Carolina Quarterly, Southern Review* and others. Sue Scalf's most recently published books, *Ceremony of Names* and *South by Candlelight*, were nominated for the Pulitzer Prize.

The Baptist Ladies Travel to the Factory Outlets

To spend two hours by bus
(plus a stop at McDonald's)
they raffle apples and shout "Apple time!"
Then take turns telling jokes over the microphone.
Minds as sweet and blithely clean
as pinafores and shiny shoes, Bible schools ago,
they munch the apples,
while sun flickers through the windows,
and autumn trees seem to part in a swath, like seas.
Sisters in the Lord, pure lambs in polyester,
do you know we are traveling a landscape
where wolves raven and rage,
where doubt writhes at the core,
philosophy and physics
meet in mystical union,
and black holes suck in worlds?
Unscathed among lions and flames,
they glide over the highway,
talking discounts and coupons,
chapter and verse.
One whispers her secret
for perfect divinity. I listen.

Genesis

They had to go,
dusty and utilitarian
with wasps and rolypolies
dangling and spinning,
and the spider rappelling down his wire.
So one hot morning the broom fell,
and a kingdom was gone,
all that geometry a chaos,
and bugs scattered like planets.
The porch gleamed, swept clean,
but, still, it seemed wanton,
so arbitrarily mean.

I've been there: through far too much,
having seen earth cover the best
I could construct. I know how much
it costs to lose a universe.
Perhaps that is why
when I saw today the gleam
of a leg weaving and flashing,
when I saw bright filaments
on fire with a dawning sun,
I wanted to applaud,
knowing how hard it is
when a world ends
and is begun.

Deborah J. Shore

Deborah J. Shore has a BA from Miami University of Ohio. She currently lives in New Jersey.

Indoor Beachcomber
—after September 11, 2001

Only driftwood will fit my mood today.
Smooth, this child's skin
is whiskered against the grain,
mindlessly runs over my face.

Smooth, this child's skin
carried by spinning waves
mindlessly runs over my face,
these seas that crash and caress.

Carried by spinning waves,
now separate from them—
these seas that crash and caress—
it rests in my left hand.

Now separate from them,
seasoned by sun and storm,
it rests in my left hand.
It is lighter than this world.

Seasoned by sun and storm,
painted by a wandering script,
it is lighter than this world
so patiently traversed.

Painted by a wandering script,
the knotted cross-section of time
so patiently traversed
where three coarse splotches lie.

The knotted cross-section of time
is whiskered against the grain
where three coarse splotches lie.
Only driftwood will fit my mood today.

The Round Glade

Meadow without stumps or brush
bounded by tall, wind-whacked pine,
both the living and the bare snags.
My hymns
know their ambit,
          bounce
back, as though
the ghost-theater of trees
hears and repeats
hears   repeats.
But those nested boughs don't listen
unless a woodland bird pecks or sings.

A bellflower rings.
Here I learn the curve of notes,
the rounding of empty.

Fall Line

An iced branch fans against
a blue-grey forest of mountains.
Beneath the snow-blanket they are hard-headed
and then boulder-strewn
where granite trades for clay and sand.

Slender trees, felled by wind
during the night, lie—
dashes on white.

I sense a brooding.
My fingers circle the glass pane.
I scan the slope for frozen falls
intent on fissures waving
like coral, the tingle of water
deep in
a snow-silenced ear.

Ernest Slyman

Ernest Slyman was born in Appalachia - Elizabethton, Tennessee, and attended East Tennessee State University. His work has been published in *The Laurel Review*, *The Lyric*, *Light: A Quarterly of Light Verse* (Chicago), *The NY Times*, *Reader's Digest* and *The Bedford Introduction to Literature*, St Martins Press, edited by Michael Meyer, and *Poetry: An Introduction*, St Martins Press, edited by Michael Meyer as well as numerous literary sites on the World Wide Web.

I'm Baggy In Because

I'm baggy in because
and snug in why,
all bundled
in my warm goodbye —
and smug in my now,
my Oh my some-how
come honey me with moon-gleam,
till I'm wild in my anyhow,
and every if's dream
a revolution of whys,
and humble never-was
slay mighty always-been
with surprise.

Therefore and Why

Therefore and why
the sense of history
of a morning sky,
and none whatsoever
not being so clever
as the blowfly
whose sense of propriety
in insect society
stands incorruptible
as the pig's appetite —
and horses white
leaping high fences
shall never die
in cold weather.

Little Piggy Everything

Oh, now there secretly
once stuffed a black kerchief
down can't tell you's mouth —
and who'll ever guess
watched little piggy everything,
in waistcoat and trousers,
lug that heavy I tell you,
with Love's dead body
snug in a bag of why nots,
upstairs where can't tell you
waited in the long, thin dark
of a last believe what you wish.

Kew Forest Park

The dark bloom watch grow,
clatter down the swell,
blanched white the meadow
on the prowl bids light farewell —-
coming to an end each pale shadow
bullied by light burn black with night
and fly high. Love quavers in the grass,
what Love made want shall pass,
quickly close the quiet dark cast
the green shout roar of insects outlast
the silver-bladed hush of moonlight
and rub the backs of stars asleep
and fleshy whirlpools dream of light,
sweep clean upstairs chamber night.

Robert Lavett Smith

Robert Lavett Smith was born in Michigan in 1957, and, after having lived on Guam and in Hawaii as a young child, grew up mostly in the New York area. He holds a B.A. in French from Oberlin College, and an M.A. in Creative Writing from the University of New Hampshire, where he studied with Charles Simic and Mekeel McBride. He is the author of four chapbooks of poetry, *The White Peacock's Throat* (1990), *Hesitant Light* (1992), *The Nob Hill Mariners* (1993), and *Jesus In Bed Between Us* (1994). His poems have appeared in many magazines including *The Hiram Poetry Review, Mudfish, Nightsun, The Pembroke Review, Poetry Northwest*, and *Visions International*. Currently employed as a Special Education Paraprofessional for the San Francisco Unified School District, he is married, and has lived in the San Francisco Bay Area since 1987.

Don't Look Now

Somewhere above us,
gargoyles cough in their gutters.
Library lions yawn and lick their paws.
In formal gardens, sundials
lean discreetly towards the light,
pliant as heliotrope.
The mirror admires
its own reflection.
Scissors dream
of a whetstone's kiss,
opening and closing
gently in their sleep.
If you listen, you can hear
the asthmatic rasp of the wine.

Walking Across The Sea Of Galilee

The Israeli government has approved plans to build a barely-submerged
foot bridge beneath the Sea of Galilee.

Our aging guide moves with surprising agility.
Ahead of me two Serbian nuns struggle to keep
their balance on the submerged path, the hems
of their habits already soaked, brilliantly white
running shoes showing under dark, heavy skirts.

On either side of the narrow span, lifeguard stations,
uncomfortable-looking straight-backed chairs bolted
to wooden rafts, sway on chains furred with algae,
like tiny islands anchored deep in opaque water.

The lifeguards listen to Berlioz on a transistor radio.
Machine guns lie across their knees, gleaming dully;
sunlight slides easily off their bare brown shoulders.

Though the land's nearly two miles distant,
the scorched hills sharpen in the morning light.
There are no railings. We must walk carefully,
gingerly, arms outspread like awkward wings.

Yet it's easy to believe in this manufactured miracle.
We follow in the footsteps of Jesus towards the new
millennium, as the rattle of gun fire carries from shore:
wobbling across a wrinkled brown sea rank with salt,
each step uncertain enough to be an act of faith.

The Skull Of Billy The Kid

"Three months after the Kid's death, a Montana newspaper reported that his body had been dug up, his head removed, and the skull polished in a manner appropriate to a relic."
—*from an article in* The New Yorker

Outlaw or not, William Bonney was a devout
Presbyterian and a former Irish Catholic
whose death elicited the usual dreary hymns.
Candles surrounded his grieving mother
like gun barrels aimed towards heaven.

Shot in the desert, miles from anywhere
last rites could be said for his soul, his body
grayed with the dust which would reclaim him.
And after his death the halo of his youth
and exploits burned ever more brightly.

But this other story interests me, the skull,
stolen by nameless admirers, rubbed until
it shone like onyx. His wanderlust outliving him
as it toured the West in some snake-oil show,
nestled in cheap velvet, five cents to see.

Why disturb its dark sleep? Murderer,
martyr, sinner or saint, Billy belongs to history now,
where the dead are restless, and never wholly themselves.

I can almost feel its weight in my hands,
the cracked surface cool and smooth, brown as a stone.
The pooled sockets which held his eyes regarding me
without apology, as if surprised to be here,
on the threshold of yet another century.

Robert Sward

A Korean War veteran and a journalist for The Toronto Star, broadcaster for CBC Radio,
Robert Sward has taught at Cornell University, the University of Iowa Writers' Workshop, and UC
Santa Cruz. A Fulbright scholar at the University of Bristol and A Guggenheim Fellow for Poetry,
he was chosen by Lucille Clifton to receive a Villa Montalvo Literary Arts Award. Widely published
in traditional literary magazines (The New Yorker, Poetry Chicago, The Hudson Review...) and
anthologies , Sward serves also as contributing editor to "Alsop Review" and "Blue Moon Review."
He has published 20 books, most recently *Collected Poems, 1957-2004* with Black Moss Press

Life is its Own Afterlife

Father:

"Enough already. Mourn,
        mourn all you want...
What good will it do?
Truth is, I feel great, son. Never better!

"So what if I'm invisible?
So what if I'm dead?
You don't need a body to be a *mensch*,
        a man of substance.
Ach, but with a body at least
you've got some privacy.
Without a body you can't conceal anything.

"There's more, son,
 and bad news for you.
God, —this will surprise you—
when you die one of the first questions He asks is,
'Did you marry?'
Turns out after God created the world, the rest of the time
He spent making marriages.
So a couple, when they meet, it's *bashert*,
        'it was meant to be.'
That's so... that's how
 together they fulfill their destiny.
But divorce, that they don't allow.
So you won't be coming.

But thank God
        for what you've got.
What are you missing? Not much. There is no afterlife,
        not really.
That's right, son.
Life is its own afterlife."

Leopard Dog in Heaven

"Bow wow, bow wow. You know what heaven is?
Dogs, dogs and people,
dogs, everywhere—and people
who can't be without them.

"bow wow, bow wow. that's right.
who do you think sees you
to the other side?
truth is, sonny, if your own dog won't put in a word for you
      you can forget the afterlife.

"heaven! you put a dog in this place
and you think he's gonna stop being a dog?
Or people? Sonny, the dead don't change.
Look at your father over there, smoking;
you think because a person's dead, he's done?
Done? Done what?

"Anyway, everything oscillates
between is and is not.
On, off. On, off.
Yes, no. Yes, no.
Aristotle said it.
There's the way things are
and the way they really are.
There's howling
 and there's howling necessity.

"so, the dead don't want to hear you carrying on.
How many times do you have to be told?
The dead don't want to hear it.
Forgive your father, Sonny, forgive him
for being dead.
Mourn
if you want to, but mourn with your mouth shut."

Dog Door to Heaven

—With thanks to David Swanger

As spirit guide, whose job it was to guide his master into the next life and then to testify as to his master's goodness, dogs of intense devotion and loyalty were needed… As pets they have been affectionately raised as loyal companions… [and] as tools in the treatment of rheumatism.
      —Ery Camara, *Looking at the Xolo,* artnet.com

Leopard dog:

I can out-think, out-work, out-fight any dog
in that world or in this.
Woof fuckin' woof. I told you before, I'm here
to look after your father. Relax, dammit!
Besides, like the man said, 'Death is an illusion.'
Bow wow, bow wow!
        But there's still shit to be accomplished
after you die,
after you shed the life that you lived.
Anyway, who else is gonna lie against him,
draw rheumatism from his body?
Leopard dog, that's who.
Even now he sleeps with his hands on me—
        osteo-arthritis.
Truth is, dogs are doctors, too.
Heaven, this "other side,"
is one big hospital and, like I told you,
 it's filled with dogs,
New Guinea Singing dogs, Xolos, Leopard dogs, dogs
        that listen to you and protect you.

People say 'Heaven is a place that cannot be found, '
but if you got a dog,
        you can find it.
Tell me, my friend, you come into life and you leave life.
What do you think
 we're here for?
And when you leave, what are you gonna leave with?

Post-Modern — A (Mostly) Found Poem

"Joan of Arc was married to the Biblical Noah."

"The inhabitants of Egypt were called mummies, and built pyramids in the shape of triangular cubes."

"The Pyramids are a range of mountains between France and Switzerland."

He graded his papers
   and went home to Honey.

   "Areas of the dessert are cultivated by irritation."

Honey and the teacher were newlyweds.
Filing her nails, she watched some Joan Crawford movie.
Handed him a joint.

"Get your papers graded?" Applying nail polish,
Honey reached for *Cosmopolitan*,
turned back to the *TV Guide*.

All pink and red she was
and full of self-esteem and bounce,
teacher's fluorescent bride.

"Now or never," Honey said, her eyes twinkling,

"Post-civilization, post-modern, post-Cracker Jack,
early unforeseeable, post paradigm.

"Now you see it, now you don't."

   "They lived in the Sarah Dessert and traveled by Camelot."

   *"In the dessert, the climate is such
   the inhabitants have to live elsewhere."*

"Come and get it," Honey called.
"Come and get it."

   "In Europe, the enlightenment was a reasonable time."

Shelby the Dog

*...all that I cared for was the race of dogs, that and
nothing else... To whom but [dogs] can one appeal
in the wide and empty world?*
——Franz Kafka

Shelby, Philosopher Dog:

"In a world of No,
dogs are a Yes.
Sixty-eight million dogs in America
and they understand
there is a fundamental human reaction
—to everything—,
and it's *No, No.*
Grrr! Dogs hate hearing shit like that.
People, it's all *No* and it's *No*
    and it's *No.*
And they look at a dog sometimes
and the dog is on its back, say,
      on someone's lawn,
          legs in the air,
               rolling and bouncing...
'This is the hand I was dealt. [Yes,] I'm a dog,'
says the dog. 'It's not a problem.'
But people—
    Look at me, Goddamnit!
'I don't have time for this,' you're thinking.
'Something better is going to come later.'
No, no it won't. As Ram Dass says, This is all there is.
This is all you get.
'All knowledge, the totality
of all questions and answers,
is contained in the dog.'
Do you know who said that? Kafka.
That's right, Kafka.
Bow wow, bow, wow. Bow, wow.
Bow wow NOW. "

Carol A. Taylor

Carol A. Taylor's poems have appeared in *Iambs and Trochees, Light Quarterly, Artemis Journal, Byline Magazine,* and *Susquehanna Quarterly.* Her growing interest in writing light verse led to her co-editorship of an anthology of classic jokes in verse form which was featured in the Fall 2003 edition of *Light Quarterly.*

Tea and Sympathy

A kindness, Deborah—is that all it was?
The way to help a faltering young man
whose doubts about himself you understood?
A gesture asking nothing in return
except the knowledge he would use your gift
to shore his confidence and then forget
an older woman's loving, or at best,
be kind, remembering? Was that enough?

Was yours a simple act of charity,
like giving away old clothes you'd never wear,
that might warm someone else, just hanging there
neglected in your closet all those years?
Or did you dream of being young, in love,
wanted again, the way you were at twenty
when you last wore them? Did you hope the thrill
of youth and passion would replace the chill
of that cold man for just a little while?

You knew, of course, the way it had to end,
but was it worth it? Tell me, Deborah Kerr.
If you could change the script of memory,
would you still offer tea and sympathy?

Chambers

Never crossed my mind that you'd be unhappy,
feeling short-changed over the hand life dealt you,
needing more grace, more than what God allotted.
I only wanted

that you'd always think of your girl with pleasure,
keeping one small chamber no grief inhabits
hidden, a sound-proof space only we could enter
sometimes together;

random hours you'd spend in my quiet presence,
not as star-crossed lovers—no melodrama;
just a refuge, knowing you seldom need one.
But I was asking

life for more gifts, more than what God allotted,
keeping unsought promises, willful, waiting,
holding one small chamber no love inhabits
ready for letting.

Houston Grows

Crepe myrtle trees are decking Houston out
in lavender and amethyst and rose
as flags parade their Easter hats and clothes
along her sidewalks. Cannas start to sprout.
A few dry months ago we cursed the drought
that choked her hedges, siphoned her bayous;
we scanned the sky for clouds. Now water flows
in rivulets from roof and gutter spout.

In February, rains (unlike the snows
that cloak her northern sisters) sluice her clean.
A trail of morning fog festoons her hair.
Beneath an incubating skirt whose flare
fans out a hundred miles in summer green,
Houston, fertile mother, grows and grows.

Don't Talk

The books you mean to write; the PhD
you're going back for in divinity;
an idea for an online magazine;
a trip abroad; one more advanced degree,
this time in medicine; a used RV
and an acre on the river near Seguin;
a dozen novel money-making schemes—

The more you plan out loud the less it seems
you have to do to garner satisfaction,
as though the word were equal to the action.
Once voiced, each goal retires and something new
claims your attention. Superstitiously
I wait to speak about *faits accomplis*.
Brave words become the things we never do.

Saving for the Future

We don't do anniversaries anymore.
Well, come to that, I guess we never did.
It mattered to a sentimental kid,
but forty years have evened up the score.
You've left the better part of life behind;
you hang on to your past. I focus through
the present to the things I've yet to do
and will, the day these fraying ties unbind.

Each day I pay my future out in gold,
a miser selling bits of real estate
begrudged from an endowment still unspent,
demanding value for each parcel sold,
saving for ventures I anticipate,
hoarding enough of me to pay the rent.

Henry Taylor

Henry Taylor is Professor Emeritus of Literature at American University in Washington, DC., where he taught from 1971 until 2003. His third collection of poems, *The Flying Change*, received the 1986 Pulitzer Prize in Poetry; his first two, *The Horse Show at Midnight* (1966) and *An Afternoon of Pocket Billiards* (1975), were reissued in one volume in 1992. His translations from Bulgarian, French, Hebrew, Italian, and Russian have appeared in many periodicals and anthologies, as well as two collections by the Bulgarian poet Vladimir Levchev. He has also published translations from Greek and Roman classical drama; his translation of Sophocles' *Electra* appeared (spring 1998) in the *Sophocles, 1* volume of the Penn Greek Drama series. Another collection of poems, *Understanding Fiction: Poems 1986-1996*, appeared in the fall of 1996, and his collection of clerihews, *Brief Candles*, appeared in 2000 from LSU Press. He is now completing work on a new collection called *Crooked Run*, titled after a creek in his native Loudoun County, Virginia; since 1999 most of those poems have appeared in journals, including *The Atlantic Monthly, The American Scholar, The Georgia Review, The Missouri Review, Shenandoah, Tar River Poetry,* and *The Virginia Quarterly Review*. He has received Fellowships in Creative Writing for the National Endowment for the Arts (1978 and 1986), a Research Grant from the National Endowment for the Humanities (1980-81), the Witter Bynner Prize of the American Academy and Institute of Arts and Letters (1984), and the Michael Braude Prize from the American Academy of Arts and Letters (2002).

You Don't Know All the Places You Take Me To

You look up from your book. "Who was Delmore Schwartz?"
So I look up from mine, say something about
the heavy bear, the bed in Plato's cave,
the sad end, and, pausing, recall a glimpse
of Delmore Schwartz walking up the left aisle
of the old Coolidge Auditorium
in mid-October of 1962,
a cigarette (not in those days forbidden)
between his fingers and between his lips,
the ember burning with such ferocity
that sparks and ash-flecks danced away from it
as if it were itself a thing alive,
almost beyond the fierce control of the poet
who meanwhile leaned his head away from smoke
and squinted ahead, proceeding to the exit.

Here Reynolds Is Laid

It can surprise you to come on a tombstone
bearing a recognized name, unless, of course,
you are looking for it. I wasn't. Just wandering
in and around an old churchyard high up
on the Blue Ridge, and wham! there it was.

I was eight when I entered third grade,
but this was back before social promotion
had taken deep hold, let alone grade inflation.
One of my classmates was twelve. A big,
dumb goon, most of us thought, including
Mrs. Pritchard, hair-triggered, squeamish,
and, as Reynolds discovered, quite helpless
against waves of out-loud disgust when he spoke
of snot, or of blisters oozing watery pus.
He invoked her desperate paroxysms
almost daily in that one-room brick schoolhouse
borrowed from the Quaker Meeting for the third grade
the year we overflowed the main building.
A coal stove heated it, and occasionally scorched
to uselessness the single wet mitten left
out of sight by the stovepipe to be forgotten,
almost inaudibly to fry, filling the room
with a scent of burnt wool, evaporating snow,
the slow decay we did not know included us,
and even, as Reynolds at last settled down
for a while, a faint whiff of powerless rage.

Metes and Bounds

The land surveyor either sets or finds.
You read this in the markings on his plats:
at such-and-such a point a pipe is set,
at older corners planted stones are found.

Still, his is not the boundary that binds.
Wandering through my native hills and flats,
I see what fields are not encompassed yet,
how little time we have to hold our ground.

A Brief Partnership

One afternoon I brought the bushhog out
to trim the ragged hill above the fork
that meanders down from the old Hatcher place,
where Foster worked his mules those years ago.
I made one cautious pass along the fence
where rotted posts and stray barbed wire lie deep
in burdock leaves and multiflora rose.
After that swath was open all the way
the old Farmall would handle second gear,
and I could drift a trifle in and out
of the tall growth on my left, and gradually
straighten some curves and round the corners off
to make the steering easier with each round.
Then in the fresh-cut section on my right,
first not there then just there, a drab red fox
that trotted beside me for at least an hour.
I wondered if he were rabid or otherwise
deprived of his inbred distrust of men,
but then supposed exhaust fumes masked my scent,
leaving him only this sudden higher power
that gloriously transformed his hunting ground.
The bushhog blades were set too high to hurt
the rodents that they brought into the light,
but what my labor furnished, he could catch.
I still suspect he wasn't at his best—
mange, if it wasn't rabies, slowed him down—
but he was quick when a fieldmouse darted out.
We worked together there that afternoon,
establishing a temporary order
that summer stays ready to overwhelm.
I looked away when I had to, and there came
at length the look back that found he wasn't there.

Hughesville Nights

υολσπχἐ̓ μ θ̂ ρμῖρμσ ὤ☐χιμσ νβζοῆπβπχβ — *Iliad* 23.753

No one now alive, I think, was ever inside. The old store
collapsed into its own basement some time around 1960,
having stood abandoned for close to a lifetime
there at the end of Bob Tiffany's driveway.
It was standing when I was in grade school;
I remember a low-hanging porch roof, a door
with an iron bar across it. All the wood
had gone gray, the paint disappeared, and the chimney
was starting to come apart at the top. Years later,
when I was living back there again, an indistinct heap
of crumpled roof and busted boards emerged
from thin spots in the briary overgrowth.
Locust trees grew from the cellar floor.

One thing that happened here, though,
probably in my grandfather's time, whenever
I think about it, makes me start putting the place back
together, making use of what materials I have.

                                                             A small

general store, mostly staple goods and work clothes,
in the back room slabs of cured pork hanging.
On one side of the room a wood or coal stove
surrounded by objects that might once have been chairs,
or only aspire to be–nail kegs, say, or apple boxes.
Across the room, on the left as you come in the door,
the cash drawer and iron safe behind the counter
of laminated walnut strips, oil-stained, dented
and nicked. A low, weak place in the floor
where you stand to pay, or to have purchases
written down in the book.
                                There are nights
after closing when men sit around for a spell,
a few loungers not quite done with the day.
A couple of oil lamps get turned up just a hair.
Squeak of corncob in crockery jug-neck,
soft boom of palm striking the stopper,
smoke in an undulant layer about even
with the tops of their heads. Somebody tells

another joke. Amid the laughter a notion takes shape
apparently in the air itself. Without a word
one of the men there reaches over and grabs an ear of corn,
shells off a good handful of kernels, and lays them
end to end, just touching, in a row perpendicular
to the counter's front edge. There is joshing
and nudging about who will go first, then
a cheer as one man steps to the counter,
unbuttons his fly, makes ready the implement,
and with it sweeps aside that part of the row
he can thus reach.
                                        By now the rest of the men
have arranged a rotation: each steps from the contest
into the committee of referees counting kernels
and calling out totals. Someone has the thought
to keep score on a slate, just a single initial
and a number. The row is rebuilt under watchful eyes.
One man sets a scale-weight down to mark a place,
another demands that two small kernels be thrown out.
The next man steps up, whips out and across,
takes the count. There are hoarse whoops
and high, loony giggles. "What color is that,
do you reckon?" "By God, you'd a got more
if you wadn't so crooked."
                                        It ended somehow,
as such evenings do, in good humor or ill,
men stepping out into the night to sniff air
and make their various ways homeward over
the very hills and hollows I have lately been walking.
Among them there may have been a winner,
possibly more than one loser, but now,
however it was, there is nobody living
who could name a single one of them. The story
reached me as a curious example
of ingenuity in the use of shelled corn,
but soon enough the laughter dies down,
and it comes now to say that what matters most
about memory is what is forgotten forever.

The Final Morbidity of the Interior Embezzler

It may seem morbid of an embezzler to keep a memorandum, yet many
of them do. It may be mere neatness.

                    —Wallace Stevens, *"Surety and Fidelity Claims"*

I've made a little sluice-gate in the flow
of cash across the spreadsheet on my screen.
Amid torrential chaos and foreseen
disasters it maintains its small and slow
on-off diversions, so my work can show
the delicacy of difference between
the beans I count and one uncounted bean,
and where the latter might invisibly go.

The hollowed shoe-tree, the hermetic jar
are gadgetry I might revert to yet.
There is the money of the thing, the far
secure retirement years, the deep-hedged bet,
but I love working where the unknowns are,
and writing down what I need to forget.

Metes and Bounds first published in *The Georgia Review*
Here Reynolds Is Laid first published in *Folio*
A Brief Partnership first published in *The American Scholar*
Hughesville Nights first published in *64*
You Don't Know All the Places You Take Me To
first published in *Tar River Poetry*
The Final Morbidity of the Interior Embezzler
first published in *Poetry*

Dianne Thomas

Dianne Thomas is a freelance writer whose work has appeared in
The Threepenny Review, Papermite, Flashquake, Octavo, and numerous other
online and print publications. She lives in Detroit, Michigan.

A Drive at Winter Solstice

The heathen inside me
knows nothing of salvation
and seeks out the lights only as diversion
on this darkest of nights

I cruise these civilized streets
comfortable in my car
an unlikely primitive
gazing at the bright displays

Yielding to another car
I pull to the curb outside
an edifice draped in glowing garlands
and pouring white light onto the snow

The other driver passes but I remain
surprised to find myself longing to belong
to know the comfort that waits
behind illuminated windows

I turn the motor off
and gaze at the house
pretending I've arrived
in a place where I am welcome

Album

My family never owned
a movie camera
Our history lives only
in a scrapbook
where we are still
and mainly black and white

The primitive color shots
have paled,
leaving only ghosts of
the grandfather
awkwardly holding the baby,
the one-year-old grinning
over a birthday cake

Early Polaroids are even eerier,
faded nearly blank with slivers of brown
where images used to be
In my mind I see
the toddler petting a dog
on a page that contains nothing but
glossy cards with crinkly edges

And so we are preserved
in grayscale tableau
Figures at a table
or in front of a Christmas tree,
couples and groups
with faces frozen into smiles,
a boy with a bike,
a girl with a doll,
a man in a hat,
a lady in a dress,
colorless people from a
monochrome past
with only an occasional blur
to hint that we were ever alive

Intensities of IV or Less

Creaking walls
a rattle of glass
the house shaking
as if a large truck
were driving past

The earth shifts and we
can feel its movements
hundreds of miles away
far above the settling layers
and beyond the epicenter
At this distance
we find only traces of the fury
a rolling pebble
a rattling tree branch
a crackling in the telephone line
How close do we need to be
and what needs to fall on our heads
before we can begin to understand
that no one is safe on the surface
when subterranean factions try to settle

Jennifer Drake Thornton

Jennifer Drake Thornton lives with her husband in Bellevue, Washington.
Her work has recently appeared in *Octavo*.

On The Occasion of My Birthday
and Iraq's New National Holiday

A year ago today, it all fell down:
dictator, statue, two-ton bombs.

Now you rise to a broken present
wrapped in smoke and steel

but this is the day that was ordained
for both of us to celebrate, so you will

have to watch the balloons go up
into a blood orange morning

where artillery still calls you
to prayer, shocking sparrows

from the palm fronds to flutter
in dark banners on the sky.

Here, my fellow citizens believe
that I should wake up happy

beneath the barrage of good wishes
and giftwrap, expect me to swallow

some sweet white cake
made festive with safe flames.

Tell them we refuse to rejoice
over any well-intended conflagration.

Professor Stephen Hawking and the Lump

The radiologist would like a closer look.
Between the spot compression
and the ultrasound, I balance
hibiscus tea in a porcelain cup,
scan the magazines for something
more remote or theoretical
than swimsuit fashions.

Stephen Hawking has radically
altered his theory about black holes;
anything (you, me, cosmic dust, the red
light of its binary twin) that falls
beyond the star's event horizon
will not be annihilated.

Holding a pose on my back,
I watch the screen as a tech
maps the margins of a mass
more hole than lump, dark
on the display, swallowing
every heartbeat. The doctor tries
to comfort me with probabilities.

If you jump into a black hole,
your mass energy will be returned
to our universe, but in a mangled form,
which contains the information
about what you were like,
but in an unrecognizable state.

At dusk, I am reluctant
to slip off the red elastic lace
holding everything together.
I attempt a sensual pose, feel
my husband's fingers pause
for a moment on my left breast.
The sun, too, hesitates before it falls
beyond the black horizon.

Notes From A Funeral on the
Hottest Day of the Year
—for Kim

I never met the man,
although his daughter is my friend.
All I can do for him now is show up

at this full house of worship
where the air conditioner he installed
cannot quite hold back the sun.

The family was wise to choose flowers
for their longevity: alstromeria, carnation,
dusky iris just emerging.

The minister speaks
of resurrection: *anastasis*,
Greek for "standing up".

Mourners in respectful clothes
fan themselves with the memorial handout;
a photo of his younger face nods agreement

to every scripture. Each breath
offers us molecules of ink, fragments
of the words recording his abridged life.

The riffle of bible pages stills,
the air conditioning whispers
along with a final prayer.

Everyone bows their heads except
a flourish of yellow carnations, standing up
straight, strong on their slim green spines.

Medusa's Great Granddaughter on the Bus

The girl was lucky to be born without
the gene that transmutes everyone to stone,
but she must wear a scarf when she goes out.
She boards the bus for work each day alone,
subjected to sly jostling and the stares
that follow every lovely-legged miss.
Her anger coils up strong where her soft hair
should be, a menace of paralysis
and pain, desiring to strike and scar.
Though she was raised to turn the other cheek,
one day a man may go a pinch too far,
and part of her will tire of acting meek.
She'll sit within a hissing whirl, serene,
and let the little vipers make the scene.

Amy Unsworth

Amy Unsworth is a Contributing Editor for *Poems Niederngasse*. Her poems have appeared or are forthcoming in various publications including *Miller's Pond, The Briar Cliff Review, The Pikeville Review* and in *Literary Lunch*, an Anthology by the Knoxville Writers' Guild. A graduate of Eastern Michigan University's English Department, she lives in Manhattan, Kansas with her husband and three sons.

Explaining Entrapment

I am a bill broken into dimes and pennies,
the granite stairs you stride
to throw another morning
 into the fountain.

And I am a kite on a string, nodding.

I am next week's paycheck, unspent.
You, who I love only while you sleep.

I am a kite on a string wet with dew,

an Ace up the sleeve
 of an amputee,
a fish frying in six inches of oil.
the runnel of the streambed.

We are turtles racing across rice paddies.
Each waterfall we tumble apart.

I am a kite rotting to strut and fin-
one wrenches
and wishes cannot fix.

You are the wind-blown leaves in a spider's web,
sunlight
diluted on a winter's day.

I am your eyes' pinprick
of black in morning,
tatters
in the net of your bare limbs.
a fish breathing what you offer me as air.

Love & War

After a month of living in Georgia
the palmetto bugs don't come
as a surprise anymore. She's steeled
to the scurry from under the bed,
the sight of six legs in the air
waving. She's learned the power of aerosol,
stopped worrying about the green house
effect. Air freshener, hairspray,
eau de cologne, all part of her arsenal.
She intercepts some mid-flight,
ambushes others on the open plain
of linoleum, wraps each in tissue,
mails him white boxes, C.O.D.,
signed love, wish you were here.

At Washington Street, With Yo-Yo Ma

Memories have no beginning; we are always in the middle
brushing our teeth or folding the laundry, turning a key
in the lock. I was working at Washington Street Station.

Yet, I can picture you on the stage, cello rich in the spotlights.
Your fingers pressed against the strings, the bow insistent.
How can I ask you to remember a girl?

One, on a night filled with the faces of the crowd,
a girl whose brown hair may have still been waist long,
or already cut to the chin. Some things are certain:
the black apron, white shirt, and green bow tie.

After hours, after the last few concertgoers
finished their coffee and flan, as I cleared the table
you were there at the window, under the streetlamp.

As I unlocked the door, laughter spilled from the bar,
your photo smiled in black and white from a discarded program.
You asked only for soup. It was Michigan,
it was always winter.

Drift

for my sons

The clock falls behind, an hour then two,
right for someplace off the coast
 where the sun is still setting.

This is the way of the glacier, the impossible
movement shaping mountains,

the manner of the hour hand—
imperceptible to the eye.

This, the way of scars, the cut closing
cell by cell to bridge the wound,

of a child growing
constrained in the sea of the womb

Benjamin Vogt

Benjamin Vogt has an MFA from The Ohio State University and is currently pursuing a Ph.D. at the University of Nebraska—Lincoln. His work has appeared in the *Cream City Review*, *Diagram*, *Southern Indiana Review*, *Valparaiso Poetry Review*, and on *Verse Daily*. Benjamin's chapbook *Indelible Marks* is available from Pudding House.

Section 117, Plot 21

This field, which weathers January warmth,
grows crows and sparrows by a hundredfold.
From under the bent stalks winged shadows rise,
harsh echoes stab the desert place before
the sky grows pointillist black. With bellies full
of hollow grain, they float through one another.
Their awkward cloud collides in distant voice
as each jackhammer beak looks down, surveys
the broken land then dives to take the combine's
once calculated route.

                The farthest rows
remain uncut. Their rotting guts hold fast
to wrapping-paper skin. This broken farmer,
whose bank has called his promissory bluff,
lies somewhere with his windows opened wide,
listening to distance. Clean hands lay folded
across his belly. Each breath lifts them slightly
higher to God. And when the empty roads
and barren trees allow the soundlessness
to come dive blindly through his house, he hears
the fields, his earth, splitting open as flocks
gorge themselves.

                He'll sell his father's Deere.
The spades as well. The home place, the Ford,
five hundred acres with the bass-filled lake—
and on Saturdays he'll cast his line into
his wife's herb garden. On his knees he'll claw
the rows and listen to his humming partner
who hovers over him, prepares the harvest.
The farthest field is slipping through his hands.

July, Just Outside of Columbus

The fireflies are hovering over corn,
young fields darkened by maple shadows swept
across the dusk line. Beetle bodies pulse.
Bright chemicals like breath released
in the cold begin to light the ground ahead,
as if a thousand searchlights were sent adrift.

Males are calling, their incandescent lust
an impatient spark, the female's waiting glow
a calm amongst this storm that binds desire
to action. Windows hover like dim suns while,
just fifty feet away, the fireflies are

like pens on paper, brief calligraphy
transposed to translucent night. Their body-light
a memory ongoing, purpose and lust
blown down to grass, then lifted up as if
a speckled hand were rising from the waters,

reformed like polished diamonds, cool and warm
against our momentary senses. How many
suns will rise and set on this frenzied hour,
work that the body needs between lost moments;
a bloodless still life when we clearly see
one-hundred lifetimes asking questions when

our mouths might have been more pensive, full
with speaking silence—not ours, not theirs—
but meeting at a time and place where neither
are gods or creatures, one and the same light,
because we need the dark to find our way.

Portraiture at Blanks' Photography
—Weatherford, OK, 1978

Her hand upon his chest like buttress, palm
In shallow rest between his tie and coat,
How its fingers curl just softly, pleading this
Is not what's kept him on his feet. With him

beside her—thinner lips and whiter skin
and the grey like panhandle snow—
the months of rest, appointments, and endless nights
refuse to linger in their steadfast smiles.

He's the husband, father of boys and land
and real estate, a dozen parcels west of town
where wind from two directions holds
the wheat erect, defiant. Where late

into the harvest night, he hears the shallow
whisper that all grown men refuse to hear.
Between the whirling thrush of dust and stalks
chipped by the combine—the time it takes

to re-approach from the distant lines of wheat—
he knows the summer night that cools his cheek
is just a careful prelude, patient push
into the friction of his aging body,

like stones pressed into a façade, the mortar
of earth and water loose against a stolid frame.
He knows that as the distant night's work
will go on until it's done—until the necessary

reaping of earth and months of dusting fields
and irrigation end—no stalk, no tree,
no God could hold him any nearer life
than the imprint of the morning's photograph,

the gentle hand still warm against his body.
He imagines, in the nearing lights of combine,
a careful way of leaving simply, without
the circling eyes, near whisper of machines

that pulse into his heart, without the thrush
of sudden memory piercing through the air.
He imagines, as the load of grain is siphoned
to the truck bed, how sudden form can falter—

how watching lifted fields now fall like rain,
that even a few firm stalks have made it past
as if threaded through the terror purposely,
released into the rush, become the silent whole.

Rural Kiss—Oklahoma, 1944

Because she's saying her goodbyes your bodies
writhe like clothesline shirts. The briefest touch
is felt deeper than her coat's arm like the clutch
of Chevy parked behind, its chrome a frieze
that cools her arching back. You push valise
away like a rusted gate, a gentle touch
to steady your expression—hers in such
untangled wonder and lusty indices.
But yours is black and white, eyes open, a search
for something past her curling hair which fades
the house, the drive, street sloped and glistening.
Today avoids you, your memory a perch
From which a distant, voiceless sound invades—
Without the war all love is just routine.

Robt. Ward

Robt. Ward is a native Soutnern Californian who reverse-migrated to Cape Cod a few years ago. A poet, photographer, graphic designer, and chef, he occupies his time editing *The Susquebanna Quarterly,* doing landscape photography in one of the great places of the earth, and trying as best he can to discharge his duties as Editor-in-Chief of *Clock & Rose Press* and staff designer for *The Alsop Review Press.*

Felipe Viejo

My first clear memory of my father's face
has haunted me for more than fifty years:
I blamed myself, as if it were my fault
I had seen him in tears.

My father wept to see me dying there,
but as a child, how could I understand?
I only knew he would not answer me.
He would not hold my hand.

What could I think but that his leaving me
was punishment for begging him to stay?
I thought, by screaming at him, I had made
my father mad that day.

I needed to believe that he was strong,
and had been taught that strong men did not weep,
so built an image of him in my heart
I could afford to keep.

I realize now how young he was, and know
he must have been mature beyond his age
to leave his son alone, in pain, to die,
and not explode in rage.

I beg forgiveness now: the child was wrong.
Though tears of grief fell from my father's eyes,
he proved, confronting my impending death,
he was both strong and wise.

Traveler

As if. Perhaps. Because. When all's been said,
we only can remember to forget,
and in forgetting, lose the thing we loved.
But simply in the losing we can find
the limits of remembrance, and forgive.

As if. Because. Perhaps it's all been said?
Yes, I remember that, if little else —
and of such else, no stuff of consequence.
And I forgive. Forgiveness is the grace
that bears me graveward in a fog of light.

As if. Perhaps. Because. It's all been said.
Remembrance is a virtue thrice ignored.
Conceive a thing, and lose it. Come to love
naked of misdirection, unabashed.
Remember to forget. The light. The fog.

They Woke From Sleep

Not all that long away, as these things go,
a certain man woke from a troubled sleep
and saw that things had changed. He wasn't sure
exactly what had happened, but he wept,
for nothing now would ever be the same.

In another country, far from his,
a woman he had never met lay down
to toss in fitful sleep — and when she woke,
she saw how nothing in the house had changed,
and wept that everything was still the same.

For each, to wake was to confirm a dream
that, in the dreaming, made uneasy sleep —
they'd slept alone, and woke alone to fear.
They never met, nor were they ever near.

My Secret Kept Alive

Familiar of soil am I.
I age more root than tree.
I wear the worm's blind mask.
I feed on twisted stone.
A bitter beast at heart,
and hollow to the bone,
become a green thing's source,
I go where blind worms go.

My secret kept alive
by bitter care and deep
pillowed against the cold
light of that world above,
couched here in soil and stone,
I make my home at last,
bitter at the bone
and fading, but not lost.

Sorrow becomes my hope.
Longing is my joy.
I make my way unwatched,
unnoticed and unheard.
Secret in my pure
attempt at staying whole,
at home where blind worms go,
I seek myself alone.

All green things know my pain.
Whatever grows, is mine.
Root, tree, leaf, bursting forth
from soil to light, wear me
as an emerging shroud
and daily grow less blind.
It is my secret, this:
the green thing has my eyes.

Now let a green force spring
from twisted stone to light,
singing for joy and pain
in blind ecstatic thrust
of what has been against
the hope of what might be,
of all things lost, now found
in flesh that twines to me...

Anniversary

From fifty years well shared, love's measure comes to this:
full eighteen thousand days, nor one without a kiss...

www.ingramcontent.com/pod-product-compliance
Lightning Source LLC
Chambersburg PA
CBHW030352020726
47493CB00003B/792